Shanghaiing Sailors

A Maritime History of Forced Labor, 1849–1915

MARK STRECKER

McFarland & Company, Inc., Publishers

Jefferson, North Carolina

LIBRARY OF CONGRESS CATALOGUING-IN-PUBLICATION DATA

Strecker, Mark, 1970–
    Shanghaiing sailors : a maritime history of forced
labor, 1849–1915 / Mark Strecker.
        p.   cm.
    Includes bibliographical references and index.

    ISBN 978-0-7864-9451-4 (softcover : acid free paper) ∞
    ISBN 978-1-4766-1576-9 (ebook)

    1. Shanghaiing.   2. Sailors—Crimes against—History—19th
century.   3. Sailors—Crimes against—History—20th century.
4. Merchant mariners—Legal status, laws, etc.—History.
5. Seafaring life—History—19th century.   6. Seafaring life—
History—20th century.   7. Sailors—Social conditions.
8. Forced labor—History—19th century.   I. Title.
II. Title: Maritime history of forced labor, 1849–1915.

VK219.S77 2014
331.7'61387509034—dc23   2014013747

BRITISH LIBRARY CATALOGUING DATA ARE AVAILABLE

On the cover: Painting of USS *Chesapeake* approaching HMS *Shannon*
during the War of 1812 by Robert Dodd, 1813 (Library of Congress)

Printed in the United States of America

McFarland & Company, Inc., Publishers
  Box 611, Jefferson, North Carolina 28640
    www.mcfarlandpub.com

Acknowledgments

As always happens with projects involving as much research as this one, a lot of people offered the author quite a bit of help. Unfortunately I did not always know their names or I forgot to note their assistance, but here I present a brief list of those who deserve special thanks: Joan E. Barney, Assistant to Curator, Librarian, New Bedford Free Public Library, Massachusetts; Emily-Jane Dawson, Reference Librarian, Multnomah County Library, Portland, Oregon; Gina Bardi, Reference Librarian, San Francisco Maritime National Historical Park, J. Porter Shaw Library; Maribeth Bielinski, Collections Access Associate, G.W. Blunt White Library, Mystic Seaport; Clarissa Dean, Museum Technician, National Museum of the U.S. Navy; and Tom Carey, Librarian, San Francisco History Center, San Francisco Public Library.

Table of Contents

The time at sea is marked by bells. At noon, eight bells are struck, that is, eight strokes are made upon the bell; and from that time it is struck every half-hour throughout the twenty-four, beginning one stroke and going as high as eight, adding one each half-hour.

—*James Lees,* Dana's Seamen's Friend, *1856*

Preface

The idea for this book came to me unexpectedly. One day my brother mentioned that on a recent business trip to Pendleton, Oregon, he had learned about the underground tunnels there, supposedly used for illicit purposes. He thought this might make an interesting article or book. It reminded me of stories I had heard about tunnels being used to move shanghaied men around in cities of the Pacific Coast. Looking into this, I found that the subject of shanghaiing had an unexpected depth rich with fascinating characters and interesting tales, and out of that came this work.

Shanghaiing, the forcing of a man to sail on a merchant ship against his will, existed because of a shortage of willing sailors, and laws that enabled landsmen to prey upon those of this profession. Tall ships required large crews to operate, and without a sufficient number of men to fill them out, the world's commerce would have stopped. Yet owners and officers treated their crews with brutality. The U.S. government made seamen wards of the admiralty as a means of controlling them.

To understand the dramatic rise and success of shanghaiing as a means of manning ships, one must also have a working knowledge of the era in which it occurred as well as the lives of its victims. This book presents not only a comprehensive history of shanghaiing, which peaked roughly between 1850 and 1915—hereafter referred to as the Age of Shanghaiing—but also examines the nineteenth century seafarer's world and the circumstances that created the perfect storm of events which made shanghaiing a lucrative business. This journey will take us into some unexpected places. Who knew, for example, that the California Gold Rush, the popularity of tea, the introduction of the steamship, and the First Opium War, between Great Britain and China, would cause the conditions that made shanghaiing so prevalent? If a person drew a chart showing all the things connected to this illicit business, it would touch such seemingly unrelated topics as piracy, whaling, and oyster harvesting on the Chesapeake Bay.

1

This book will also shatter a lot of myths. Popular culture usually places shanghaiing on America's West Coast, but in reality it occurred in nearly all the world's major ports, even in the city of Shanghai itself. Although those who shanghaied men—called crimps, landsharks, or sea pimps—did hit men on the backs of their heads and drugged their drinks to get them onboard ships, the majority of them employed nonviolent coercion. They favored economic blackmail made possible by laws that allowed creditors to throw those who owed them money into debtor's prison or to sell their debt to others.

Merchant mariners did not remain passive about their lot in life or lack of power. Tired of the economic blackmailing perpetrated by crimps, they gathered together and formed powerful seamen's unions that used collective power to force their wages up so as to get members out of perpetual debt. These unions successfully lobbied Congress to repeal the draconian laws against them. They also exposed their persecutions in newspapers and other media outlets to make the public more aware of their hardships. This helped, but it ultimately took a major tragedy involving women and children to end shanghaiing altogether.

1

A Conspiracy of Events

The merchant ship *Baltic* out of New York City arrived safely in San Francisco on October 8, 1873, despite having a crew of landsmen consisting of carpenters, tinkers, clerks, brewers, cobblers, tailors, and greengrocers— men who had been procured with drugs and threats. The *Baltic*'s captain did not have much choice in the selection of his crew because New York City's boardinghouse masters controlled the manning of all departing ships, so he had taken who they had offered. Certainly he would have preferred experienced hands. No ship's master wanted to undertake the 18,000-mile voyage around South America via Cape Horn with no one but landsmen manning the ship. With a kindness virtually unknown in that era, the captain ordered his officers to train his green crew without the use of physical coercion or verbal abuse, a technique that worked. The *Baltic* made the trip without the loss or injury of a man, an amazing feat considering even experienced crews had trouble accomplishing this.[1]

One Bell

The word "shanghai"—the kidnapping and forcing of a man to serve on board a merchant ship—first appeared in print in 1872.[2] While most etymologists believe it originated from the fact that many victims of this practice sailed to the city of Shanghai,[3] Portland historian Edward C. "Spider" Johnson disagreed: "In the old days in England a guy might come along and offer you a shilling to buy a drink or a flop [a place to rent a bed]. You took the shilling, if you were broke, and then you were told that you had enlisted in the queen's navy or army, either one. The guy, of course, was a recruiting agent in civilian clothes. But if you took the queen's shilling you were immediately taken on board a ship or put into a barracks for the army. That's where 'shanghaiing' comes from."[4]

The *Oxford English Dictionary* backs Johnson's assessment. It defines "queen's shilling" as "a shilling formerly given to a recruit when enlisting during the reign of a queen.... To enlist as a soldier by accepting a shilling from a recruiting officer (a practice now disused)."[5] Although a study of the total number of shanghaied seamen who found themselves on ships destined for that city as opposed to others would likely prove difficult if not impossible to execute, the mass of anecdotal evidence this writer uncovered suggests very few victims went there, another point in Johnson's favor.[6]

Those who perpetrated the act of shanghaiing became known as "sea pimps," "landsharks," or "crimps." This last appellation, the most frequently used in accounts of shanghaiing, probably derived from the British slang term for "agent."[7] Crimps did not discriminate. They kidnapped men regardless of race, social status, or vocation. One crusader against shanghaiing, Reverend William Taylor, summed up their philosophy: "Get all the sailors' money, honestly if most convenient, but get it." Seamen called the fee that crimps received from captains "blood money."[8] Some captains and masters who willingly paid this went even further by allowing crimps to shanghai their entire crew in exchange for half the proceeds.[9]

Crimps frequented the places where seamen gathered, such as saloons, shipping offices, brothels, and especially sailors' boardinghouses. Although they used drink, drugs, coercion, and trickery to shanghai men, most preferred to employ financial blackmail. It worked like this: seamen chronically lacked money, so a crimp extended them far more credit than they could possibly repay. The crimp then offered those indebted to him the choices of debtor's prison—something many American states and territories had—or taking a berth on a ship of the crimp's choosing. Most did the latter. The crimp took what they owed him from their advance, the wage paid after signing onto a ship and money seamen did not receive until the third day out to sea to prevent them from spending it. The loss of this portion of earnings caused the affected to have short wages at the voyage's end. To make up the difference, they had to get credit from another boardinghouse master, starting the whole process over.[10] Since experienced mariners learned to avoid this trick, boardinghouse crimps usually targeted landsmen and green sailors.[11]

Shipping agents often stole advances when signing men even if no previous debt existed. This happened to John Owen. He needed to get out of New York City as fast as possible, thanks to trouble with the law, so he asked a shipping agent named Mr. Williams to get him a berth on a vessel bound for Sydney. Williams charged a $35 fee for this service, the amount he said Owen would earn for his advance. In no position to negotiate, Owen agreed. Upon boarding the ship, he learned he had earned an advance of $50, not $35, meaning Williams had pocketed the $15 difference for himself. Owen's captain compensated him with two pounds of tobacco.[12] Mr. Williams resorted to violence when trickery failed. Thomas Anderson of New York City came into his office drunk and asked for a berth onboard a ship bound for Sydney because he had missed his own. Taking advantage of Anderson's inebriated state, Williams signed him up for the *Alexander Yeats*. Before boarding, Anderson learned the ship would sail to Shanghai, not Sydney as promised. When he refused to board, Williams threatened to blow out his brains, convincing him to sail to Shanghai after all.[13]

In America a seaman had to sign a contract called the ship's articles before getting under way.[14] The Shipping Commissioner's Act of 1872 required all seamen to sign this in front of a shipping master, but the law got ignored, especially in New York City, where the crimps had so cowed captains they dared not go through the commissioner's office. Britain passed a similar law in 1854 called the Merchant Shipping Act. Seamen who signed articles became indentured servants because they could not break these contracts. Captains had the right to ask law enforcement officials to track down, arrest, then throw deserters into jail until needed. Authorities did not always care if a man had signed under duress or because of trickery.[15] John Collins and Frederick Moss told a judge their captain had shanghaied them. The captain responded by producing articles with their signatures, and the court ruled against them. The judge had them returned to their ship under guard, then deducted two days from their wages to cover court costs.[16]

Ship's articles stipulated a starting and ending port. Vessels with lengthy voyages typically had multiple stops, usually picking up a cargo in one and selling it at the next. The wait for more freight to come along could last for months. During this downtime the crewmen dared not leave because they would not receive their earned wages until reaching the agreed-upon final port of call. Those who did so lost all their pay. By law a captain had to feed and provision his crew during such lulls, but if he chased them off, he kept their wages for himself. This prompted many unscrupulous masters to make their men's lives hell in an effort to entice them to desert. If successful, captains contacted a crimp for replacements when they needed to sail, then repeated the process in the next port.[17] A captain named Joe Rich liked to do this. During a two-year trading voyage to Brazil, he ran off several crews by terrorizing them. His first officer, Bob French, did not fear him and refused to go, forcing Rich to pay him his wages in full.[18]

Shanghaiing occurred in every major seaport around the globe, including the city of Shanghai itself. One Sunday night a seaman named Patrick Grant went carousing along that city's waterfront. The next morning he awoke on a strange ship as the newest member of her crew. Feeling ill beyond the effects of a hangover, he informed the second mate he could not work because he had a nasty fever. During the four days it lasted he received not a morsel of food. Somehow his plight caught the attention of Mr. Brown, a British vice-consul, who charged Grant's master, Captain Murphy, with illegally bringing a man on board without first having him sign the ship's articles, a violation of the Merchant Shipping Act of 1854. For his defense, Murphy produced articles with Grant's signature, saying he had put it there himself as Grant could not write. Grant proved his literacy and went free. The judge fined the captain a mere £10 for his violation because he felt Murphy had meant no harm.[19]

American crimps operated not only along the Pacific and Atlantic coasts but also on the Great Lakes. Some of them, such as shipping agent "Big" Jack McQuade, became quite infamous in their own right. One story about him occurred a few days before Christmas 1888 in his home city of Chicago. When the 1,000-ton schooner *C.C. Barnes* broke free of her icy imprisonment in the Chicago River with the help of a tug, she needed extra hands before getting underway to Buffalo, New York, with a cargo of "38,000 bushels of grain." McQuade headed to the Sans Souci Bar and told its owner, Olaf the Swede, to give him six men. Olaf protested that he could not find mariners right before Christmas. McQuade threatened to arrange for the rescinding of the saloon's license. That night Olaf rolled up with a wagon carrying six unconscious men.[20]

Olaf had served as McQuade's "runner," a person charged with finding new victims and bringing them to a landshark. To accomplish this, some runners rowed out to ships just coming into the harbor and, once on board, promised high-wage jobs, cheap liquor, or women to those who returned with them to shore. On ships where captains forbade shore leave, runners covertly returned at a prearranged time and picked up those willing to come. Along the wharves, runners lured men into the places in which their employers operated. At this point crimps typically liquored up unsuspecting victims to make them so drunk they passed out, or handed them cigars laced with enough opium to lull to sleep those who smoked them.[21] New York City's crimps preferred the use of chloral hydrate, or "knockout drops," for this purpose. While twenty grains would render the average person unconscious, crimps regularly used between thirty and forty, and sometimes up to sixty for a particularly "robust customer." The drug paralyzed the heart and lungs—too much and a victim died. It created a distinctive taste in a drink, so most crimps waited for a victim to get drunk before using it.[22]

Hollywood and other purveyors of fiction have created the myth that some crimps used trapdoors as a means of procuring men. The author of this work could not find a single reliable source showing this ever occurred. It makes little sense to use such a technique because it had too many variables for consistent success. A crimp would have had to repeatedly corral his victims into a relatively small area in a very specific place, then hope that as they fell through none of them knocked their heads against the trapdoor's frame or suffered a major injury upon landing below, a likely outcome considering that even a relatively short fall produces a considerable amount of force. A 150-pound person falling ten feet, for example, will hit the surface with 1,500 pounds of force.[23]

The idea of crimps utilizing underground tunnels for the purpose of shanghaiing has some merit. Portland's crimps may have moved victims using a system of tunnels that connected the city's "saloons and other businesses in the north end and terminated near the present-day Burnside Bridge." In the 1970s historian Mike Jones excavated some of these, determining these "brick-lined passageways ... may have originally been constructed for drainage or flood control," yet they contained "intriguing artifacts such as pill bottles, a turn-of-the-century shoe, part of a peg leg, bullets, meat hooks, and ... a man-sized cage."[24]

Reliable accounts of crimps passing dead men off as drunks do exist. One such incident occurred in Quebec. A boardinghouse master named Dick Ward needed to procure five seamen, a difficult thing to do at the time because most ships in that port leaked so badly men refused to sail on them. Ward found four men but not a fifth. A fellow boardinghouse owner told him he had a lodger who had just died, so the two hatched a plan to use this to their advantage. They poured rum all over the deceased and told the captain he had fallen into a drunken stupor. The captain duly paid for him, and the partners split the proceeds.[25]

Shanghaiing occurred in all parts of the world. Upon arriving in Rio de Janeiro on the British ship *D.S. Morris,* a Swedish seaman named Gustav Johnson went to shore to procure medicine. "As he was leaving the chandler's shop he was set upon by four negros, directed by a short, thick-set white man. They knocked him down and bound him, carried him to a wharf, threw him into a small boat, [and] rowed him" back to their bark, the *Canvas-down.* On the Filipino island of Cebu, Johnson tried to go to shore, but his captain prevented him from doing so. He protested. The captain took him to the British consulate and had him locked up until departure, then audaciously deducted this cost from Johnson's pay. The Swede secured his release in New York and used that city's courts to successfully sue his captain for $150 in damages.[26]

Captains did not have a monopoly on perpetrating or enabling shang-

haiing. Some people used it as a means to achieve ends having nothing to do
with the theft of a seaman's earnings. E.M. Byers, who owned a successful
Pittsburgh iron business with his brother, disappeared. His wife asked her
brother-in-law to help locate him, but he refused, so she hired a team of detectives. For a year they looked in the United States but found no trace of their
man. Then a lead took one of them Japan. Here he picked up Byers' trail. This
he followed for a year, going "to Australia, China and to the Hawaiian Islands."
Finally he returned to Japan and there found his man in a state of mental tur-
moil and under the care of Doctor Samuel A. Boyd, paid for by Byers' brother.
The detective whisked Byers away. In Hawaii, another set of detectives hired
by Byers' brother tried and failed to stop them. They made their way to San
Francisco, where Byers' wife awaited them. She took him for treatment at a
hospital. At one point she stepped out of his room for a few minutes and upon
returning found him missing. She later learned her brother-in-law had her
husband shanghaied to take control of "between $1,000,000 and $2,000,000"
in assets.[27]

A similar thing happened to Jacob Wilson, Jr., a wealthy but, unfortunately, deformed man whose father owned a significant amount of property
in New York City, including a saloon on South Street. At this establishment
Jacob became infatuated with Mary Keane, daughter of its manager. After the
two married, Jacob's new father-in-law, Hugh J. Keane, kept his son-in-law and
friends perpetually drunk. Wilson, Sr., died soon thereafter, leaving $50,000
worth of property to Jacob. The rest of the inheritance went to the father's
second wife and the children they had together. Mary sued Wilson's estate,
claiming Wilson, Sr., had promised her $15,000 to marry his son. Smitten
with Mary, Jacob testified to that effect on her behalf, helping her win. Next
she convinced him to sue his stepmother for a percentage of her property.
Although the widow won the case, the legal wrangling devaluated her assets.
Greedy for more, Mary persuaded the endlessly inebriated Jacob to give her
his entire inheritance as well.[28]

With that secured, she asked her friends to steer Jacob into the company
of other women, a gambit that gave her the grounds she needed for a successful divorce. Knowing if he ever sobered up he might contest what she had
done, she decided to take care of this loose end by making him disappear altogether. In December 1888 she arranged to have him shanghaied and shipped
off to a desolate outpost in western Australia at which he arrived penniless.
She remarried but died soon thereafter in June 1889, leaving her ill-gotten
gains, totaling about $60,000, to her second husband. Jacob made his way to
San Francisco and there retained a good lawyer to help him recover his lost
inheritance.[29]

Two Bells

In December 1848 President James Polk made his annual speech to Congress. About this *The Stars and Banner* newspaper of Gettysburg, Pennsylvania, editorialized: "There is nothing of striking importance in the message—it being mainly devoted to a defense of the policy of the Administration. The President argues the beneficial results of the Mexican War—alludes to the discovery of the large Gold mines in California, and recommends the establishment of a Mint on the spot."[30] The paper's dismissive attitude toward Polk's mention of gold in California greatly understated the reality soon to unfold. His speech had verified the truth of the rumors of a great gold discovery there that sparked the California Gold Rush.[31]

Countless Americans decided to go there by land or by sea. Because the land route involved negotiating rough terrain, facing hostile Indians, and dealing with Mexicans still bitter about losing the recent war, those gold seekers who could afford it took one of two hazardous sea routes. The first brought them around South America to the Pacific, a trip that lasted between six and eight months depending on the wind, weather, and point of departure. Those who took the second route reduced their travel time to just a few weeks by landing on the Caribbean side of the Isthmus of Panama and crossing overland to the Pacific so as to sail on an awaiting ship to San Francisco.[32]

This route had its own risks. Those who chose it disembarked at Chagres, a village containing a Spanish-built castle and a few thatched huts in which lived a hodgepodge of native people, Africans, and a few officials from the Colombian government whose country ruled Panama at this time. During the peak of the California Gold Rush, thousands of Americans flooded this village, devastated its ecology and overwhelmed its few buildings to the point where travelers slept anywhere they could, even on the beaches. In its early years, the Isthmus contained no highways or coast-to-coast railroad, so travelers had to hire canoes for an inflated sum to take them as far as the continental divide. Here the navigability of the waterway gave out, so gold seekers negotiated the next disease-ridden thirty-nine miles overland, using beasts of burden to cross a mountainous tropical terrain covered with a thick jungle, a journey made still more difficult from June to September by unending rain. Those not killed by tropical ailments such as yellow fever boarded a ship bound for California.[33]

In 1851 Cornelius Vanderbilt established the Accessory Transit Company in Nicaragua in an effort to cash in on the popularity of the Isthmus route. He controlled the transportation to, through, and from Nicaragua, advertising it as a more comfortable alternative to the Panamanian crossing, an assertion with which not all passengers agreed. Vanderbilt's company shipped 8,000

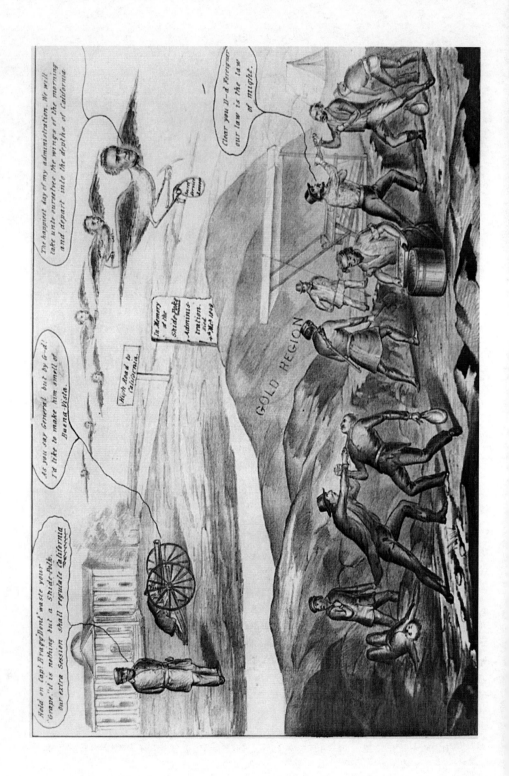

gold hunters in 1853, ten thousand in 1854, and 11,000 in 1855, but the completion of the coast-to-coast Panamanian Railroad (which started running in 1855) and political instability in Nicaragua soon caused Vanderbilt's route to fall out of favor.[34]

Ships sailing around South America had two ways to get to the Pacific side: go around its tip, Cape Horn, or through the Strait of Magellan. The Horn route involved tackling perpetually cold, rough seas whipped up by strong winds. The constant, churning ocean made a ship roll so violently many passengers could not get any rest as their vessel struggled to make way against contrary currents and winds, all the while avoiding icebergs. During the winter months rigging iced up and snow fell onto the decks so high crewmen had to shovel it off. Rounding the Horn took anywhere from a few days to six weeks, depending on the volatile weather. Many of those who made the journey swore never to try it again.[35]

The Strait of Magellan, about two hundred miles to the north, had its own dangers. Although shorter than the Cape route by several hundred miles, contrary winds, extreme tides, and strong currents made sailing from east to west difficult to say the least, and its narrowness created dangerous navigational hazards. Once around the Horn or through the Strait, ships sailed north until they reached between the thirteenth and twenty-fifth parallels, at which point contrary winds and currents forced them to strike west, often all the way to the Sandwich Islands, known today as Hawaii. From there they headed northeast to San Francisco.[36]

The gold rush quickly changed this city's makeup. By 1851 the Hispanic ranchers who traditionally lived in and around it had for the most part all fled, replaced mainly by Americans as well as a significant minority of French, Chinese, Mexicans from the state of Sonora, Chileans, Germans, and Italians. Together they swelled the population to about 30,000. The environment remained unimproved. Sand drifted in from the surrounding hills and covered the streets in the dry season, then turned into mud during the wet season, the latter problem being dealt with on the major thoroughfares by covering them with planks. Chronic fires ripped through all this tinder repeatedly.[37]

Most ships arriving here dropped anchor at Yerba Buena Cove, at which a vast sea of derelict ships gathered, a circumstance caused by the multitude of crews who had followed their passengers to the goldfields.[38] Even military vessels like the U.S. Army's *Anita* suffered from this fate; upon reaching San

Opposite: **This lithograph,** *Things as They Are,* **outlines some of the troubles prospectors experienced when they arrived in California during the 1849 gold rush (Library of Congress Prints and Photographs Collection, Henry Serrell & S. Lee Perkins Lith & Pub, 1849).**

Francisco, her entire crew decided they liked gold better than their country and deserted en masse.[39] The cove contained an estimated 150 abandoned ships in May 1849. There were 308 in October and 635 by June 1850. Salvagers brought some of them to shore to serve as housing, saloons, wood for buildings, and even a prison. Despite the fact that an 1851 fire swept across and destroyed a significant number of these vessels, they still choked the cove's entrance. To remedy this, between 1854 and 1859, city officials arranged for the breaking up of 200 deserted ships.[40]

Captains who lost their crews to the goldfields so desperately needed replacements to get back to sea they would pay a premium for them. A runner named Bill Thomas recalled that the crimp for whom he worked, Tom Brewster, received between $50 to $75 a man from captains. Brewster mainly targeted failed miners returning from the goldfields, some of whom willingly took a berth on a ship to get back home; others had problems with the law and therefore needed to escape in a hurry. Brewster built a boardinghouse to lure in those disinclined to sail for him of their own free will. He built it in front of a hill, constructing its front half out of wood and its back out of canvas, which he stretched tightly against the hillside. Into this he dug a cave reinforced by timber and there within imprisoned his victims (whom he usually got drunk before corralling them there) until such time as a captain needed them. He called it "the hold," and only he and Thomas knew about it. Those who spent time in it never had a chance to reveal its existence, as they went directly to waiting ships and on out to sea.[41]

About 300,000 gold seekers from America and around the world headed to California, a massive number of people for ships to move around the globe. In 1849 the number of American ships alone that sailed to California amounted to 775. As the demand for ships and crews to man them increased, the number of those inclined to sail decreased because they could not resist the lure of quick riches versus toiling away at one of the hardest jobs in the world.[42]

Two more gold rushes would have a similar effect on the seafaring world within the next twenty years. The first occurred in Australia when Edward Hammond Hargraves and a companion named John Lister found gold at Lewis Pond Creek at New South Wales on February 12, 1851. Lister moved on and, with a different partner, made another strike at nearby Yorky's Corner. Hargraves christened the area Ophir, the gold-filled region mentioned in the Old Testament. The population of Sydney drained almost overnight as its citizens rushed to strike it rich. People from other parts of the world soon followed.[43] In 1861 a gold rush occurred in New Zealand when Gabriel Read, a Tasmanian miner, found the precious metal in Otago, followed by more discoveries in 1864 on the west island.[44]

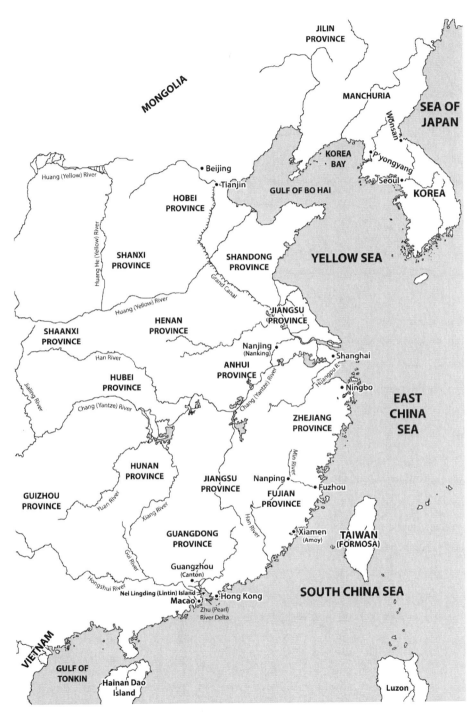

China, based on the CIA map "China Railroads and Selected Roads, May 1959" (redrawn by the author).

Three Bells

The European traders who first made their way to China found a bonanza of goods to sell back home for incredible profits, including silk, porcelain, and especially tea, at least during times when they could gain access to the country.[45] Although one emperor eased trade restrictions in 1684 by allowing foreign merchants access to some southern ports, another, Emperor Qianlong, reversed this in 1760 by limiting trade to the single port of Guangzhou (Canton) because he feared foreign infiltration. He decided upon this city because of its remoteness, which he figured would isolate his subjects from contamination from outsiders.[46]

He also created the so-called Canton system. Excluding women altogether, it issued a limited number of passports to foreigners each trading season, containing them on Guangzhou's island of Shamian. Here they lived and operated in a narrow strip of thirteen buildings that served as warehouses, sleeping quarters, and offices, all run by twelve foreign trading companies. Foreign exporters could deal directly only with those Chinese merchants who belonged to a monopolistic group called the Cohong, its members having gained this privilege by agreeing to guarantee the "barbarians'" debts, which it insured with a pool of money called the *consoo*. In the rare cases when a foreigner went beyond the designated area, he had to travel with one of eight specially appointed Chinese translators.[47]

The British had a special interest in the city as it provided the only viable source of tea they could obtain, a commodity introduced into England in the 1660s as part of the dowry paid to King Charles II. It became so popular that by the eighteenth century it outsold beer. Only one British corporation, the East India Company (later renamed the United Company of Merchants of England Trading to East Indies), had the right to sell it because Queen Elizabeth had granted it a monopoly when she chartered it in 1600. Tea would make its fortune.[48]

Independent British merchants hungered for greater access to China. Unable to obtain passports, they set up floating warehouses off the shores of the island of Nei Lingding (Lintin) in the Gulf of Guangzhou, buying and selling about £2 million worth of smuggled goods a year.[49] Called "country traders," their presence irritated the Chinese government so thoroughly the East India Company feared retaliation in the form of banishment. Since the government could not stop the country traders, the president of its Board of Control gambled that eliminating its monopoly and allowing country traders full access to Guangzhou might ease the situation. The president introduced a resolution to Parliament on June 13, 1833, to effect this.[50]

That governing body not only complied, it also dismantled some of Britain's oldest trade laws dating back to just after its mid-seventeenth century civil wars, when it had reasserted control over England's overseas colonies by passing a series of new navigation acts forcing colonists to limit their trade to English merchants and their ships. All cargos from the colonies, no matter what their destination, had to at some point stop in the home country.[51] The complete repeal of these trade laws in 1849 eliminated all tariffs on incoming foreign ships, allowing them to bring commodities into the country duty free.[52]

The American company A.A. Low & Brother of New York City decided to start transporting tea directly from China to Britain and to that end ordered the construction of the two-deck clipper *Oriental.* Launched on September 10, 1849, she sailed from Hong Kong to New York City in a record eighty-one days in the spring of 1850, demonstrating that her design, a recent development in ship technology invented by the British but perfected by American shipwrights, fit the needs of the Chinese tea trade more than any other type of vessel.[53] Clippers could attain speeds that far exceeded previous types of tall ships as well as that of contemporary steamers. The clipper derived its superior velocity from its three masts, style of rigging, and unique hull design, a narrow affair that produced a deep draft with low water resistance.[54] (The first American clipper known to sail, the *Rainbow,* was launched in New York City in 1845 and later carried some of the first passengers from the East Coast to California during the California Gold Rush.)[55]

The *Oriental* set another record in 1850 when she brought a cargo of tea from Guangzhou to the West India Docks in England in a record ninety-eight days, far outpacing the much slower British ships leaving about the same time. The *Oriental* being one of the first traders of the season to arrive, her cargo of tea was sold at £6 a ton; ships coming in later made only £3 10s a ton.[56] Britain could not build a rival clipper fleet because it lacked the cheap lumber to which American shipwrights had ready access.[57]

The *Oriental*'s record prompted shipping companies to demand that their captains significantly reduce sailing times. Companies also start ordering new clippers built with iron and steel frames so as to increase their size yet still survive the stresses of the sea. Clippers of this construction adopted taller masts to compensate for the extra weight, making the ships difficult to handle in heavy seas and thus more likely to founder.[58] Some captains feared losing their command if their voyage times did not meet expectations, while others desired to beat existing records. In either case, masters recklessly pushed their crews to take dangerous risks and did not mind if a few seamen died because of it.[59]

In 1851 the clipper *Surprise* made a record journey from New York City to San Francisco via the Horn in ninety-six days and fifteen hours. In that same year a rival shipping company launched its own clipper, the *Flying Cloud,* under the command of Captain Josiah Perkins Creesy. Because his vessel would follow an identical route, he obsessed over beating the *Oriental's* time. Setting sail on June 3, 1851, he began in a foul mood, an ominous state of mind foreshadowing things to come. Three days out the weather got bad, but Creesy did not reduce sail, an order most masters would have given because excessive winds strained sails, masts, yards, and rigging, causing them to rip or break.[60]

The *Flying Cloud's* main topgallant mast snapped, taking the topsail yard and a good deal of its upper rigging with it. Creesy ruthlessly ordered the crew aloft to remove the wreckage—a very risky thing to do in foul weather—then refused to take in any canvas. During another storm along the coast of Argentina, high winds and Creesy's continued unwillingness to reduce sail caused the mainmast to spring (the development of a horizontal crack). Creesy ordered his men aloft to cut away all its yards. His first mate, Thomas Austin, told him he did not like executing this order, although he obeyed it. The crew cut down all the main mast's upper sails. This limited the *Flying Cloud's* maneuverability and would

The clipper *St. David* (Library of Congress Prints and Photographs Collection, Detroit Publishing Co., 1905).

have induced most captains to stop and effect repairs before rounding the treacherous Cape Horn ahead. Creesy had no such intention. He pushed through and, remarkably, did not lose a man. Upon rounding the Cape, he relieved Austin from duty, allegedly for slacking and fraternizing with the passengers.[61]

During the last part of the voyage, still another storm erupted. Creesy predictably did not reduce sail, so it ought to come as no surprise that the fore- and topgallant masts snapped off. Again he forced the crew to go aloft and make repairs during nasty weather, and again he followed this up by keeping full sail. His gambit paid off. The *Flying Cloud* broke the *Surprise*'s record by making the voyage in eighty-one days and twenty-one hours.[62] Yet his recklessness did not go unpunished. Austin sued him for wrongful dismissal, and several other seamen did so for his excessive cruelty. The *Flying Cloud*'s owner, Grinnel, Midturn & Company, did not want to deal with such legal entanglements, so it shipped Creesy out on another of its vessels before the case went to trial, then falsely announced his death. He had the unsettling experience of reading his own obituary.[63]

Four Bells

Upon securing its monopoly in Guangzhou, the East India Company found the Chinese wanted none of the finished goods from Britain it sold. Chinese merchants demanded payment in Spanish silver, the international currency of that era and the supply of which the company had little of after the American Revolution. It needed to find something to sell to the Chinese to readjust its balance of trade. Thanks to a series of events it did not cause but happily exploited, it found one.[64]

Around 1620 Spanish traders introduced tobacco into the East Indies. Chinese seafarers then brought it home from Siam, Java, and Bengal. Its popularity soared. Dutch seamen who came to the region brought with them the practice of mixing a pinch of opium in with their tobacco because they incorrectly believed it prevented malaria, and this practice made its way into Taiwan. When China sent troops there to quell a rebellion in 1721, its soldiers brought this back with them. At first, smoking opium remained the exclusive purview of the Chinese elite, who used it as an aphrodisiac. Soon enough its use trickled down to the lower classes, who embraced it because it helped to ease the mental and physical pains of their everyday lives.[65]

The East India Company gained control of a massive supply of opium in 1783 with its conquest of Bengal, India's biggest producer of this narcotic, giving it control of a massive yet cheap supply. East India Company's sales of the drug went from £39,000 in 1773 to £250,000 in 1793. This generated a tidy profit and restored the company's balance of trade with China. The Chinese paid a staggering seven million Spanish silver dollars for the drug between 1806 and 1809. The number of opium-filled chests brought into Guangzhou spiked from 18,000 in 1830 to 30,000 in 1833, causing the flow of silver into China to reverse. Opium sold at four times the cost of producing it, an amazing profit margin considering that only human labor could effectively harvest it through a grueling process mechanization could not replicate.[66]

Only one poppy species in the world, *Papaver somniferum,* produces opium with a strong enough dose of narcotic to induce mind-altering effects. This plant begets raw opium as a "cloudy, white, fairly mobile substance." When exposed to air, it turns "into a dark brown, vicious substance, sticky to the touch with a distinctive, delicate [smell of] perfume." To collect it, a farmer pierces ripened pods with a specialized knife and bleeds each one. Done correctly, these heal themselves, producing opium up to three more times. Harvesters dry the liquid in the sun, cook it in boiling water, drain it through a sieve or cheesecloth, bring it to a boil again, then simmer it until it becomes "a thick, brown paste."[67]

Despite the fact "the East India Company kept the price artificially high" until 1820, opium's popularity continued to infiltrate the Chinese masses, so much so that in 1800 their emperor banned both its importation and its growth domestically. Those caught smoking it for purposes other than medicinal suffered a punishment of 100 strokes from a bamboo cane. This proved no deterrent, so in 1813 the emperor banned opium smoking altogether no matter what the purpose. Its use became a national crisis: the Chinese government now had a nation of opium fiends on its hand.[68]

The prohibition prompted the company to avoid selling it directly in China, as it feared continuing to do so might prompt the emperor to initiate a reprisal by banishing it from Guangzhou. The company auctioned its supply off in Calcutta to private businessmen, letting them find illicit ways to get it into China. Smugglers sold it to the merchant houses operating in Guangzhou itself, such as the American owned and run firm Russell & Company. This company dealt in opium for years after officially declaring it would no longer do so, making many of its principles exceedingly wealthy, including Warren Delano, whose fortune ultimately benefited his grandson, Franklin Delano Roosevelt.[69]

Many Chinese subjects hated opium and its effect on their fellow countrymen, so much so that they protested its use through songs, poetry and religion.[70] In 1839 Emperor Daoguang heeded this call and decided to rid the nation of it. He appointed Lin Zexu, one of his provincial governors, to the rank of high commissioner with the charge of achieving this goal.[71] Lin, officially known as the Imperial Commissioner for Frontier Defense, arrived in

Guangzhou in 1839. There he confiscated opium pipes, arrested dealers, and demanded foreign merchants turn all their stocks over to him without any compensation. At first they refused, but threats of expulsion prompted them to give up 20,000 chests of it, a total of 2,376,254 pounds.[72]

To dispose of it, Lin had a large force of workers break it up, dig three deep trenches, throw the offending narcotic into them, then add a mixture of water, salt, and lime to ruin it. That accomplished, they "flushed [it] out into a neighboring creek," through which it made its way out to sea.[73] The British government demanded reparations. The emperor dismissed Lin for his failure to eradicate opium from the empire, then commanded his grand secretary to smooth things over. This effort failed to get anywhere, so the peeved British government ordered the Royal Navy to blockade Guangzhou in 1841. They threatened to destroy it if the Chinese government did not pay a ransom that

Shanghai's French Concession (Library of Congress Prints and Photographs Collection, publisher/creator unknown, 1900).

equaled six million Spanish dollars. Incapable of defeating the Westerner's technological superiority, the emperor agreed.[74] To end what became known as the First Opium War, the Chinese signed the Treaty of Nanking on August 29, 1842, a document negotiated by scholar-bureaucrats who did not understand the mindset of the Western "barbarians."[75] The treaty opened up four new ports to foreigners: Xiamen (Amoy), Fuzhou, Ningbo, and Shanghai. It also gave Britain the island of Hong Kong.[76]

For European and American traders, Shanghai would become the jewel of the new ports. British missionaries arrived as its first foreign residents in November 1842, followed the next year by the Crown's new consul to the city, Captain George Balfour of the British Army. He found the city to be unpleasant and overcrowded, its authorities uncooperative. They refused to provide him housing within the city walls, claiming they could find nothing for him. An enterprising Chinese merchant named Yao approached the captain and offered him a lease for a house there. Balfour quickly seized upon this unexpected opportunity, not realizing Yao would then proceed to sell his fellow countrymen tickets to come inside and watch the "white devils" in their daily lives, an enterprise Balfour quickly stopped.[77]

Unlike the modern city, Shanghai in the nineteenth century did not stretch to the East China Sea. Rather it stood where the Suzhou and Huangpu rivers meet and was reachable only by sailing fifteen miles up from the mouth of the Chang (Yangtze) River, then through the narrow, dirty, crowded Suzhou another twenty miles. Ships struggled up it during high tide and dropped their anchors at low.[78] Westerners living in Shanghai (save for the French) founded the International Settlement and built it outside the original city walls. Here even a low-paid agent of an American trading company could afford servants.[79] Shanghai quickly became the port of choice for Chinese merchants to take their goods because connecting interior waterways allowed for transportation on boats, whereas reaching Guangzhou involved a grueling overland trek.[80]

The Treaty of Nanking had an unexpected effect on America's seafaring world, especially along the Pacific Coast. Until that time most American shipping companies did little trade in China. Although the Continental Congress had sent the *Empress of Asia* there in 1776 to establish a trading presence, American merchants made few inroads. The moment the British forced China to open its ports, President Tyler sent Caleb Cushing there to negotiate for the same rights. The emperor signed a treaty to that effect in 1844, an unnecessary document as he considered all nations tributary to his own and therefore equal. Thus what he had already granted Britain applied to all others.[81]

Now that it made economic sense to expand their trade routes to China,

Opium traders in Hong Kong (Library of Congress Prints and Photographs Collection, H.C. White Company, 1901).

American shipping companies financed world-circumnavigating voyages that could last for several years. Ships leaving West Coast ports now sailed to China and the East Indies, then returned by going around the tips of Africa or South America, stopping in a number of places along the way. At this time many American seamen working on the Pacific Coast sailed only part-time, limiting themselves to coastal trade. They made their primary livings in other occupations, especially lumbering, mining, and farming, and sailed only in their off seasons. Such workers had no desire to sail around the world.[82] With so few men willing to commit themselves to long voyages, desperate captains paid crimps blood money in exchange for a crew of shanghaied men.

Five Bells

The first steam-powered boat ever to operate in the Western world appeared in France upon the Seine in 1772, although its prospects as a viable alternative to wind or human power did not look promising: it sank. A few years later the French tried again. This one foundered at its own dock. The first steamboat to sail on American waters made its maiden voyage on the Delaware River as members of the Continental Congress watched. Designed by a silversmith named John Fitch, its steam engine powered twelve oars, six to a side, which rowed the vessel in an inefficient manner.[83]

The paddlewheel quickly replaced this awkward system, and while it worked well for flat-bottomed riverboats, adapting it to oceangoing vessels with a V-shaped hull proved much more difficult. The earliest deep sea steamships came equipped with two paddlewheels, one to each side, and a full set of sails to maintain stability. The sails made steering difficult and the rolling of the ocean prevented both wheels from biting into the water at the same depth, greatly reducing their effectiveness. In heavy seas the wheels became useless, forcing a steamer to rely exclusively on its sail power. Although the screw propeller ultimately replaced both sails and paddlewheels, it did not make a favorable impression when it first appeared on the *Great Britain* in 1836. It propelled her at an even slower rate than paddlewheels, prompting engineers to ignore the innovation for many years.[84]

Steamers had one danger tall ships carrying benign cargoes lacked: they

This drawing by Alfred R. Waud, created between 1860 and 1865, shows the side-wheel steamer *S.R. Spalding* (Library of Congress Prints and Photographs Collection).

exploded. One infamous incident occurred on the Mississippi River in Memphis, Tennessee. While eating their breakfast on the morning of February 24, 1830, passengers on board the *Helen McGregor* heard the sound of artillery fire just as the boat got underway, not realizing it had come from their vessel's exploding boiler. Moments later a crewman stumbled into the dining room and tore the remains of his clothes off to reveal his flayed skin and blackened face. The explosion of steam whitened everything, threw the boilers out of place, collapsed part of the deck, and blew those caught by it into pieces. One witness estimated the total number of dead as between fifty and sixty, but no one knew for certain as the blast had tossed many victims into the river, from which they never emerged.[85]

Despite this danger, steamships became good enough by the 1860s to pose a commercial threat to their wind-powered counterparts. The net tonnage of Britain's fleet of steamships, for example, grew from 168,474 in 1850 to 948,367 in 1869. The next leap in steam engine technology, the compound engine, produced superior compression, giving more power and improved fuel efficiency so that by 1870 steamers could travel nonstop for about 7,000 miles before refueling. To go farther they had to fill precious cargo space with coal, an uneconomical alternative. Steamers departing for China from Europe or America could not readily refuel along the way because an insufficient number of coaling stations existed along Africa's west coast, a problem competing tall ships did not have.[86]

The French and Egyptians formed a partnership with the goal of solving this limitation by digging a canal across the Isthmus of Suez to link the Red and Mediterranean seas. This they accomplished. On November 16, 1869, the Suez Canal opened. In its first full year of operation, fewer than 500 ships, with a total of about 400,000 tons, used it, far fewer than the five million the Suez Canal Company had projected. The next year offered little improvement. By 1875 the company faced bankruptcy. British prime minister Benjamin Disraeli, seeing its potential, ordered his government to buy a 44 percent stake in it at a cost of £4 million, despite the fact the British people did not approve of the purchase. This influx of cash failed to keep the company from defaulting, so the British seized it, then solidified control by occupying all of Egypt with its military.[87]

Disraeli's gambit paid off. When British shipping companies with steamer fleets realized going through the canal shaved 5,777 miles off the trip to China, they started to use it in increasing numbers. Tall ships for the most part avoided it because they had to rely on expensive towing to get through, plus the Red Sea was difficult to negotiate. This allowed steamers to overtake the tea trade by the end of the 1870s, forcing tall ships to reduce costs as much as possible

This photograph by Francis Frith, taken between 1856 and 1860, shows the Suez Canal connecting to Lake Timsah (Library of Congress Prints and Photographs Collection).

to keep competitive and causing the already poor conditions on board them to worsen.[88]

Shipping companies with fleets of tall ships achieved savings by manning their vessels with reduced crews, a very dangerous thing to do when dealing with the whims of the sea. Many professional mariners gave up the business altogether because they refused to sail on undermanned ships. Others took work on steamers because they offered improved working conditions. This forced captains of tall ships to turn to crimps to find them crews any way they could. These landsharks usually obtained society's dregs, whose lack of experience and motivation to work made the already dangerous conditions on board a tall ship even worse.[89]

Six Bells

In summary, no single factor caused shanghaiing to become a worldwide problem in the seafaring world between 1849 and 1915—the Age of Shanghaiing. Rather, a variety of circumstances, some related, others not, created a conspiracy of events to make the seafarer's life one of the hardest and most dangerous in the world, exasperated by chronic debt, undermanned crews, and excessive ill-treatment by captains. The California Gold Rush created the first major worldwide shortage of seamen by motivating crews to abandon their ships for the goldfields. This forced the wages of those willing to sail to spike, a windfall the unscrupulous crimps decided they wanted for themselves.

The United Kingdom's repeal of its navigation acts allowed American ships to trade in the British Isles without having to pay extra duties, giving U.S. shipping companies the opportunity to get into the lucrative tea trading business. The clipper *Oriental* made a record run from Hong Kong to New York City, and another from Hong Kong to London. This showed that faster tea trade voyages yielded higher profits and enticed shipping companies to demand their captains reduce the time of their runs. To meet this goal, masters recklessly put their crews in danger. Shipping companies also tried to increase profits by purchasing clippers made with iron and steel frames, unwieldy vessels on which professional mariners did not like to serve because they sailed poorly in heavy seas. Competition with steamers, particularly in the tea trade, forced shipping companies to man their tall ships with reduced crews, not a wise thing to do when sailing upon the open ocean.

The British forced China to open more of its ports to foreigners at the conclusion of the First Opium War, allowing U.S. shipping companies to expand their trade routes there. The resulting globe-circumnavigating voyages, which often lasted between one and two years, were a commitment many mariners used to the seasonal coastal trade refused to make, a situation that exacerbated the already existing shortage of seamen caused by undermanned ships, gold rushes, and tyrannical captains obsessed with making faster runs. This confluence of events produced the perfect environment in which shang-haiing prospered.

2

A Mariner's Life

Captain William Morris Barnes' body told the tale of his life better than his autobiography, *When Ships Were Ships and Not Tin Pots.* By the time he reached his last years, he stood five feet six inches and had only tufts of gray hair remaining. The back of his head showed the scars from a hammer strike and a bullet wound. A hit from a stone had left a nick in the bridge of his nose, a wound hardly noticeable compared to the scar running from his lip down to the bottom of his chin. He could not remember the exact cause of the now-healed holes on either cheek, though he believed either a bullet or shrapnel had done it, taking two molars with it. "A seven-inch scar" meandered across his belly. Scars from stab wounds decorated a spot just below his left knee cap, as did two on his right thigh, while his left hand bore the mark where a man had pinned it to a seachest.[1]

One Bell

Life at sea took a terrible toll on sailors. The average seaman sailed until his body could stand no more, which in the waning days of the Age of Sail might last just a few years. Sailors might suffer disfigurements such as missing digits or limbs, bad kneecaps that never properly healed after breaking, and scars caused by lacerations, frostbite, or any number of other things. Disease, too, left its mark, such as the loss of teeth from scurvy.[2]

Seamen looked startlingly different from landsmen. Covered with far more disfigurements than the average laborer, men of the sea walked with a rolling gait and wore clothes designed for their trade, usually consisting of loose-fitting shirts, caps, and white duck trousers made of tarpaulin, "a water-proof cloth impregnated with tar ... [that] was just about the first truly water-resistant fabric and so was often used by old-time sailors for [their] ... articles of clothing." The British and Americans often referred to sailors by the nickname "Jack Tar," an appellation that derived from the fact they coated their clothes with this substance as well as the rigging, wood, and canvas of their ships.[3] Landsmen tended to refer to all men of the sea generically as "sailors" without realizing that while naval enlistees did not mind this sobriquet, those in the merchant marine did, much preferring the appellations "seaman" or "mariner."

In the early days of the United States few except sailors had tattoos. Tattoo artists used India or Chinese ink if available, gunpowder and even urine if not. To make a tattoo, an artist stretched the subject's skin tight, dipped a needle into ink, and pricked it into its recipient's dermis. It usually took multiple sessions to finish and caused much "pain and swelling" in the bargain. Some did not survive the ordeal: dirty needles could cause infections or diseases such as tetanus.[4]

Most historians believe the modern association of the sailor with the tattoo dates to Captain Cook's discovery of Tahiti and New Zealand during his first scientific voyage to Oceana from 1769 to 1770 when he and his men first saw tattoos covering the local people. Many of his crewmen, commoners and gentlemen alike, received them. Cook also returned home with two tattooed Tahitians named Omai and Tupaia. Cook rendered the Tahitian word for this skin decoration—*tatau*—as "tattow," causing it to enter the English lexicon as "tattoo."[5]

One scholar, Ira Dye, traced the tradition of Western sailors receiving tattoos all the way back to the ancient world, making the compelling argument that those of this profession never gave up the practice during its lull in the Middle Ages. Certainly the Romans and Greeks tattooed slaves and criminals, and the Byzantines used tattoos to mark their soldiers to make desertion more difficult. The practice fell out of favor in medieval Europe because the Roman Catholic Church forbade its use. This did not stop those who went to Jerusalem during the era of the Crusades from getting one to show they had visited.[6]

Professional seamen of all races chose an eclectic mix of images for their tattoos, often ones that reflected their politics, religion, or important symbols. Some came home with Polynesian designs because they looked pretty. Naked women also proved quite popular. The U.S. Navy passed an ordinance in 1908 banning this last type of image on enlistees, creating an unexpected boom in the tattoo business because merchant mariners who wanted to enlist had to first stop at a parlor to have clothes put on their nudes.[7]

The electric tattoo machine made tattooing much easier. This invention, created by Samuel O'Reilly in 1891 and based on Thomas Edison's 1876 autographing machine, speeded the process up considerably. A former seaman, O'Reilly called himself "Professor" and opened a tattoo parlor in New York in 1875 in which he trained apprentices. As the popularity of tattooing increased, its artists created "flash books" containing all their designs so clients could look through them before deciding what they wanted. The earliest known examples of these came from travelling tattoo artists C.H. Fellowes and C.V. Brownwell and date to around 1900.[8]

Two Bells

Two types of merchant ships existed: the liner and the tramp. Liners took passengers and mail along set routes from which they rarely deviated. Tramps hauled mainly cargo and went wherever they could find or sell it. Because these latter vessels touched a wide array of places all around the globe, they tended to carry crews that included a diverse range of races and ethnicities.[9] When, as an example, Anton Otto Fischer, a Bavarian, signed onto the Welsh-owned, Liverpool-based ship *Gwydyr Castle* at Hamburg for $15 a month, only one other German joined him. Of the others who took a berth on her, one came from Finland, one from Sweden, and one from France. Two hands jumped ship at Cardiff and an Englishman and Irishman replaced them. A black man from Argentina served as the ship's cook.[10]

No one on board thought much of the presence of this last man. Despite the notorious second-class citizenship given to blacks in the Age of Shanghaiing, they often served as professional seamen. During the years in which slavery thrived in the American South, the United States produced a surprisingly large number of black mariners. In the early nineteenth century along the Atlantic Coast they made up about 20 percent of the approximately 100,000 sailors working there.[11]

A slave named Frederick Douglass—one of the greatest, if not the greatest, of the abolitionist orators and writers—became familiar with the seafaring business in 1837 when his master rented him to Baltimore shipwright William Gardner. Here four white apprentices started a fight with Douglass. His dignity compelled him to hit back, an offense punishable by death under Maryland law. He fled to his master and explained the circumstances of the brawl. Although his master believed him, he nonetheless rented Douglass out once more, this time to a shipyard where he learned the trade of caulker. For this work he earned pay but his master took every last cent. Deeming this unacceptable, he decided to make his escape to freedom.[12]

Maryland required all free blacks to carry papers containing a detailed description of their physical characteristics. To escape, a slave often borrowed papers from a free black they resembled, then returned them in the mail upon reaching the safety of the North. Douglass borrowed a set from an acquaintance he dared not mention by name in his autobiographies for fear of a reprisal against this benefactor. Douglass' physical characteristics did not match the papers very well, so he disguised himself as a seamen, knowing their commonness in the South would allow him to move freely without attracting attention. If questioned, he felt confident of a successful bluff because he knew the parts of a ship as well as any professional mariner. On September 3, 1838, he boarded a train for Philadelphia. The conductor asked to see his papers. He replied that he never took them to sea. The conductor accepted this without fanfare and moved on. With that danger past, Douglass made his way to freedom, a status he would enjoy for the rest of his life.[13]

Many freed black men took up the life of a sailor because they had few other opportunities open to them. Skin color meant far less on board a ship than on land, although this did not cause racism to vanish altogether. Blacks rarely became officers, suffered worse hazing than whites, and experienced harsher punishments. Racial slurs abounded. Blacks usually wound up working in the nastiest jobs, especially as the ship's cook, although some earned more than their white counterparts because of their skill level. Others served as stewards, a position that

African American sailor (Library of Congress Prints and Photographs Division, Ball & Thomas Photographic Art Gallery, ca. 1861–1865).

called for the one who filled it to take charge of the stores, act as the captain's servant, and work on whatever part of the ship demanded his attention.[14]

At the peak of the whaling industry in the early to middle nineteenth century, many blacks signed onto whale ships, a process helped along when

Massachusetts, one of the centers of the industry, amended its state constitution to outlaw slavery in 1780, although blacks rarely did anything more than the lowliest of jobs on board. Native Americans also sailed in significant numbers on these vessels until drink and disease wiped most of them out.[15] In 1820 Native Americans made up about one-eighth of the whaling crews, while blacks and mulattoes consisted of somewhere between one-fourth and three-eighths. So many blacks took to this profession they formed significant communities in whaling centers such as New Bedford and Nantucket.[16] By 1861 the number of blacks serving on whalers numbered nearly three thousand.[17]

When the whaling brig *Alexander* departed from San Francisco for the Arctic in December 1890, she carried several black crewmen, including a third mate named Gabriel, two boat-steerers from the Cape Verde Islands, and a mulatto from Barbados. Before heading north, the *Alexander* sailed west to the Hawaiian Islands to pick up the captain. During this part of the voyage all officers assumed the duties of the next higher rank, allowing Gabriel to serve for a time as the second mate.[18]

Other minorities took berths in significant numbers as well. Between 1876 and 1906, many American shipping companies operating along the West Coast made extensive use of Chinese seamen, a move adding fuel to the anti–Chinese movement that prompted the passing of the Chinese Exclusion Act of 1882. This forbade all Chinese entry into the country for the following ten years save for those with a certificate, something rare and granted only to professionals and students. Because the measure did not remove those Chinese already living and working in America, their continued presence and willingness to accept low wages sparked white resentment, especially during the economic depression of the 1880s.[19]

Two San Francisco–based shipping companies, Pacific Mail and Occidental and Oriental Steamship, became well known for employing Chinese crews. Between 1876 and 1906, one estimate lists the combined number of Chinese employed by them at 80,523, although this count likely includes the same men multiple times because they frequently changed ships.[20] Reaction to their presence, both on land and at sea, culminated in 1885 when the city of Tacoma expelled them, an event repeated the following year in Seattle. Congress passed the even more draconian Geary Act in 1892, a law forbidding all Chinese from entering the country and forcing them to wear photo identification around their necks, something around 100,000 refused to do.[21]

Another oppressed class in America, women, also sailed on ships, some as members of the crew. Eleanor Creesy, wife of the infamous Captain Josiah Perkins Creesy, served as the navigator for her husband, a skill she had learned from her sea captain father.[22] Hattie Atwood Freeman also learned to sail from her sea captain father during a world-circumnavigating voyage from New York to Hobart, Tasmania, on the merchant bark *Charles Stewart.* Just seventeen, this petite five foot five girl initially suffered from terrible seasickness, but after this passed she learned seamanship. Her father offered to buy her a new black silk dress if she correctly answered sixty-seven questions about sailing and navigation, the number needed to qualify as a steamship captain. She passed.[23]

Because captains who went to sea on whale ships sometimes did not return for years at a time, a few brought their wives with them. Mary Brewster married a whale ship captain in 1841 at the age of eighteen and found his lengthy separations so unbearable that four years into marriage she took to the sea with him and continued sailing with him for the rest of his career. The privilege of taking a wife and children on board did not extend to the other officers and certainly not to the hands.[24]

Some women sought to stay with their loved ones by disguising themselves as men and sailing with them as members of the same crew. Other women went to sea incognito for a lack of better economic opportunities. Anne McLean, born of poor Irish parents around 1829, found her stout stature allowed her to pass for a boy. She joined an East India Company ship twice. Back on land, she tried her hand at factory work, porting coal, and working in the fields but, disliking these trades, went to sea again. On the voyage back, though, someone saw through her disguise, forcing her to admit to being a woman.[25]

In 1882 Georgiana Leonard disguised herself as a young man and signed onto the whale ship *America* using the pseudonym George Weldon. She told the captain she had served in the Confederate cavalry. Her short temper soon got the best of her. In one incident she beat up the burly black cook who had caused her trouble. In another she tried to kill the second mate, Robert G. Smith, while under his command in a whaleboat. Tasked with rowing, she became tired and stopped for a rest. When he wacked her with an oar prompting her to resume, she responded by whipping out her knife with the intent of stabbing him. She failed because others in the boat subdued her. Back on board the *America* she faced being stripped to the waist and flogged as punishment for this act of mutiny, so to avoid this she revealed her identity. The incident did not deter her from sailing in disguise once more.[26]

One wonders how she and other women masquerading as men managed to keep their sex hidden so well. In his book *She Captains: Heroines and Hellions of the Sea,* David Cordingly pointed out that it took little effort for a woman to bind her breasts and don loose-fitting clothing, the sort mariners wore anyway. A woman relieving herself at the head drew little attention because men sat over the holes, too, when they needed to defecate. The intensity and amount of physical labor demanded each day may have stopped the menstrual cycle like it does with some female athletes. Even if this did not occur, no one would question the presence of bloody rags considering the large the number lacerations and a variety of ailments from which working hands suffered on any given day.[27]

Although culture, ethnicity, race and, in some cases, gender, as above, created differences and possible animosity among crews, one thing did unite them: an almost universal belief in maritime superstitions. Examples abound. Seeing a shark portended a bad voyage. Sharks that circled a ship sought the souls of the sick on board. Whirlpools contained spirits that a ship's crew could appease by throwing salt or bread into it. Seamen from the Shelton Islands believed mermaids could sing up a storm.[28] Davy Jones' Locker had a darker meaning than just being the place to which men went when they drowned. "Davy" represented the devil and "Jones" Jonah, the Biblical figure swallowed by a whale. The evil souls within the locker tortured any sailor unlucky enough to end up there.[29]

Superstitions provided mariners with hope of overcoming the over-whelming number of dangers sailing presented. Some seamen, as an example, had a pig tattooed on top of their left foot and a rooster on their right to keep them from drowning, an idea based on the belief that pigs and roosters escaping from a sinking ship always got to shore first. Naked or scantily clad female mastheads had the purpose of quieting the water. Whistling helped to bring a breeze during a calm or reduce the wind during a storm.[30]

Ghost stories such as that of the Flying Dutchman complemented super-stitions. In one version of this tale, the evil captain of the *Voltigeur,* a man who believes neither in God nor the supernatural, refuses to head for a safe harbor during a storm at the Cape of Good Hope. A goddess comes out of the water and curses him so he can never again enter a port. The Dutchman thereafter only appears in heavy seas with the goal of leading another ship to her doom. If the Dutchman's captain sends the master of another vessel a letter, the recipient will go mad and his ship fly violently into the air.[31]

Three Bells

A ship's victuals and water went into wooden casks for storage, a poor receptacle into which to place them. Meat quickly went rancid and bread became infested with bugs. Sailors joked that such contamination caused biscuits to walk on their own. Fresh water became tainted with algae and other unwanted contaminants. Even after the introduction of refrigeration and industrial can-ning, shipowners continued to purchase subpar victuals to save money.[32]

Pollutants infected just about everything. A seaman on the whaler *Atkins*

Adams, William Abe, reported finding molasses filled with between two to three inches of cockroaches, making it an unappetizing, smelly muck. Contaminated food caused many crews to starve.[33] Whaling captain George Fred Tilton, who had worked his way up through the ranks and so remembered the food he ate while still a hand, wrote in his autobiography that a mariner's daily fare consisted of "salt beef, salt pork ... flour, hard tack [a type of biscuit], molasses, tea, coffee, and potatoes. The beef was saltier than Lot's wife, and had to be soaked in a 'steep-tub' overnight before it was cooked." Once a week the crew received a ration of soft bread.[34]

Needless to say, seamen tried to supplement their diet with any fish or birds they could catch. The rare "treat" came in the form of duff, a mixture of flour, lard and water that sometimes had raisins or plums added. Duff usually appeared on Sundays, the only day seamen got off, or at least the one on which they needed to do only the minimum to keep the ship operating and sailing on course.[35]

Hattie Freeman recalled no instances of bad food, and in fact had fond memories of its quality and variety. As the captain's daughter, she either had no knowledge of the food fed to the crew, decided only to record what she had personally eaten, or her father served better fare to his men than the norm, not an unheard of thing. She ate donuts, apple dumplings, a large variety of canned meats, cheese, assorted vegetables, bacon, butter, smoked herring, and plum duff.[36]

She also noted that the medicine cabinet included a large variety of liquors and lime juice, the last of which cured scurvy, which is caused by a lack of vitamin C. The disease's symptoms include lethargy, rough, dry skin, wounds that will not heal well, and, after about thirty weeks, swelling of the gums, which turn purple and cause teeth to fall out. A good dose of vitamin C, or ascorbic acid, cures it. Historical evidence suggest the disease did not afflict ancient European mariners and became a problem only during the Renaissance when ships began sailing for months at a time without stopping.[37]

As early as 1601, some western Europeans knew citrus fruit could cure this ailment although they had no idea why. Sir James Lancaster prevented outbreaks by feeding his men lemon juice on a long voyage from Britain to Sumatra. The cure also made its way into a 1617 book by John Woodall, *The Surgeon's Mate,* for use by the East India Company, although such knowledge did northern European seafaring nations little good because they lacked ready access to citrus fruit. The Dutch corporation Vereenigde Oost-indische Compagnie tried to remedy this by growing citrus orchards on its way stations at St. Helena and the Mauritius Islands.[38]

European navies, with their large complements of crews, did not adopt it even after it became common knowledge that citrus fruit could prevent scurvy. In 1754 a Scottish naval doctor named James Lind published *A Treatise of the Scurvy* outlining an effective treatment. Despite these works, the Royal Navy refused to use known cures until 1795, when an administrator named Gilbert Blane arranged for the issue of lemon juice on all naval vessels. Within twenty years scurvy virtually disappeared from the service, although it did crop up from time to time. At least until the end of the nineteenth century, it remained a problem on merchant ships.[39]

On March 22, 1897, the *T.F. Oakes* came into New York Harbor with twelve of the her eighteen crewmen, including the captain, incapacitated by scurvy. This ship's tale began 259 days earlier when she left Hong Kong for America on July 4, 1896, with a crew of twenty-four. Her master, Captain Reed, decided that rather than take the normal route into the Atlantic via the Cape of Good Hope, he would sail west with the expectation of picking up "more favorable trade winds." About six days later, a typhoon hit, springing his ship's fore and main topmasts. Before he could get her into a port to make repairs, a second typhoon hit, forcing her to endure another twenty-four days of foul weather. Once out of it, Reed decided to make for the Cape of Good Hope after all.[40]

While on this new course the wind died, becalming his ship for several weeks, during which time six men died. The food started to run low and scurvy struck nearly everyone, forcing Reed's wife to take the wheel. The first mate died and the second became incapacitated with painfully swollen feet. The *Oakes* shined her blue distress signal as she approached Philadelphia, attracting the attention of the British oil tanker *Kasbek*. The vessel's chief officer, C.P. Helshem, took three men in a boat to get within speaking distance, then asked if the *Oakes* needed a tow. She did. Helshem asked, "Where to, and what will you pay?" To this extortion the *Oakes* agreed. The *Kasbek* towed the *Oakes* to New York City. Once docked, those in need of treatment went to the Marine Hospital on Staten Island.[41]

Scurvy presented seamen with just one of many hardships and miseries. Crews chronically suffered from general malnutrition, overwork, exposure to foul weather, and a lack of hygiene. They lived in the cramped quarters of the forecastle, usually located beneath the main deck. This looks roomy when empty but becomes quite cramped with a full complement of men. Here no one had privacy and little in the way of personal possessions except for what would fit in a sea chest. About this the New York agent for the Atlantic Coast Seamen's Union commented: "According to the law, a man is allowed [a space of] 6 feet long, 2 feet 8 inches wide, and 6 feet 3 inches high. It is larger than a coffin, but smaller than a grave."[42]

Filth prevailed, made worse in the first few weeks of a new voyage by vomiting caused by seasickness. Fleas, bedbugs, and other vermin infested every sleeping place, including the aftercabin in which the officers slept. Whaling ships often had a problem with excessive numbers of cockroaches and rats. In cold conditions the forecastle had no heat and, when the hatch closed during foul weather, the only light came from an oil lamp. Conditions such as these motivated many men to jump ship at the first opportunity or caused them to leave tall ships altogether in favor of the better conditions found on steamers, which had electricity to power lightbulbs and provide heat.[43]

Work on tall ships involved a daily, unending effort of a backbreaking nature. Never did a seaman on duty have a moment of rest. Officers allowed no hand to stand idle, usually not much of an issue since ships rarely lacked for things that needed to be done, such as swabbing the decks or tarring cables and canvas. On the rare occasions when the crew completed its tasks for the day, officers usually created work, such as having the men scrape rust off chains.[44]

Two things brought order and routine to the mariner: the watch and the bell. At a voyage's start the crew divided into two groups known as the "starboard watch" and "port watch" (except on whalers, in which case they used the older term for the left side of the ship, "larboard"). The first mate commanded the port watch and the second the starboard. Those on it worked on the main deck and aloft. Watches changed every four hours except between one and four in the afternoon, at which time all men worked on deck in a "watch and watch," really a four-hour shift during which each one worked only two hours so as to create a total of seven to make it so neither had to work the same shifts each day. On some ships this switch, known as the dogwatch, ran it so that one two-hour shift came before and another after a full four-hour one. During the night shift the men did not have to labor as hard as they did during the day.[45]

The ship's bell rang at half-hour intervals to mark the time, the number of strikes increasing until they reached eight. The count reset every four hours. Eight bells represented four, eight, and twelve o'clock in the morning or night. Even bells marked the hour, and odd ones the half-hour.[46]

Such routine contributed to the monotony and boredom at sea, exacerbated by the repetition of work and a lack of diverse company.[47] To help alleviate it, the men amused themselves with a variety of activities. Some whittled away their time with scrimshaw, an engraving usually carved into walrus tusk, whalebone or whale teeth. To get this last, whalers sometimes towed the jawbone of a sperm whale behind the ship for about a month, then dried it out on deck to loosen the teeth, which they stored in brine. Those who wanted to etch a particularly detailed picture preferred walrus tusk.[48]

Although scrimshaw subjects often had a nautical theme, they also included portraits of famous politicians, military figures, and (not surprisingly for men at sea for months and years at a time) nude women. Those who wanted to add color used dyes and ink. The often breathtaking detail and craftsmanship of these works certainly makes many worthy of display in the world's greatest art museums. Some excellent scrimshaw sculptures exist as well. One artist created a pie crimper that, when rolled across the dough, said, "Good Pie Watt Made." Others produced baskets, cane ends, the canes themselves, a miniature tripod table, and a miniature oil lamp. Seamen also created sculptures with ropes.[49]

They took much pleasure in smoking, often keeping tobacco in their hats. If it ran out, some tore out the lining and chewed it, thus inspiring the phrase "I'll eat my hat!"[50] In the nineteenth century, most sailors smoked pipes rather than cigarettes or cigars. Presuming their stock did not run out altogether, tobacco tended to dry and lose its flavor quickly at sea. To compensate, sailors boiled it in brines of sugar or rum to keep it moist and give it flavor, then removed and compressed it into a block. Once it was dried, they cut it up for smoking or chewing, the origin of the term "Navy cut."[51] Tobacco also served as a means of exchange, particularly when betting on card games, but this caused so much trouble captains often forbade bringing cards on board.[52]

Prohibitions like this undoubtedly included another favorite of the sailor out to sea for a long period of time: pornographic images. Although illegal in many ports and nations, acquisition of them did not pose a great problem. In New York City, as an example, a man could find peddlers on the docks selling lewd illustrations, usually sold in the guise of something else, such as tracts on moral reform. The introduction of cheap photographs in France led to the creation of pornographic stereoscopic images in 1857. These prints contained the same image side by side that, when viewed through a stereoscope—a device not unlike the modern View-Master—took on a three-dimensional aspect. The compact size of such images made them easily concealable.[53]

Seamen also entertained one another. Some brought on board and played musical instruments. Because of the space constraints of the forecastle, mariners favored compact instruments such as harmonicas, fiddles, penny whistles, pipes, and the concertina, an instrument invented by a fellow named Sir Charles Wheatstone in 1829 that resembled, and worked similar to, an accordion. As musicians played, others "sang and danced" along with them. Some crews put on theatrical productions, although certainly with few, if any, props or scenery.[54]

Seamen also liked to read. Those who could not often asked, or paid, others to read for them or to teach them this skill.[55] Libraries created specifically for seamen existed, although the benevolent societies that founded them usually had the underlying motive of bringing God, and therefore morality, to sailors. The American Seamen's Friends Society, as an example, introduced floating libraries in 1837 on a ship leaving from New York City. By the end of the next year their libraries traveled on eighty ships, but the system abruptly ended. It restarted in 1858.[56]

At first the man in charge of the libraries' collection development, John S. Pierson, favored mainly religious works, such as John Bunyan's novel *Pilgrim's Progress*. He later aimed more on recreational reading with a focus on humanity, culture, and general knowledge, although works with religious themes and instruction never completely disappeared. For poetry Pierson preferred William Cowper and Longfellow. The secular works of which he approved had to have a moral message and included *Ben-Hur, A Christmas Carol,* and *Uncle Tom's Cabin.* Pierson wisely made sure books came in different languages to cater to the international makeup of crews.[57]

Four Bells

Many dangers existed for those who sailed upon the world's oceans, seas, and great lakes. Water presented one. A leaky vessel whose crew could not pump water out faster than it came in meant abandoning ship. Presuming an affected vessel had enough boats on board to accommodate everyone, they still could not carry sufficient supplies for a trip that might, depending on the location, span thousands of leagues and last a month or more.[58]

George C. Bugbee, who sailed as a hand on the merchant ship *Premier,* nearly learned this firsthand. While on course for the Cape of Good Hope during a voyage from Asia to America, his ship sprang a bad leak. Her captain ordered the crew to man the pumps, sure he could make Simonstown. The leak worsened and the seas became heavy. The pumps could not keep up, so the captain had casks thrown overboard to lighten the load and thus raise the ship in the water. This worked, but barely. At Simonstown he had to have the cargo completely unloaded to effect repairs.[59]

Few things caused more fear on board a ship than fire. The ship's dried wood and the tar that coated ropes and canvas acted as the perfect tinder when the ship went up in flames. This happened to the cargo vessel *Logan.* On December 19, 1832, while sailing from Savannah to Liverpool with a cargo of cotton bales, she caught fire, the flames making their way into the hold. The men tried to throw the bales overboard but abandoned the effort when the smoke started to overwhelm them. They fled to the deck, closed the hatches, and drilled holes below the ship's waterline with the hope that the water would extinguish the fire. This, too, failed. By morning the main deck had caught on fire, so the crew abandoned ship and took refuge in a long-boat.[60]

During heavy seas no one person held life and death in his hands more than the helmsman, always a hand rather than an officer on a merchant ship. So terrible did this task become during foul weather that the time served at this post, called a "trick," decreased from two hours to one. In a particularly hard gale two men took the wheel at once to keep it under control.[61] Turning at the wrong moment in heavy seas could cause the swamping of the main deck, sweeping anyone not clinging onto something into the sea. For this reason the captain sometimes strapped the helmsman to the wheel to keep *him* from washing out to sea. Few who went overboard survived.[62]

Turning wrong into a wave or the wind could also make the ship violently pitch, yaw or roll, potentially causing men working aloft to fall.[63] The log of the merchant ship *Chelsea* noted that on December 10, 1839, a man fell from the maintop. Although another aloft seaman noticed, no one below could hear him yelling because of a gale, and by the time he climbed down to the deck to report it eight minutes later, no one could do a thing for the victim.[64] Officers, too, sometimes went overboard in this way. On the whaler *Sharon* the second mate went over the side, disappearing forever.[65]

One helmsman just getting off duty lost his balance when the ship rolled and caused him to fall onto the edge of an open circular tin, its sharp edge scalping him. A friend, Hiram Bailey, rushed him to the captain's cabin for surgery. The captain, performing this duty, told Bailey to go back to the deck and recover his friend's scalp, which he did. The captain sewed it back on and the helmsman fully recovered.[66]

Five Bells

During the Age of Shanghaiing pirates presented a very real threat to European and American seamen working in Asian waters. The number and boldness of Chinese pirates expanded in the late eighteenth and early nineteenth centuries as their nation suffered great economic and political upheavals. With the Chinese navy in disarray, these pirates prospered, boldly targeting opium runners because they carried such valuable cargo. The first known attack of this type occurred in 1783.[67]

In 1806 a hydrographer in the Royal Navy, Alexander Dalrymple, estimated that about 200 pirate vessels operated along China's southern coast and another 400 to 500 did so off the island of Hainan Dao. Chinese pirates also based themselves on an island south of the Zhu (Pearl) River Delta called by the Portuguese Ladrão, which in their language meant "thief." English speaking people corrupted this into "Ladron," and it entered the English language as "ladrone."[68]

Many ladrones lived and operated on the island of Macao, from which they launched attacks on American ships bound for the port of Guangzhou. In 1802 the brig *Ohio* scared some of them off by firing grapeshot at them, but this did not always work.[69] In May 1817 Chinese pirates captured the Baltimore-based ship *Wabash*, killing several crewmen and robbing her "of $7,000 in specie ... [as well as] thirty-five cases of opium." Chinese authorities caught the pirates and returned the specie, but refused to pay repartitions for the illegal opium.[70]

Possibly one of the most detailed—and certainly exaggerated—accounts of a Chinese pirate attack came from a Scot named Robert Fortune, the man who disguised himself as an ethnic Chinese (a Han) to aid in his infiltration of China so he could steal the secrets of cultivating and processing tea as well as the plants themselves. After spending time in China's southern regions, he decided to head north to Shanghai, a trip he figured would work best if he sailed to the city of Fuzhou in Fujian Province, and from there up the Min River because this waterway connected to other navigable rivers leading to his destination. To that end he found passage on a junk headed to Fuzhou that, upon reaching the city, would head up the river to Nanping.[71]

The Chinese government would not allow merchant ships to arm themselves against pirates, probably out of fear the merchant ships might one day turn these weapons on its navy. This left China's merchant marine defenseless against ladrones. Nor could Chinese ships legally carry foreign passengers. Fortune speculated that the captain who agreed to transport him had done so because Fortune possessed personal firearms that might prove useful against pirates. The junk on which Fortune sailed joined a convoy of 170 merchant ships whose captains did not want to pay the Chinese navy for an escort. A contrary wind kept the fleet from reaching the Min's mouth for several weeks, causing it to break up into groups of three or four and keeping them about fifty or sixty miles from their destination. During this time Fortune came down with a nasty fever from which he nearly died.[72]

One day the captain and pilot came to his quarters and begged him to come to the deck with his guns to fend off an impending pirate attack. Fortune, disbelieving this and still seriously ill, nonetheless loaded his weapons and came up on deck. From here he saw more pirates than he and the crew could possibly fight off; yet knowing his possible fate if apprehended (probably death), he decided to make a stand, prompting the reluctant crew to do so as well. They gathered up stones—probably from the ship's ballast—to throw at incoming pirates.[73]

Most ladrones used junks, the largest vessel the Chinese built at this time and readily identifiable by a large rudder and mast made from a single piece of wood and often armed with "small naval cannon and swivel guns." Some ladrones used a *tymung,* a vessel with both sails and "forty or more sweeps (long oars)."[74] Their ships doubled as homes and often carried family members. Ladrones rarely used their cannon because they lacked the practice and skill to employ them with much effect, instead preferring to run alongside their prey and throw upon its deck stink bombs made from earthenware pots filled with gunpowder, gin, and charcoal.[75]

Fortune did not see these in use. Those who attacked his ship fired a broadside, which prompted all but three of the men on his ship to flee below. He convinced those who remained to stay on deck by threatening to shoot them if they tried to go below. He returned fire with a double-barreled gun when the pirate ship came within twenty yards, causing most of her crew to flee below. A second pirate junk approached, so Fortune fired at her as well, this time killing a helmsman. No other pirates molested his ship that day, although within the same week six more attacked. These, too, Fortune fended off with his firearms.[76]

Ladrones who caught western seamen often killed or tortured them unless they had some ransom value (and most did not).[77] Even those with worth might not necessarily escape harm. Ladrones, for example, outright killed Captain Robert Funter of the *Leebow* in 1795. They likewise frequently threatened the life of, and tried to press into service, a British officer named Robert Glasspoole of the East Indiaman *Marquis of Ely.* This incident began in September 1809 during a time when the *Marquis* stood anchored off an island in the South China Sea. Her commander, Captain Kay, ordered Glasspoole to take a boat to Macao to procure a pilot. He and seven armed seamen took a cutter on the twelve-mile journey there without incident. Finding a qualified candidate, they started back but got lost when squalls and a thick fog moved in. At one point pirates chased after them, but their furious rowing effected an escape. By now the boat had started to take on water, so Glasspoole sought refuge with what looked like several fishing boats. Only upon reaching them did he realize they belonged to pirates.[78]

Having captured Glasspoole and thrown him into chains, the ladrones commanded him to write a ransom letter to Captain Kay demanding $100,000 for his release. They warned him that if he refused they would kill him and his men. Glasspoole convinced the pirates to lower the ransom to $70,000, knowing Kay would never agree to the higher sum. As the letter went to Macao via boat, the pirates sailed through the night to another bay where the ladrone captain brought the Westerners to his admiral. Having managed to intercept Glasspoole's letter to his captain, the admiral commanded Glasspoole to write a new one asking for a "loan" of $70,000. Glasspoole told the admiral if the ransom issue was not resolved soon, Captain Kay would just sail away. The admiral retorted if that happened, he would either make his captives fight for him or put them to death.[79]

The admiral commanded one of seven massive squadrons, each with its own colored flag, that belonged to a pirate fleet under the command of Zhèng Yī Sǎo (frequently transliterated as "Cheng I Sao"), one of the most notorious Chinese pirates in the history of that people. Born around 1775, she became a prostitute and in that capacity met the pirate captain Zhèng Yī, whom she married in 1801. Her husband ruled the ladrone fleet in the province of Guangdong, which "by 1805 ... included 400 junks and between 40,000 and 60,000 pirates."[80] Each squadron had "a different sea lane to patrol, usually located near the squadron-leader's home base." Zhèng Yī commanded the Red Flag Squadron.[81]

At one point Zhèng Yī took his fleet to Vietnam and became embroiled in its internal affairs. Around 1620 this nation had split into separate northern and southern kingdoms, the latter being ruled by the Nguyen family. In 1868 the debasement in the southern kingdom's copper coinage with tin caused massive inflation and made food too expensive to purchase, causing a famine. One of the southern kingdom's tax collectors, Tay Son a Ho Nhac, got caught skimming off his collections to pay off gambling debts, so he fled into the mountains to escape apprehension. There he became a true Robin Hood. This so endeared him to the poor they became his soldiers when he launched a rebellion against the ineffective king in 1771.[82]

Taking the name of his mother, Nguyen (Ho Nhac had bad connotations because it reminded people of the usurper Ho Qui Ly), he became known as Tay Son Nguyen, the surname being the same as the ruling royal family's. He, with the support of his two brothers, successfully conquered the northern and southern kingdoms, creating a reunited nation. Upon his death in 1793, his realm started to crumble, giving the last survivor of the legitimate ruling family of southern Vietnam, Nguyen Phuc Anh, the chance to start a counterrevolution. Lacking sufficient forces, he hired Zhèng Yī and other pirates to fight for him.[83]

By 1802 Nguyen ruled all of Vietnam. No longer needing his pirate mercenaries, he stopped paying them, prompting Zhèng Yī to return to southern China in July of that year.[84] Upon his death in 1807—possibly he washed overboard during a typhoon—Zhèng Yī's wife took over his pirate fleet. This she accomplished in part by marrying her husband's loyal lieutenant, Zhāng Bǎozǎi, a man kidnapped by ladrones at the age of fifteen.[85]

An excellent organizer and businesswoman, she created "penal sanctions as well as elaborate provisions for sharing booty," expanded protection and extortion rackets to include the lucrative salt trade, and kept meticulous records of the capture and sale of plunder. She required the villages along several southern rivers to pay annual protection money. Those who defied her did so at their own peril. When, for example, a village on the Zhu River refused to pay in 1809, she unleashed a hoard of pirates who overwhelmed the village's meager defenses and burned it to the ground. Her men hanged the heads of eighty inhabitants from a banyan tree as a warning to others with notions of defiance.[86]

Glasspoole witnessed two similar incidents. The first occurred when his kidnappers took him up an unnamed river on an extortion cruise. Along the way they encountered a town that refused to pay its tribute of 10,000 Spanish dollars. It negotiated a reduced payment of $6,000, pledging to hand this over when the pirates passed by on their way back. Upon their return, the pirates found themselves facing a couple of cannon erected by the townspeople. This did not deter the pirates from attacking and chasing those who resisted them into nearby hills. They killed or imprisoned those who could not escape, taking "two-hundred and fifty women and several children," and treated them cruelly. Those who had fled into the hills had to pay for their kin's safe release.[87]

Not long after this, a fisherman delivered a letter from Captain Kay containing his reply to the ransom demand. He commanded Glasspoole to offer $3,000, giving him permission to go as high as $4,000 but not more than that. The ladrone admiral considered this amount too little and again threatened to kill Glasspoole and his men unless Kay paid what he demanded. While pondering that, the admiral combined his force with the Black Squadron for another river cruise to collect protection money. Along the way the combined force encountered a defiant town, this one defended by a small fort and several vessels belonging to the Chinese navy. The ladrone admiral demanded Glasspoole and his men fight for him. Glasspoole refused despite the threat of losing his life over it. The admiral asked if he and his men would at least commit to assisting with the firing of the ship's cannon. To this Glasspoole agreed, but unfortunately one of his subordinates died during the battle.[88]

As the pirates emerged from the river back into the bay from which they had come, they saw a flotilla of ships from the Chinese navy accompanied by a few Portuguese vessels blockading their way out into the open sea. A nine-day action ensued during which Glasspoole came under fire and narrowly escaped death twice from passing cannonballs. The Chinese navy attempted to burn the pirate fleet with eight fire ships—vessels filled with straw and set alight with the idea of burning any ships they touched—but these failed to reach their target, the ladrones intercepting and towing them to shore. In the

The heads of executed pirates hang over this wall in China (Library of Congress Prints and Photographs Division, publisher/creator unknown, 1900).

end the pirates prevailed, chasing their enemy away without losing a single ship. This incident only reinforced what most Westerners already knew at this time: the Chinese navy could do nothing about the ladrones.[89]

Zhèng Săo threatened Guangzhou itself in 1809. To defend it, the Chinese borrowed a British vessel, the *Mercury,* manning her mainly with Americans. They also acquired the temporary use of six Portuguese men-of-war, but even this modern technology could not stop the pirates. Admitting defeat, the Chinese government tried a different approach. It offered the pirates amnesty if they surrendered. Săo boldly visited the governor of Guangzhou to negotiate this. She agreed that in return for breaking up her fleet, she and her men would retain any booty they had gathered *and* earn ranks in the Chinese military. The governor consented. She decommissioned her fleet and retired, dying in peace at the age of sixty in 1844.[90]

Glasspoole never mentioned Săo, so one must presume he did not meet her, although he did report initially sailing with the Red Squadron, which her husband had once commanded. On December 2, 1809, he received a letter from a Lieutenant Maugh, the commander of the East India Company's cruiser *Antelope,* to inform Glasspoole he possessed the ransom. This he would present to the ladrones in whatever way Glasspoole could arrange. Glasspoole replied with some brief instructions.[91]

The ladrones transferred their prisoners to a gunboat that sailed within a few miles of the *Antelope*. From this boat several pirates took a launch to retrieve the payment. The ladrone admiral planned to release his prisoners upon his boat's return, but a ship belonging to the Chinese navy appeared and gave chase, so the ladrone fled before doing so. The next morning he examined the ransom, which consisted of "two bales of superfine cloth; two chests of opium; two casks of gunpowder ... a telescope," plus the requested amount of Spanish dollars. Although he complained he had not received a brand new telescope, he loaded his prisoners into two boats that took them to the *Antelope* and freedom.[92]

Six Bells

While indentured servitude and other hardships made life as a professional merchant mariner one of the worst career options in the world during the Age of Shanghaiing, this ought not diminish the fact that other people suffered conditions just as bad if not worse. Chattel slaves, for example, did not regain their freedom at the end of their usefulness but instead died in bondage. Mariners lucky enough to retire at least retained the dignity of doing so as free men. Although the Civil War had supposedly ended slavery once and for all in America, it really had not. Many of its states still had statutes of artificers on their books that, where enforced, compelled a man capable of working to do so or he would face imprisonment or a fine, and never mind if the economy had collapsed and he could not find work. Such laws existed for the sole purpose of giving powerful business interests the ability to control their labor forces and ensure that those at the bottom of the social ladder remained there.[93]

Workers' strikes horrified employers as well as local and state authorities so much they reacted with draconian measures. In 1880, for example, former slaves working on sugar plantations in the South demanded higher wages by going on strike and threatening to head to Kansas if they did not receive them. They wanted a raise from seventy-five cents to one dollar a day. Plantation owners had them arrested for trespassing. The next year 10,000 workers, 90 percent of them black, went on strike. Backed by the union Knights of Labor, which had started in 1869, this standoff ended when the militia arrived and started gunfights with the strikers.[94]

Corporations in the South leased prisoners from chain gangs "to depress the general level of wages and also to break strikes." In 1891 the Tennessee Coal Mining Company tried to get its workers to sign an "iron-clad contract" committing them to never strike, take their pay in company-issued script, and give up their right to weigh coal, this last demand a serious issue because at this time mines paid men by the pound rather than hourly or daily wages. The men refused, so the company had them evicted and replaced them with chain gang labor. The workers freed 500 convicts and won the right not to sign the contract.[95]

Most American mining companies did everything possible to lower their workers' incomes so as to increase profits. They built a mining camp, or possibly a somewhat better settlement, and compelled all workers to live in them, and for this privilege the men paid rent. To ensure such dependency, companies refused to hire anyone who owned a home. Their stores offered the only place in which miners could purchase goods (at inflated prices) using the company script, which also covered rent, utilities, school fees, and taxes. Deductions often exceeded the amount earned. To remedy this, miners had to purchase necessities on credit, throwing them into even deeper debt.[96]

Miners often died or found themselves incapacitated because of the many dangers their work presented, including cave-ins, explosions, and deadly gases. In such cases their loved ones faced immediate eviction, often with as little as ten days' notice. The mining company used local law enforcement officials or in-house security to enforce this and to suppress union organization. The Pittsburgh Coal Company, for example, spent more than $670,000 in two years to employ more than 300 policemen for this purpose.[97] Small wonder miners formed secret societies such as the infamous Molly Maguires—the violent Irish-American union movement—to fight such oppression with deadly violence.

3

Rebellion on the Open Water

The seamen of the whaler *Sharon* out of Fairhaven, Massachusetts, chafed under the brutality of its captain, Howes N. Norris, as their ship sailed through the Pacific. On December 13, 1841, Norris flogged his steward. On September 1, 1842, he became, for reasons never made clear, upset with a black man named John Babcock, and for this whipped him about three dozen times. Thereafter he decided to dress his subordinate's recently scalded foot, but while doing so started to kick him in the face and temples.[1]

He told Babcock to fill a 100-gallon tub with water. As Babcock did this, Norris continuously hit him across the back with a whale-line (a heavy rope), demanding he go faster. Once the tub was filled, he ordered Babcock to wash the bulwarks. As Babcock did this, Norris continued hitting him on the back with the whale-line, causing Babcock to fall off the larboard side of the try-works. Norris commanded him to get up, but he could not. Norris grabbed his subordinate and made him stand up, then realized he would not live long. He told his officers to get a blanket to sew around the dying man and, once Babcock expired, he had his corpse thrown overboard with no ceremony or anything else said.[2]

On November 25 of that same year, the second and third mates took two whaleboats out to hunt. After their departure, three crewmen slit Norris' throat with a spade. The steward frantically waved the signal flag that ordered the boats to return. The mutineers, whose number exceeded more than just those responsible for this killing, tried to get the ship under way, but they could catch no breeze. As the whaleboats closed in, the mutineers repulsed them with readily available missiles such as belaying pins, axes and spades.[3]

Under the cover of darkness the third mate, Benjamin Clow, made his way on board and to the ship's store of muskets. These he began to load. A mutineer happened upon him and attacked him with a cutlass, causing a minor wound. Clow wrested the cutlass from the man and tried to decapitate him with it. His blow missed and instead gouged his adversary's eye, killing him all the same. As other mutineers came to investigate, Clow picked up a loaded musket and killed one of them. Another slashed him with a spade, cutting his arm to the bone. Despite this, he fought his way free and called for the men in the boats to come aboard, which they did. The second mate arrived, grabbed a loaded musket, killed another mutineer, then dressed Clow's arm. The two officers and their loyal men cast the captain to the sea, then hunted down the remaining mutineers to retake control of the ship.[4]

One Bell

Some of the most notorious petty tyrants in the world served as sea captains, an assertion corroborated by the large number of accounts from those who served under them. The captain, or ship's master, had absolute power and answered to no one on board. Although legally responsible for the treatment of his crew, the captain often circumvented this by having his officers mete out harsh punishment because they did not have the same accountability. Ill-treated seamen rarely had recourse in the courts. A survey of cases against officers in a New York federal court, for example, showed that between 1835 and 1861 only three convictions resulted out of twenty-seven trials.[5]

The captain performed no manual labor, stood no watches, and did not even have to enforce his orders. This fell to the first officer, or chief mate, who acted as the boatswain, the man responsible for carrying out the captain's sailing orders. He also kept the ship's logbook and ledgers for the owners and insurers.[6] The second officer, or ship's mate, served as the pilot and navigator. He had a hybrid status of both officer and hand. He had "to go aloft to reef and furl the topsails, and to put his hands into the tar and slush ... with the rest" of the men. He lived in the officers' quarters and received wages "double those of a common sailor" but had to stay on deck at all times while on duty. The steward, the captain's servant, also had a similar hybrid status in that the first mate had no control over him, yet the steward had no authority over any others.[7]

Seamen not of the officer class had two official ratings: ordinary and able-bodied. Ordinary seamen possessed a limited ability to perform most shipboard work and could understand commands, although landsmen with no knowledge of seamanship whatsoever also received this designation. Able-bodied, or AB, seamen possessed a mastery of the specialized language of the sea as well as an ability to execute all on board tasks with great skill. Many vessels also carried ship's boys, apprentices who earned no salary. Theoretically they signed on to learn seamanship and perhaps one day become officers, but most just worked as servants performing menial tasks. A hand who worked his way into the officer class became known as the "bucko mate," the most despised person on board because he usually exhibited exceptional brutality toward the crew to maintain his authority over it, and to show he had become better than a mere hand.[8]

Officers often resorted to violence to control the crew. Of all the punishments they could inflict, few caused as much fear and physical damage as flogging, a sentence often employed for the most minor of offenses. The power of flogging gave captains the ability to force men to agree to anything.[9] A stenographer in Washington, D.C., named J. Ross Browne witnessed this during his time sailing on a whaling ship. One day the captain asked the helmsman the heading. He replied, "East." The captain accused him of lying, despite the fact the compass verified this assessment, and warned he would have this man flogged if he continued to contradict him. The helmsman told the captain what he wanted to hear. Browne commented, "There was no answering such an accusation as this; for, if the captain says black is white, it must be so."[10]

The process of flogging involved whipping a man using the cat-o'-nine-tails, a device that had nine cords with three knots tied near and at each strand's end, bound together by a rope or other type of handle and usually about "half a yard long."[11] Today flogging qualifies as a form of torture under international law. Its overuse once caused a mutiny on board the British vessel *Hermione*

This 1840 woodcut by Henry Howe shows flogging on board a ship (Library of Congress Prints and Photographs Division).

and nearly did on the American ship *Constitution,* an event that would surely have tarnished the latter's prestigious reputation.[12]

An officer had a man he intended to flog "seized up," a process in which someone stripped him to the waist to expose his back, then secured his wrists to the shrouds. The crewmen dared not complain because doing so qualified as an act of mutiny, and unless they wanted to take over the ship and become pirates, they had no choice but to watch this horror in silence.[13] Before the whipping began, someone placed a bullet in the victim's mouth to prevent him from screaming, the origin of the phrase "bite the bullet." Those who cried out became known as a "nightingale," another form of humiliation.[14]

One eyewitness who watched the flogging of a 20-year-old Welshman on board a ship of the Royal Navy for attempted desertion found the scene quite distasteful despite the fact he considered this victim "a blackguard." Upon the first strike, "the prisoner gave a smothered cry, and nine blood red streaks appeared on his back." The witness "turned [his] ... head aside, and ... saw ... the chief engineer bury his face in his hands." At the tenth lash "the Welshman uttered a yell that was heard by the sentry on the forecastle of the flagship, at anchor two miles off." A total of forty-eight lashes left the prisoner's back "a miserable, bleeding spectacle."[15]

Before the Civil War, American lawmakers debated the outlawing of flogging along Northern and Southern lines, their arguments for and against mimicking the debate over slavery. Some believed white men should not receive the same punishment as black slaves. Abolitionist Senator John Parker of New Hampshire frequently added amendments to prohibit corporal punishment on the high seas in naval appropriation bills because he felt it and slavery contradicted America's democratic and capitalistic principles. Southerners opposed the abolition of flogging in part because they used it as a means of punishment against more than slaves, but also such miscreants as thieves and counterfeiters. Southerners dominated the Navy's officer corps and, like many of the their states' legislators, feared eliminating it as a deterrent would result in an outbreak of insubordination. Despite this resistance, public outcry pushed Congress to outlaw the practice on the seas in 1850.[16]

But this failed to eliminate other types of shipboard brutality. Officers turned to alternatives such as withholding food, sleep deprivation, or giving a man harsh duties. Some captains ignored the prohibition altogether.[17] Hiram P. Bailey, shanghaied in the 1890s along with several others, including a Norwegian named Fenn, saw one of these substitute punishments firsthand. One day upon entering the forecastle he saw Fenn in a peculiar position: "And there, in the sombre [sic] light, he was swaying. Upon his bent head his blood-stained lips moved in torture. From the drooped corners of his distorted mouth blood oozed unheeded. And from his filmy eyes great tears were trickling down his pale, wan cheeks into his beard." This for committing the "crime" of trying to escape on a barge. Bailey feared he would suffer the same fate if he interfered, but he nonetheless kicked a piece of dunnage under the poor fellow's feet to help ease his suffering.[18]

Despite the horrors thus far chronicled, not all captains and officers acted as tyrannical sadists. Captain Joseph Bates of New Bedford, Connecticut, did not, and for this he gained the allegiance of his crew. Determined to retire from the sea to pursue other things, he set off on his final voyage out of New Bedford on August 9, 1827, as the master of the brig *Empress* with the commission of delivering goods to the east coast of South America. None of the men he commanded save for one had ever sailed with him, so they had no idea what type of discipline to expect.[19]

On their first night at sea he issued some standing orders. The men could address one another only by their first full names; he would have no one using "Bill," "Jack" or "Jim" on his ship. No man could swear (surely a difficult thing for a seaman to do). On Sundays they could not mend or wash their clothes (Sunday was the traditional time for this), although Bates promised to allow them to do so on Saturday night instead. While ashore, the men would appear in their best clothes. He forbade drinking both on board and ashore except alcohol used for medicinal purposes. He did not allow shore leave on Sundays. Each morning he held a brief prayer service, which he encouraged the men to attend.[20]

He administered no harsh punishments and treated the men so well that only one left the ship during the voyage. Upon their return to New Bedford, all hands decided to stay on board for the next voyage despite Bates' departure, possibly because they expected his replacement, Bates' younger brother Franklin, to have a similar command style. The elder Bates committed himself to the temperance movement, and later became an "itinerant preacher." He died in 1872.[21]

Two Bells

According to early U.S. law, any man who even questioned an order from an officer while at sea committed an act of mutiny.[22] This gave those beset by tyrannical officers no legal recourse while on board, forcing them, if they did not want to find themselves hanged, to find alternate means of resistance. Although illegal, some turned to sabotage. During the maiden voyage of the *Flying Cloud* under the command of the infamous Captain Josiah Perkins Creesy, two disgruntled men chose an out-of-sight place to drill holes through the main deck and the one below it. This would allow saltwater to seep through in heavy seas and thus foul the cargo in the hold, costing their hated captain money because he received a percentage of its sale. One day a man opened the door to the forecastle and water gushed out. An investigation resulted in the discovery of the holes. Creesy quickly caught the culprits and threw them into irons, although he kept them chained only for a day because he lacked a sufficient number of men and needed their services.[23]

If the entire crew became disgusted with the captain or his officers, they might show their displeasure by performing a work slowdown, often effected by decreasing the tempo of the sea chantey accompanying their work. A particularly peeved crew might even attempt a work stoppage, such as one did on the *Rambler* upon learning about the cancellation of shore leave. Under the law this defiance qualified as mutiny, but fortunately the first officer acquiesced to the crew's demands and work resumed.[24]

Desertion offered another form of resistance. In a friendly port this might work well, but for those who attempted it in some far-off place, things might not go as hoped. Take the story of Melville Kelsey, Thomas McGuire, Dave Barnes, and Edward A. Brailey. These four young Americans, all landsmen, signed onto the whale ship *Two Brothers* in New Bedford on June 13, 1854. They found it not to their liking, complaining about insufficient food, beatings, and a lack of clothes. In addition to this, Barnes had received a flogging for some sort of infraction in the forecastle, probably a fight.[25]

The *Two Brothers* sailed around Cape Horn into the Pacific. While in the Sea of Japan, the four stole a ship's boat on the night of June 26, 1855, and for six days made their way through a gale. They landed in Korea, a nation known at this time as the "Hermit Kingdom" because it had closed its borders to all foreigners save for the Chinese. The Americans made their way to a hospitable village in the vicinity of the city of Wŏnsan, located on the east coast of modern North Korea.[26] The Koreans treated the strangers well, but had no idea what to do with them. After twenty days, a local government official decided to send them north to China as part of Korea's annual tribute to that nation's emperor, a tradition that had started after China sent troops to Korea to save it from two Japanese invasions in the last decade of the sixteenth century. In gratitude, Korea's ruling dynasty, the Chosŏn, acknowledged the Ming emperor as its diplomatic superior and agreed to seek his permission before making any dynastic changes.[27]

In 1644 the foreign Manchus toppled the Ming Dynasty and replaced it with their own, the Qing. The new Machu emperor, Shunzhi, demanded the Koreans give him the same diplomatic acquiescence they had the Ming dynasty, but the Koreans refused. So Shunzhi invaded Korea with 100,000 troops, forcing its king to flee his sacked capital and, forty-five days later, to kowtow to the emperor. Thereafter the Koreans had to make biannual trips to Beijing to give the reigning Qing emperor his due recognition.[28]

A Korean official had the Americans put onto horses and sent them north under the charge of a messenger named Li Jin-yih. At this time bandits known for decapitating those they caught infested the border between Korea and China, but fortunately none molested the travelers. In Manchuria they met with an official Chinese escort. To get to Beijing, the combined group had to go over the Great Wall and through one of the most vicious peasant insurrections in Chinese history, the Great Taiping Rebellion, a conflict that had erupted in reaction to China's humiliating defeat by the British in the First Opium War.[29]

The rebellion started when a disgruntled and probably mad schoolmaster from Guangzhou named Hong Xiuquan became so disgusted by his inability to pass the civil service test he declared himself the second son of God and started a quasi–Christian Protestant missionary-inspired cult rebellion against the ruling Manchus. His movement escalated into a greater rebellion sparked by the economic woes caused by China's loss of the First Opium War. Grievances included ire against the government's mismanagement of the nation, excessive taxes and rents, and the Manchu rulers themselves, whom ethnic Chinese (the Han) did not like because of their masters' foreign origins.[30] "Red Turban" armies formed to restore the Ming Dynasty. Muslim separatists took over the province of Yunnan in 1855, while others of that faith revolted in the provinces of Shaanxi and Gansu in 1862. Peasant armies banded together and roamed freely. Secret societies appeared. As tends to happen during such turbulent times, nature also contributed. The Huang (Yellow) River flooded, causing terrible damage as well as the shifting of its path.[31]

Despite such dangers, the travelers made their way to Beijing without incident. There the Koreans turned their American guests over to the Russian Orthodox mission school, the Russians being the only Europeans with diplomatic relations and allowed to reside in the city. The Americans, not at liberty to see the city, stayed with the Russians for twenty days while their new hosts negotiated with the emperor and his court to figure out what to do with them. China's Board of Rites, the bureaucratic body that dealt with the Russians, recommended the Board of War issue the Americans an escort to take them to Shanghai. It also awarded them a stipend of silver for expenses, money, to the Americans' annoyance, they only received from their minders as needed.[32]

Their trip to Shanghai involved a wide variety of transportation types, including boats—one of which sailed upon the famous Grand Canal—wheelbarrows, carts, and by foot. The trip took them fifty-one or fifty-three days to complete. Although the Americans felt they had received too little water and food, it otherwise went well because they did not come across any fighting.[33] They entered Shanghai shortly after its liberation from a rebel group, the Short Swords, who had taken its walled city in 1853. The French, with the unofficial aid of the Americans and British, had helped the Chinese Imperial Army retake control of it in February 1855.[34]

The Americans' journey to get there from Korea took a total of six months. The deserters fell into the custody of the city's governor-general, I-liang, who, after a brief interrogation through an interpreter, turned them over to the American consul, Robert C. Murphy. Murphy debriefed them, then sent them home on the first available ship to America.[35]

Three Bells

Mutiny served as the most severe and desperate form of resistance against tyrannical captains and officers. Causes varied, although mutiny commonly occurred when the men felt they had not received enough food. Mutinies had serious social connotations for the Americans and British. In their merchant marines and navies, those who served as officers usually came from the upper classes, while the hands came from the lower ones. Crews that openly rebelled therefore represented the poor rising up against the rich, something few American and British newspapers wanted to report.[36]

Possibly the most famous mutiny in history occurred in 1789 and involved a ship of the Royal Navy, the HMS *Bounty,* during her voyage into the Pacific on a mission to bring breadfruit from Tahiti to Jamaica. Led by Fletcher Christian against commanding officer Lieutenant William Bligh, the mutineers forced their captain and eighteen men loyal to him into a twenty-three-foot boat. The exiles' food and drink consisted of "150lb. of bread, 16 pieces of pork, each piece weighing 2lb., 6 quarts of rum, 6 bottles of wine, [and] 28 gallons of water." For navigation Bligh had nothing more than a quadrant and compass. The boat did have a sail and oars, but with no wind to catch, its occupants had to use the latter to start their journey for the island of Tofua (part of modern Tonga), about ten leagues to the northeast of their starting position.[37] Here they stayed for several days gathering some food and water. Then the natives turned on them. During their escape the castaways lost one man and most of the food they had acquired. Back at sea Bligh did not stop again until reaching his final destination, the island of Timor, 3,618 miles away. This he accomplished in forty-one days without the loss of another man, an incredible feat of navigation.[38] The Royal Navy did not doubt Bligh's side of the story and allowed him to continue to serve. Because those in authority came from the same social class as ship's officers, they tended to believe their peers about such matters.

During a voyage from Aberdeen, Maryland, to England, the crew of the *Jefferson Borden* mutinied and killed several officers before the captain subdued them with his revolver. He told English authorities his men had had no reason whatsoever to mutiny, and his assertion went unquestioned. The captain found replacements and headed home. Upon arrival there, the new crew signed a grievance against him complaining of his brutality, the withholding of their wages, and his refusal to feed them sufficient amounts of food. Upon hearing this, English authorities reconsidered their earlier judgment and reopened their investigation into the mutiny.[39]

The reporter who wrote the article about the *Jefferson Borden* noted that a captain had to push his crew pretty hard to get it to commit mutiny. Although this journalist thought little of the sailor as a person, he acknowledged the hard life a seaman had, comparing his treatment to that of a slave on a Louisiana sugar plantation. He pointed out that "however capable of murder and robbery a sailor in the Atlantic trade may be, he is perfectly aware that unsuccessful mutiny means death from the captain's revolver, and that a successful mutiny means death on the gallows if he succeeds in reaching an American or a European port. He therefore submits to almost any degree of cruelty rather than resort to the hopeless remedy of mutiny, and it is this certainty that the sailor will not strike back which encourages brutal captains to oppress and maltreat their men."[40]

This print shows the August 18, 1845, mutiny that took place on the bark *Oscar* against Captain Isaac Ludlow (Library of Congress Prints and Photographs Division, publisher/creator unknown, January 1846).

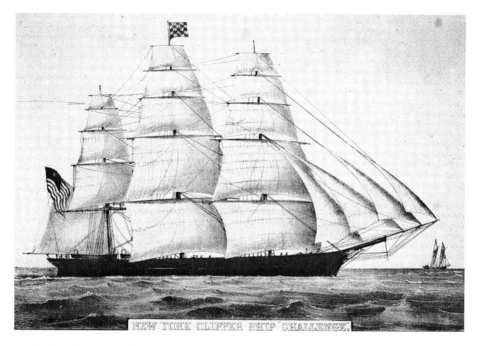

NEW YORK CLIPPER SHIP CHALLENGE.

Challenge (Library of Congress Prints and Photographs Division, N. Currier, ca. 1835–1856).

Some captains pushed their crews hard for personal gain. The owners of the clipper *Challenge* offered her captain, Robert H. Waterman, a bonus of $10,000 if he made that vessel's maiden voyage (and his final one before retiring) from New York to California in ninety days or less. The *Challenge,* the largest American clipper built in 1851, stretched a bit over 230 feet long, had a beam of just over forty-three feet, a draft of nearly twenty-seven feet, and a mainmast that rose to an impressive 197 feet. Brothers Nathaniel and George Griswold, owners of a tea trading company, had her constructed as a means of capitalizing on the lucrative trade to California sparked by the gold rush. Waterman rigged her differently than other clippers of the day, adding a massive amount of extra canvas his next three successors dared not emulate.[41] He had a well-deserved reputation of never losing so much as a spar while pushing the ships he commanded to make record-breaking voyages. From 1837 to 1846 he served as the master of the cotton packet *Natchez.* Under his command she sailed from Guangzhou to New York in a mere ninety-two days on his very first run between those ports, an accomplishment manageable in part because of this vessel's exceptional qualities.[42]

He took the *Challenge* to sea on July 13 with a green crew mainly procured by crimps. Better types of work on shore plus Waterman's fearsome reputation had kept experienced seamen from signing on, so he took who he could get. Only ten of his sixty-four-man crew knew anything about sailing. Of this minority, only six could take the wheel, and just four spoke English. Waterman swore he would make them into seamen or else. While barely out to sea, he performed his first characteristic outburst by attacking a black steward with a carving knife, gashing his head.[43] Writer Kenneth Giggle called Waterman "bestiality personified. He took the marvellous [*sic*] *Challenge* and made her name a poisonous stench in the nostrils of seamen throughout the ports of the world."[44]

As the *Challenge* made her way to and around Sandy Hook, she passed the incoming *Guy Mannering*, upon which sailed another bully, James Douglass, who transferred to the *Challenge* to escape his crew because he feared it planned to lynch him upon docking. Waterman, acquainted with Douglass, made him first mate knowing he would whip the green hands into shape. Douglass did not disappoint.[45]He hit the men relentlessly, considering them lazy and unwilling to learn how to sail. As the *Challenge* made her way into the tropics past Brazil, she frequently fell into calms. The terrible heat facilitated outbreaks of disease. Several hands died, probably of maladies but some possibly murdered by the officers' cruel punishments. Late in the morning on or about August 17, Waterman ordered Douglass to have the men come to deck with their possessions. He had a thief on board and intended to catch the fellow. Douglass took a belaying pin to those he felt emptied their chests too slowly. When he struck Fred Birkenshaw, this fellow jumped up and attacked him, probably because Douglass had broken his arm with a piece of wood earlier in the voyage.[46]

Several others, including George Smith, joined in. During the altercation someone, probably Birkenshaw himself, stabbed Douglass in the thigh, inflicting an inch-long gash. Waterman weighed into the fray with a belaying pin and subdued those who resisted. He had Smith thrown into irons, but Birkenshaw escaped and disappeared. Some said he had jumped overboard. He managed to evade capture until September 18, when two men betrayed his hiding place in the lower forecastle. Douglass found him and took him on deck, forcing him to his knees. Waterman, who struck him twice with a stick, got him to confess he had plotted mutiny.[47]

The *Challenge* arrived in San Francisco on October 29, a 109-day voyage, short of the ninety for which Watermen would receive his bonus. When word of the state of the crew reached shore, a mob of angry seamen rowed out to the *Challenge* to take the offending officers by force. Douglass barely made it off before their arrival by escaping on a friend's boat.[48]

Waterman had already gone ashore to visit the Alsop building, where he met the man who would replace him as the *Challenge's* master, Captain John Land, and the agent representing the firm that owned the *Challenge,* Charles Griswold. As the three conversed, a mob intent on lynching Waterman arrived. Griswold delayed them long enough for Waterman to make his way to the roof and jump to the next building, in which he took refuge until the mob dispersed. He then went into hiding. Sailors continued to roam the streets in search of him and Douglass. On the afternoon of November 3, some newspaper boys created an effigy of Waterman and hanged it on a pole in a plaza.[49]

Authorities apprehended the alleged mutineers. They also charged the second mate, Alexander Coghill, with assault, then issued arrest warrants for Waterman and Douglass for the murder of nine crewmen. Douglass tried to flee and got about eight miles south of the city "in a covered wagon" before someone caught him. The local U.S. marshal offered a reward of $500 for Waterman's capture, but he surrendered himself.[50]

A jury failed to convict the mutineers. A different jury convicted Coghill of severely kicking a hand named John Brown, Waterman for beating a Fin named Jon Smiti, and Douglass for the assault on several hands as well as the murder of an Italian hand known only as Pawpaw. Only Coghill received jail time, a mere thirty days, fifteen of which he had already served. Waterman and Douglass paid fines and went on their way.[51]

Four Bells

Men who mutinied had two choices: go to port and turn themselves in with the hope authorities would rule on their behalf—an unlikely thing—or become pirates. Few Americans or Europeans did the latter after 1825 or so. But during the Golden Age of Piracy, which lasted from about 1695 to 1725, unprecedented numbers of them did so, a phenomenon that occurred upon the conclusion of the long-running War of Spanish Succession. This conflict lasted from 1701 to 1714, and its end caused thousands of seamen on naval ships and privateers to lose work. Those who found it usually did so on merchant ships.[52]

Many took up the career of piracy not so much out of greed as from a desire to escape the persecution of a ship's discipline. Most European seamen came from the lower classes and therefore knew nothing but oppression by their so-called betters. Such men wanted a kind of fair treatment they had never known either on land or at sea. To that end, pirates created a form of grassroots democracy in which they voted for their captain and retained full power to remove him if he failed to serve their best interests.[53]

Pirates shaped their ships' articles into a sort of primitive constitution that outlined the powers of the officers, the distribution of plunder, and stipulated rules and punishments. Pirate captains had absolute authority only during a fight. The men could remove and in some cases execute those who showed cowardice, refused to attack a ripe prize, or just acted too much the tyrant. The quartermaster, another elected officer, had the task of seeing to the crew's needs. He arbitrated minor disputes, made sure everyone got a fair share of the booty, distributed food, and so forth. A council voted on where the ship would sail next and what kinds of prizes she would take. The articles also provided for the crew's welfare. Men wounded in a fight, for example, received compensation beyond their share of the plunder.[54]

For British pirates in particular, their bitterness against the upper classes resulted in several manifestations. A number of their ships had "revenge" in their names, such as Blackbeard's *Queen Anne's Revenge.* As an outlet for their loathing of merchant captains, sometimes when they boarded these vessels they held a "Distribution of Justice." This involved questioning the crew as to how the captain had treated them. If the assembly found a captain to be cruel, the pirates might whip, then "pickle" him by throwing seawater onto his bloody wounds. Sometimes they just killed him. If they found a captain had treated his crew well, they might award him some of their plunder.[55]

The last major outbreak of piracy in North American waters occurred in the 1820s and consisted mainly of out-of-work privateers left over from the Latin American wars of independence against Spain as well from the War of 1812. The pirate ships sailed primarily in the Caribbean, and one Baltimore newspaper estimated that between 1813 and 1823 pirates had attacked about 3,000 American ships in that body of water, with the effect of insurance rates rising hirer than during the British blockade of 1815. The public and press demanded someone do something about this menace.[56]

The Royal Navy, also concerned, focused its antipiracy efforts around Jamaica, rooting out the American privateer-turned-pirate Charles Gibbs from Cuba, although he remained active for another ten years. President Monroe initiated an antipiracy force known as the Mosquito Fleet. Based in Key West and commanded by David Porter, a veteran of the War of 1812 and the U.S. Navy's battles with the Barbary Pirates, the squadron of sixteen ships had difficulty executing its mission because many of the pirates it pursued retreated to Cuba, still Spanish territory and therefore out of U.S. jurisdiction. Fortunately, Cuban merchants convinced Spanish authorities to cooperate with Porter and

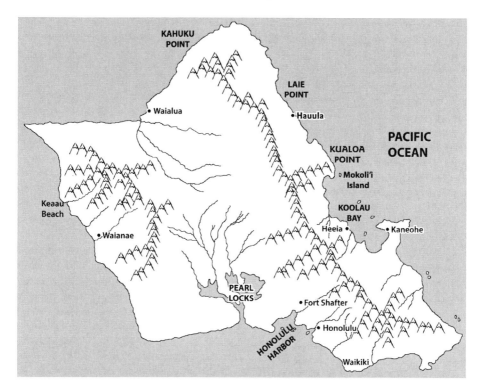

Oahu, based on the "Topographical Map of the Hawaiian Islands from Government Data Kindly Furnished by Dr. R.H. Davis" published by Linton & Garrigues in 1893 (redrawn by the author).

allow him to decimate the pirates there. The combined British and American efforts made pirates in the Caribbean nearly extinct after 1825.[57]

As European and American piracy receded into memory, it took on the sheen of romanticism. Books like *Treasure Island* and plays such as *The Pirates of Penzance* and *Peter Pan* glorified and humanized pirates, excusing or ignoring the sadistic tortures they often inflicted upon their victims.[58] This version of going a-pirating induced two men to do just that, and, in a strange twist, they exhibited all the characteristics of the idealized pirate in popular culture.

On the morning of June 6, 1908, Captain Frederick C. Miller, proprietor of Miller's Salvage Company, found his yacht *Lady* missing from her berth in Honolulu's Rotten Row, a natural slip between two reefs. The local watchman had not seen this schooner depart, yet her severed mooring lines and cast off hawser clearly indicated someone had taken her without Miller's permission. Three week's worth of provisions and a recent remodeling made her fit to sail around the world. Miller speculated Japanese sailors had stolen her and had headed either to the South Seas or to California.[59]

The next morning a native boy named Kamoku saw from a distance two masts just offshore of Keaau Beach in Oahu, the same island from which the *Lady* had disappeared. Upon closer inspection, he found her breaking up on a reef and saw two white men apparently leaving her and heading into the nearby hills. Kamoku contacted the deputy sheriff at nearby Waianae, who in turn sent out three officers to investigate. They identified the wreck as the *Lady,* then went looking for the men Kamoku had seen. Miller, upon hearing of the loss of his yacht—valued between $2,000 and $3,000—sent a salvage steamer out to try to tow her back to port, but this effort proved futile. She had broken up and her pieces either sank or washed onto the beach.[60]

About twenty-six miles to the southeast of there as the crow flies stood Fort Shafter, the first permanent U.S. Army base in the Hawaiian Islands. Built upon a spot once used by a dairy and with two ponds, the U.S. Army had finished constructing it the year before, changing its name from Kahauiki Military Reservation to its present sobriquet in honor of Major General William Shafter, a man who had distinguished himself in both the Civil and Spanish-American wars.[61] At this base two British subjects, Stephen Smith and his good friend Charles "Cockney" Dusebury, served as privates in the Twentieth Infantry. Smith had previously worked as a mule driver in the Quartermaster's Department in the Philippines. Dusebury had once sailed as a common seaman before joining the army, although he never learned navigation.[62]

On the night of the Thursday before the *Lady* crashed upon a reef, Dusebury abandoned his gun and guard post, then met with Smith. The two headed down into Honolulu with the idea of finding a boat to get off the island and therefore away from the monotony of army life. Possibly inspired by the romantic tales of piracy, they saw themselves "as pirate princes" or perhaps kings who would rule the South Seas. (The local papers played this up but failed to print quotes of either man declaring this specifically as their intention.) The two combed the harbor for just the right vessel and fell in love with the *Lady* upon seeing her.[63]

Delighted to find the schooner well stocked, they climbed on board and made themselves at home, leaving only once to buy a thirty-pound bag of rice. The weather prevented them from departing until about one-thirty on Sunday morning. Considering neither knew much about taking a vessel out of a dangerous slip in the dead of night, their success qualifies as somewhere between amazing luck and a minor miracle. In the short term they had in mind just to get away from Oahu, and to that end sailed southwest because the wind took them in that direction. Or so they thought. They had little time ponder it because seasickness overcame them, forcing them to spend the rest of the night being ill.[64]

In the morning they sighted land. Thinking they had come upon a deserted, or at least a sparsely inhabited, island, they dropped the anchor. Before deciding upon their next course of action, a wind whipped up the sea and sent the *Lady* crashing onto a reef. Realizing their predicament, the two swam ashore. They returned to raid the sinking vessel of all they could find useful, then went inland and set up a sailcloth hut. Over a campfire they made a meal. During an after-dinner smoke they heard the unexpected sound of a loud horn. It belonged to a train with "Oahu Railway" printed on its side.[65] This told them they had not only failed to get off of the island, they had not even gone that far from Honolulu itself, because the Oahu Railroad, the first passenger service on the island, had only thirty-five miles of track at this time and went no farther than Waianae.[66] At about two in the afternoon authorities found them, an incident colorfully recalled by Smith:

> We was sitting down when we heard what we thought was birds whistling and then about twenty kanakas [the generic term for natives of the South Seas and surely a gross exaggeration] came up all around us, each with a gun. One feller had a great long gun and they was all a-trembling and scared and calling "hands up." I had my hands up but they was scared. I guess they thought we had guns an' say if we had had a gun and fired a shot I bet we would have sent 'em all up the line. All we had was big fat cigars.... An' what dye thing of that? Twenty big kanakas with guns coming after us innocent people with nothing but cigars. I saw them guns but they had the triggers down. I reckon they was afraid them guns might go off.[67]

The two initially concocted an implausible defense. They claimed not to have deserted from the army but rather to have taken absence without leave in an effort to enjoy themselves around Waianae. While there, they had happened upon the wreck of the *Lady* and, thinking her a derelict, swam out to see what they could salvage.[68] The district attorney, meanwhile, found that charging Smith and Dusebury with piracy had no legal basis because it applied only to professional seamen. He instead charged them with larceny with the possibility of adding looting a sea vessel, which had a more severe penalty.[69] *The Hawaiian Gazette* thought little of their escapade: "Their adventure seems one of the most stupidly conceived and worst executed things of the kind that could be imagined. Both men are of a low grade of intellectuality, ignorant and hair-brained."[70]

Smith and Dusebury dropped their defense and pled guilty to the charges against them. Their oddball manner and a humorous speech given to the court by Smith convinced the judge neither man qualified as a hardened criminal but rather that they were misguided adventure seekers. He fined each one a dollar and sentenced them to a month of hard labor.[71] Upon the completion of this, the army took charge of them, bringing them back to Fort Shafter for a court-martial on charges of desertion, which had a severe penalty. Placed into a guardhouse, by five the next morning they had escaped by climbing through the door's transom, a pivoting window built into the doorframe above the door itself to let in air. This particular transom spanned about a foot in length, just enough room to allow the prisoners to worm their way through.[72]

By this time Captain Miller had begun refurbishing another schooner, the *Luka,* to replace his lost yacht. Upon hearing of Smith and Dusebury's escape, he placed a guard on the vessel because, as *The Hawaiian Star* put it, "Captain Miller is not in the business of supplying amateur pirates with vessels to wreck." The *Star* further suggested "perhaps they are under the impression that they may find some wondrous cave with treasure and the usual providentially gurgling crystal spring from a convenient rock where they could establish their lair."[73]

At six in the morning on the same day of their escape and a mere three blocks from the police station, the fugitives walked into the popular Honolulu restaurant Royal Café and ordered breakfast. Dusebury asked its proprietor, "Scotty" Meaton, for a loan, but he refused because he did not know him. About an hour later Meaton saw the fugitives' faces in a newspaper and reported their recent appearance to the police, who would find locating two white men in Honolulu at this time no easy task. The city had an eclectic mix of whites and other ethnicities with a population of over 39,000.[74]

The fugitives remained on the loose for ten days until tracked down and arrested by Detective Joe Leal on the afternoon of July 14.[75] Once back in the Army's custody, they faced a double charge of desertion. At court-martial they were found guilty and sentenced to Alcatraz for three years, the designated prison for those tried under the jurisdiction of the Pacific Branch of the War Department. While there, they would have would have watched, and possibly contributed to, the construction of that iconic penitentiary best known for holding civilians such as mobster Al Capone.[76]

4

The Crimps and Their Business

When three men from a rowboat came on board the British vessel *Cavalier* in late September 1877 as she lay anchored off of Staten Island, the man in charge on deck, a carpenter named George Paulsen, confronted them. They told him they had come from a boardinghouse and wanted to leave their business cards with the crew. Paulsen tried to refuse them entry into the forecastle, but one of the trespassers pulled out a gun and insisted on passing. Paulsen, having a natural aversion to bullets, let them go by. Five willing hands accompanied these runners to shore. Paulsen reported this to the authorities, but it would do him little good.[1] He had witnessed one of the many shanghaiing techniques used by runners and crimps, who did not limit themselves to violence such as this, but also used blackmail, trickery, and drugs.

One Bell

Bill Thomas, a San Francisco runner who worked for the crimp Tom Brewster, needed men, so he took a boat out into San Francisco Bay and waited for an incoming ship. He boarded the first one that arrived and told her captain not to give his men shore leave because San Francisco's many temptations would probably induce quite a few of them to desert. The captain asked the pilot if he could get him back out to sea, but the fellow, bribed by the city's crimps, said he could not. The captain dropped his anchor in the bay for the night. Thomas next made his way to the forecastle and there told the men they really ought to go to shore, telling them about many pleasurable diversions there. He promised to return around midnight to pick up those who wanted to come.[2]

For this he used a Whitehall boat, a vessel popular with runners and one often used in San Francisco Bay.[3] These rowboats, which originated in New

63

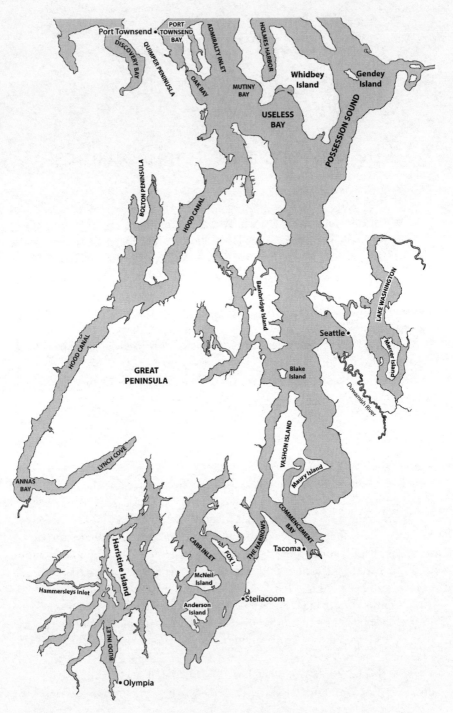

Puget Sound, based on the 1889 U.S. Coast and Geodetic Survey map "Puget Sound, Washington Territory" by A. Lindenkohl (redrawn by the author).

York City as water taxis, typically had a length between sixteen and twenty feet with a design that allowed them to cut through the water in a straight line no matter the weather conditions.[4] Thomas, accompanied by Brewster, returned at midnight as promised, but no one appeared. He climbed up the anchor cable and, once on board, quietly called to one of the hands, asking him if he and his friends wanted to come or not. Eight did. As he rowed away with his catch, Brewster passed a bottle around to the deserters and told them about the fun they would have once ashore.[5]

But before reaching shore, Brewster and Thomas stopped at another ship on the pretense of delivering oilskins. Shortly after the men boarded, someone on deck invited the others to come on board as well with promises of liquor. Unable to resist, the men did so. As they imbibed the drinks offered, Thomas and Brewster quietly returned to their boat and headed to shore, the captain having paid $400 for those they had left behind. Brewster's landshark career ended abruptly one night as he rowed an unconscious man out to a ship. His victim unexpectedly awoke from his drug-induced slumber and blew out Brewster's brains.[6]

In Puget Sound, about 650 miles to the north of San Francisco, the competition to snatch men from incoming ships became so fierce it made runners persistent if not aggressive, despite the large area in which they had to work. One nineteenth century writer described it as encompassing over 2,000 "miles of zigzag shores, running south and running north, branching east and branching west ... [and containing] bays within bays, inlets on inlets, seas linking seas,—over twelve thousand square miles of surface, the waters come and go, rise and fall, past a splendid succession of islands, promontories, walls of forest, and towering mountains."[7]

In the winter of 1902 the bark *Gwydry Castle* entered the sound bound for Tacoma, a city located at its southern end roughly sixty miles as the crow flies from its entry point. To get there, her captain hired a tug with a pilot well-versed in this waterway. As they got underway, a speedboat carrying three men came alongside. Its occupants asked for and got permission to board. They tried to lure crewmen to come to Tacoma with promises of large steaks at the boardinghouse they represented as well as the possibility of getting them better paying jobs than they had now. Although no one went away with the visitors, a few men expressed interest. The runners pledged to meet those responsive to their temptations at Tacoma's docks when the *Gwydry Castle* came into port. This they did because the more seamen they could strip off of incoming ships, the more their crimp masters could make by selling them back.[8]

The *Gwydry Castle* had to wait for three days before docking upon arriving in Tacoma. During this time one of the runners returned as promised, entering the forecastle with free cigars and a swig of whiskey. He repeated what he had said before about the quality of food and entertainment one could find ashore. Three men went with him. Not long thereafter a beautiful young woman boarded and told those who wanted to come that she had rooms and food at the Seaman's Mission, a boardinghouse where they would receive Christian charity and preaching rather than inflated prices and bad liquor. The man from whom this account comes, Anton Otto Fischer, went with her.[9]

As a rule, runners and crimps took anyone they could get their hands on, and never mind who might miss them. In May 1882, for example, a New York crimp boldly snatched an enlisted man serving at nearby Fort Hamilton, an army base established in 1808 along Fifth Avenue in Brooklyn at which Robert E. Lee and Thomas Jonathan "Stonewall" Jackson once served. At first the enlisted man's superiors thought he had deserted, but soon enough a lieutenant received a note saying someone had shanghaied and taken his man to the British merchant ship *William Cochran*. The ship's master, Captain Dornier, had a reputation of treating his crew poorly, so no one would willingly sign onto his ship. He had therefore gone to a crimp to procure him enough men to allow him to set sail from his anchorage off of Staten Island. The crimp he employed had found, or gotten, the missing soldier drunk, then shanghaied him.[10]

The lieutenant went to Brooklyn's U.S. assistant district attorney for aid. He in turn sent a U.S. marshal out in the revenue cutter *William E. Chandler* to retrieve the lost man, but too late. The *William Cochran,* bound for Hamburg, had already gotten under way. The cutter gave chase but could not overhaul her prey before she reached the nine-mile limit of jurisdiction. The U.S. secretary of state, upon hearing of this incident, said he would demand the soldier's return when the *Cochran* arrived in Hamburg.[11]

Crimps did not respect a person's social rank or personal achievements. Charles Cheesboro, captain of the three-masted schooner *Bell Holliday,* went ashore in Baltimore to procure a new steward from a shipping agent, but the fellow had none to offer. A stranger overheard his conversation and approached Cheesboro on the street just outside the agent's building. He said he knew of a steward in need of a berth. The captain followed his new benefactor into a house. Asked to sit down, he waited while his new acquaintance left the room to fetch the fellow he had in mind. A few minutes later Cheesboro's benefactor returned and asked him to meet the steward in the next room. As the captain passed through the doorway, something crashed down onto his head, knocking him unconscious.[12]

He awoke three days later at sea onboard a ship out of New York City

This 1897 photograph by A. Ludden shows Tacoma with Mt. Rainer in the background (**Library of Congress Prints and Photographs Division**).

bound for the Barbados Islands. He had no recollection of his transportation from Baltimore to New York nor did he ever know the fate of the large sum of money he had carried on his person. Upon arriving at Barbados in February, he wrote to his wife to tell her of his location and plight, then made arrangements to get back home. There he arrived in May with his health much poorer.[13]

Two Bells

Many colorful crimps worked along the navigable parts of the Columbia River between Astoria and Portland, most of whom operated boardinghouses and commanded the exclusive manning of all ships between these two cities.[14] Shanghaiing along the Columbia had started in earnest in the 1870s upon the arrival of British-born James "Jim" Turk, a former seaman and veteran of the Mexican-American War. He had come to Oregon overland from the East and in 1876 settled first not in Portland but rather Pendleton, a town about 189 miles to its west. Here he worked for a fellow named Bill Daly, who established a saloon called the Big Bonanza, a place patronized mainly by cowboys. Daly and Turk claimed to have worked as professional pugilists and staged exhibition fights for the entertainment of the guests.[15]

This business venture ended when authorities arrested Daly for beating his wife and children. He sold his bar and left town for Portland. Turk followed, establishing his own boardinghouse on Coach Street, where he got into the business of shanghaiing. He later expanded into Astoria by opening legitimate businesses such as hotels. Turk weighed 200 pounds, stood five feet eleven inches, was always well dressed, had a clean-shaven face, and usually carried a gold-tipped cane. He married three times, and legend has it that when his youngest son got involved with drinking and loose women, Turk shanghaied the boy for a profit as punishment.[16]

By 1890 the crimps' monopoly along the Columbia had raised the average fee for each man shipped to $87.50, forcing captains to pay between $1,200 and $1,500 for a full crew. An 1890 federal law limited the advance a seaman received to a maximum of $40 to prevent him from spending all his earnings before he went to sea, but Columbia's crimps just added this amount to their overall charge, then pocketed the extra as a bonus. Astoria's crimps forced captains who found crews in Portland to replace that crew with one from them. Those who refused found themselves unable to leave because Astoria refused them permission to depart, charging $100 for each day they stayed.[17]

This just demonstrated the immense amount of political power the crimps wielded, influence that allowed them to keep Astoria from appointing a harbormaster in 1891 as well as preventing Portland's harbormaster from doing his job. Crimps gained such influence by getting themselves or their families involved in local politics, as Astoria's notorious Grant family did. Its matriarch, Bridget, ran "one of the [city's] most successful boardinghouses.... [Her] brother Nace (short for Ignatius) held influential civic posts ranging from grangemaster [the head of an organization of farmers] and volunteer hose-team chief to sheriff and chief of police." He served the public until 1918, "when he was charged with graft in his capacity as chief of police."[18]

Jim Turk dabbled in politics as well, even running for mayor of Astoria at one point.[19] During his residency in Portland, one of the city's reform-minded newspapers, *The Morning Oregonian,* began a relentless attack on him that included calling him a pirate. He sued for libel but lost. Chafing under the reforms in Portland's laws designed to crack down on shanghaiing, he moved to Astoria permanently.[20] The *Oregonian* attacked Astoria as well, accusing it of supporting its crimps because of the revenue they generated, and chided its newspapers for praising Jim Turk as a great businessman without pointing out his shanghaiing enterprises. It predicted allowing people such as Turk to operate along the Columbia would induce shipowners and captains to stop using the river altogether and shut down its commerce.[21]

Certainly Turk deserved such accusations. Those who crossed him paid for it. While moored in Astoria, Captain Dagwell, master of the British ship *Oberon,* found he needed five more men to fill out his crew before he could get underway. To that end he arranged to bring them from Portland on the boat *R.R. Thompson,* hiring a sixth "big man" to ensure they made it. Turk brazenly boarded the boat and convinced all five of Dagwell's men to come with him with the promise of a better deal. Dagwell could do nothing about it because a federal court had recently ruled American citizens did not have to honor articles signed for a British vessel. Dagwell took his loss and made other arrangements.[22]

A similar thing happened on another British ship, the *Howard D. Troop,* upon her arrival in Astoria. Runners came aboard offering drinks and promises they could get the crew easier work at $3.50 a day. Twenty out of the *Troop's* twenty-six hands deserted. With that many men gone, her master, Captain Corning, could not depart. He refused to pay Astoria's crimps blood money for replacements when he learned they wanted $160 per man and an additional $7.50 per night to hire someone to keep watch to ensure they did not jump ship.[23]

He sent for a crew out of San Francisco, having them sign their articles before they boarded the *Columbia,* the steamer that would take them north to Astoria. It took Corning ten days to make these arrangements and cost him dearly. He paid $800 for the men and fee for their transportation, $100 a day to remain docked in Astoria, and still more for insurance, the total of all this amounting to $3,000. The crimps sent runners to San Francisco to try to entice the men Corning had signed to desert, but they had no luck.[24]

Corning arranged for a U.S. marshal to detain his twelve new men to ensure they neither deserted nor fell into the hands of Astoria's crimps when the *Columbia* came into port. The crimps retaliated by having Corning arrested on the charge of kidnapping. Taken into custody, he appeared before a magistrate the next day. In the meantime Astoria's boardinghouse land-sharks had a writ of habeas corpus drawn up to force the release of the men detained by the marshal on the grounds that an 1892 treaty with Britain forbade American citizens from being forced to serve on British ships. The court ruled the release of only those men with American citizenship, which amounted to four. It also dismissed the kidnapping charges against Corning.[25]

In 1903 the state of Oregon passed a law creating a commission responsible for issuing licenses for boardinghouses. Portland decided it would allot just one, so Bridget Grant, in partnership with the powerful crimp Larry Sullivan, obtained it. Another boardinghouse master, Harry White, sued them for creating a monopoly. He won only after his case went all the way to the state supreme court. Thereafter he merged his boardinghouse with Grant's and Sullivan's, preserving the monopoly.[26]

Portland produced its share of notable crimps. Nancy Boggs served mainly whiskey on a scow she operated along the Willamette River. In 1881 or 1882 the police tried to raid the vessel. She kept them from boarding by pouring boiling oil onto them. They returned a few hours later with reinforcements, but she escaped in a rowboat and later established a new place onshore, out of which she shanghaied men from time to time.[27]

Joseph "Bunco" Kelley, an Englishman born in 1847, had started on the waterfront as a runner, then opened the Mariner's Home boardinghouse on Davis and Third streets in Portland.[28] In his autobiography he claimed to have served in the Confederate navy during the Civil War and to have worked afterward as a merchant mariner for a few years. In 1873 he signed onto the infamous side-wheeled steamer *Virginius.*[29]

Originally built by a Clyde, Scotland, shipyard in 1864 to serve as a Confederate blockade runner and christened the *Virginia,* she fell in 1870 into the hands of Cuban rebels who bought her incognito, rechristened her the *Virginius,* and had her refitted in New York Harbor. For the next two years she sailed under several American captains with the purpose of aiding Cuba's rebels, causing so much trouble (including a revolution in Venezuela) that Spanish authorities designated her an outlaw vessel. In 1872 ex–Confederate naval officer Joseph Fry took command of her and launched an expedition to land men and materials in Cuba. To man it he hired unemployed seamen without informing them of his mission for fear they would refuse to sail. He departed on October 23, 1873, for Port-au-Prince, Haiti, to pick up weapons and powder.[30]

On October 30 the Spanish corvette *Tornado* sighted the *Virginius* and set off in pursuit. Fry tried to get away, pushing his vessel so hard he ran out of coal and had to burn other combustibles such as oil, fat, and grease to keep sailing. After a day-long chase the *Tornado* finally stopped the *Virginius* by shooting her stack. The Spaniards took their prize and her men to Cuba, where

This 1879 lithograph by E.S. Glover, *Looking East to the Cascade Mountains*, shows a view of Portland (Library of Congress Prints and Photographs Division, A.L. Bancroft & Company, 1879).

authorities put them on trial for piracy, finding them guilty and executing all but four.[31]

Kelley claimed to have sailed on this last voyage and survived only because he had gotten off the *Virginius* shortly before she met her end. He next supposedly got involved in a Chilean revolution while serving on the rebel ship *Wanda,* although he left the details of his involvement so vague the year in which it occurred remains unknown. He worked for a time as a steamboat pilot on the Columbia, then established his boardinghouse in Portland. He insisted he never shanghaied a single man in his life, embellishing this lie with the assertion that he often went to court to defend the rights of British seamen by suing for wages not paid to them.[32]

His ability to shanghai men became more legend than truth. Once he supposedly took a wooden Indian from Wildman's Cigar Store and sold it to a captain as a drunken sailor. A fisherman later caught it in the Columbia and returned it to the store, which then chained it to the ground. This incident supposedly earned Kelley his nickname "Bunco," which means "swindler."[33]

Another time a group of forty men broke into the basement of Johnson & Sons Undertakers and tapped a keg of formaldehyde. Drinking it, they died or became so ill they could not function. Kelley happened upon them and took both the living and the dead to the captain of the *Rosecranna* with the claim he had gotten them all into drunken stupors. The captain initially wanted to pay him $50 per man, but Kelley said it had him cost $2 a piece to get them drunk, so he received $52 a person instead.[34]

In 1890 Kelley promised a landsman named Albert Armstrong easy work on a British ship for $30 a month. Armstrong, along with two other landsmen procured by Kelley, boarded the *Noddleburn* only to find out they would earn between £2 and £10 a month. Before sailing out of the Columbia, one of the shanghaied men stole away on the steamer *Reed* and from there made his way to shore. Armstrong jumped overboard into the river at night, and the crew of the steamer *Volga* fished him out. The *Noddleburn*'s master, Captain Hall, uncovered the escape and demanded Armstrong's return. The *Volga*'s commander, Captain Church, refused. An officer on board took Armstrong to the city prison, where he gave the details of the incident to Deputy U.S. Marshal Smith. Armed with this intelligence, Smith boarded the *Noddleburn* and retrieved the last of the three men shanghaied by Kelley, none of whom had signed the ship's articles.[35]

Marshal Smith telegraphed the details of the incident to Portland and there another marshal arrested Kelley for kidnapping. Smith arrived later and took Kelley back with him to Astoria for a trial. Astoria's authorities also locked up the three victims to ensure these witnesses did not flee before the trial. Kelley directed his lawyer to file a motion demanding his return to Portland for a trial, well knowing he had important friends there who would aid him. And at a separate hearing about the matter in that city two men did just that: both a deputy U.S. marshal and a board of trade officer testified they knew for certain the three men Kelley had allegedly shanghaied had in fact signed the ship's articles.[36]

Kelley, who claimed other boardinghouse masters in Portland had framed him because he refused to participate in their monopoly, got off because authorities had failed to secure an arrest warrant when they took him into custody.[37] He would not be so lucky a few years later during another trial. On October 5, 1894, his life changed irrevocably. Police arrested him and an associate named X.N. Steeves for the murder of George William Sayres (Kelley spelled it as "Sears," probably its phonic equivalent) during a failed shanghaiing attempt. A jury found them both guilty of second degree murder, although Steeves later received a retrial. For this crime Kelley served thirteen years.[38]

He maintained his innocence, pointing out that a little fellow like him— he stood a mere five feet three and a half inches and weighed 135 pounds— could hardly have beat the man in question to death because of the fellow's superior size and weight. Moreover, Sayres had died on Fulton Street, but someone had discovered his body along the shores of the Willamette River. Kelley could not have managed to move such a large body that far by himself. As a habit, Sayres also carried a big stick with him—one never found after his death—and how could Kelley have overcome that? Kelley failed to mention the possibility that his accomplice, Steeves, could well have helped him in this.[39]

When the police had arrested Kelley, they found him with a broken collarbone and ribs, circumstantial evidence that helped in his conviction. He maintained these injuries had resulted from a fight he had with boardinghouse master and ex-pugilist Larry Sullivan. Enough of Oregon's citizens believed Kelley to sign a petition asking the governor to pardon him. He did so in 1907.[40]

Despite strong circumstantial evidence, Kelley had a good case for his innocence. The murdered Sayres, a saloon owner, had owed a contractor named W.O. Allen a considerable sum of money for which Allen had sued, the matter staying in litigation for several years. Upon the discovery of Sayres' body on September 26, 1894, many presumed Allen had killed him. Even more suspicion fell on Allen the next year when he committed suicide by taking an overdose of laudanum. One newspaper article obliquely suggested he had killed himself because of a guilty conscience.[41]

Three Bells

In Canada the city of Quebec became infamous for the aggressiveness of its crimps. Built along the hilly confluence of the Saint Lawrence and Saint Charles rivers, it consisted of narrow streets and architecture uniquely suited to the rugged terrain upon which it stood. A natural divide separated its Upper and Lower towns, the former of which hosted the city's main buildings and military fortifications and the latter its warehouses, banks, customs house, and other buildings necessary for the functions of a port. In 1843 one travel writer described Lower Town as "a narrow strip of land extending from Diamond Harbour to the suburb of St. Roch ... [that] possesses no object of particular attraction to strangers."[42]

Quebec served as a major timber and shipbuilding port and yet, despite both activities, it had no native population of mariners. Sailors who came from elsewhere often jumped ship when they learned they could find landsmen jobs that paid an average of £10 a month as opposed to the £3 a month they earned at sea. To entice men back on board, captains paid inflated wages, a revenue stream the city's crimps could not resist tapping.[43] To that end they set up boardinghouses on Champlain Street, which ran along the St. Lawrence's northern bank. From here runners or the crimps themselves boarded incoming ships, by invitation if possible and force if necessary. Of the latter technique, they pulled out revolvers to gain access to the forecastle, telling those within tales of vast quantities of available liquor to induce

A photograph of Quebec taken between 1890 and 1901 (Library of Congress Prints and Photographs Division, Detroit Publishing Co., ca. 1890–1901).

them into deserting. If that did not work, sometimes they took crewmen at gunpoint.[44]

Because the Saint Lawrence froze annually, its crimps became quite aggressive so they could make a year's worth of money in less time. Examples of such audacity abound. In 1856 crimps boarded the *Juno*. When her captain, John Henry, ordered them off, one of them pulled out a pistol and threatened to kill him if he did not stand aside. He did, and they left with several of his men. Crimps who boarded the *John McKenzie* with stones hit those who defied them, including the captain, J. Tilby, whom they beat down when he resisted.[45] Some captains kept crimps from boarding by dropping grindstones and pig iron ballast into their incoming boats, refusing to rescue anyone in them from drowning.[46] Captain David Price of the *Rhea Sylvia* shot two runners who climbed onto his deck in 1854. Captain Napoleon Pelletier of the *Rivoli* killed a crimp named James Dillon with an ax in 1873.[47]

A captain in the Royal Navy, E. Smith, complained that the seamen on ships coming into Quebec often went to shore and filed complaints of abuse with "petty-lawyers" to get out of their obligations. Smith believed they lied about their mistreatment, insisting few captains handled their men poorly. The high price and shortage of seamen forced many captains to leave the city with inadequate crews, a dangerous thing to do on the open sea when sailing through foul weather.[48] Although most captains disliked crimps, some would, for a fee, allow one to spirit away his entire crew and place it on board an outgoing ship.[49]

In 1856 Henry Fry, a Quebec-based agent of the Lloyds of London insurance company, wrote a letter to London's influential newspaper *The Times* in which he complained that Quebec's crimps had gotten so bold their presence put the lives of British sea captains in danger. The authorities either could not or would not do a thing to address the problem. Fry mentioned, among several examples, an incident that occurred on the brig *Regina*. Sometime after she arrived on August 20, 1856, four boats filled with crimps armed with clubs and pistols surrounded and boarded her, daring the mates to resist. The crimps beat one who did, then stole his clothes.[50]

When Canada's governor-general, Sir Edmund Walker Head, read these accusations, he became indignant, refusing to believe them. Despite his doubt, he instructed one of his secretaries to send a letter to the superintendent of Quebec's police, John Maguire, to investigate the matter.[51] Maguire sent letters to prominent people living in Quebec, including diplomats and merchants, asking them to report what they knew about the city's crimps and their activities. While none of the diplomats had firsthand knowledge of such incidents and few had heard any complaints about them from their citizens or subjects in the city, a reply from the owner of one of the city's shipping firms, David Gilmour, gave Maguire a frank and dire assessment of the situation.[52]

Gilmour complained that the seamen who came into Quebec from other ports made between £2 and £3 a month, but when they learned of the inflated wages outgoing seamen made, they immediately jumped ship and found a crimp to aid them in finding a new berth.[53] In times of surplus, crimps in Lower Town often hid these deserters until such time as a shortage made their wages go up.[54] Mass desertion caused much financial damage to shipping companies. In 1854 alone Gilmour's own ships lost 483 crewmen to desertion, costing his firm about £4,000.[55] He cited an incident to illustrate this. Once, he needed to get two vessels on their way by November 20. The ships in question had lost, within just a few days in port, forty men, and now neither vessel had enough hands to safely depart. Gilmour's firm could not find a man who would take less than £15 a month because of the interference of crimps. Realizing his desperate need to get his ships out to sea before the river froze, the crimps raised the price to £17 a month. Disgusted, Gilmour arranged to bring forty men up from New York. Upon learning this, the crimps offered to ship their men at £4 a month.[56]

Another letter from one of the governor-general's secretaries went to the city's shipping master, J.W. Dunscomb, to ask for a report on the matter. Dunscomb admitted that crimps operated in the city but did not think their activities had worsened of late. Like many of those in a position of authority, he blamed the problem on its victims rather than the unscrupulous men who exploited them: "I feel quite sure that desertion, robbery and even murder, will be committed amongst such a number of sailors, wherever they may be; but add to this, that the immediate locality entertains and exercises a direct and active interest in the desertion of seamen, it should not be a matter of surprise that outrages such as complained of do exist and require strong measures for their suppression."[57]

Information like this forced Governor-general Head to admit the problem of shanghaiing existed. He asked Gilmour for his ideas on stopping this practice. The police chief suggested, among other things, that the city's river police ought to have two more boats (for a total of six) with at least forty-two persons to man them. He felt the existing 1853 law against crimping needed amending because, while it imposed penalties on men who deserted from their ships, it failed to punish those who induced them to do so. He also pointed out that the city's many shipbuilders found their crews by stealing them off of incoming vessels, so there should be a law forcing them to get the builders from somewhere other than Quebec.[58]

Dunscomb had some proposals of his own. He thought captains should obtain crews only through his office so it could verify all the men signing their articles had not deserted. He also suggested the city of Quebec build a sailor's home in which unscrupulous crimps could not bilk the men of all their money, then get them indebted and therefore into their power.[59] In the year that Dunscomb put forth his ideas to the governor-general, one of Quebec's most notorious crimps, Jim Ward, arrived in town. He had reportedly begun his criminal career by kidnapping men during the U.S. Civil War and selling them to the Union army to serve "as cannon fodder." He set up a boardinghouse on Champlain Street near Diamond Harbor and did not usually resort to shanghaiing because he had little trouble finding volunteers. When, for example, the brig *Cerces,* an old timber-hauling ship falling apart at the seams and leaking badly, came into port, most of her men asked him to shanghai them so they could get off. Doing so may have saved their lives. *Cerces* returned to England loaded with lumber but before reaching port broke up on a sandbar by Appledore, a seaside village on the shores of Barnstaple Bay, Devonshire, where the Rivers Taw and Torridge meet.[60]

Ward did resort to shanghaiing when necessary. In 1869 he kidnapped a fifteen-year-old boy from Liverpool named Thomas Turner and forced him to ship out on the *Atlantic.* Fortunately for the boy, the weather became so bad the crew refused to sail any farther than Halifax. There Turner told his story and escaped his fate. Ward left Quebec with the passing of the 1873 Seamen's Act, which made his business practices a felony. He died in Savannah, Georgia, in 1891.[61]

Four Bells

Shanghaiing became big business in San Francisco. Some of the city's boardinghouse crimps took in $50,000 a year even after paying their runners an average of $500 a month. Crimps operated all along San Francisco's waterfront, especially in the tenderloin district known as the Barbary Coast in which stood disused warehouses converted into brothels, saloons, and boardinghouses. Many of those buildings along the wharf had floor hatches through which crimps could drop their victims into waiting rowboats below.[62] In this vice district operated Miss Piggott, whose infamous concoction of rum, whiskey, gin, and opium or laudanum became universally known as a Miss Piggott Special. She ran a boardinghouse on Davis Street and had an enforcer from one of the Nordic countries who employed a slingshot to render his victims unconscious.[63]

The crimp James Kelley used, in addition to Miss Piggott Specials, opium-

This lithograph, *Vue de San-Francisco* by Isador Laurent Deroy, shows the city as it appeared around 1860 (Library of Congress American Memory Map Collection).

laced cigars to lull asleep those who smoked them. For those disinclined to drink or smoke, he or one of his runners whacked them in the head with a blackjack.[64] A native of Ireland, Kelley received his citizenship in 1848 in Philadelphia and moved to San Francisco shortly thereafter. He set up a boardinghouse on the corner of Chambers and Davis streets.[65] A short fellow "with flaming red hair, a bristling red beard, and an irascible disposition," he gained a fearsome reputation among seamen and became known to them as "Shanghai Kelley." Despite his notoriety, his three-story boardinghouse, which stood in part over the harbor's water and thus allowed him to drop men into boats below it, still attracted sailors because of its large quantities of liquor and loose women.[66]

Stories about Kelley's boldness abound, such as the time he needed men for three ships that included one out of New York, the *Reefer,* whose captain had a reputation for harshness. Kelley did not have a sufficient number of lodgers to fill out these crews, so he rented an old steamboat, the *Goliah,* and announced his intention of taking her to a picnic where he would celebrate his birthday. He promised plenty of liquor and said anyone could come. Ninety did.[67] Giving these men Miss Piggott Specials, he sailed his little vessel to the side of the *Reefer* and unloaded some of the now drugged men onto her, then repeated this process with the other two vessels in need of men. On his way back he came across a ship that had just wrecked, the *Yankee Blade.* From her he rescued about ninety men, coincidentally the same number he had just unloaded, allowing him to return without anyone taking notice of what had happened to the men who had departed with him.[68] Although this account has certainly come down to us with exaggerations, it rings true because other crimps used this same trick.

Kelley employed a number of runners. Of these, at least one, Johnny Devine, met his end with a noose around his neck. Born on June 19, 1840, and sometimes known by the nickname "the Chicken" or "the Shanghai Chicken," he came from Waterford, Ireland. He first visited California in 1861 and stayed permanently the next year. He came to the notice of the public when he participated in an 1864 bare-knuckled prizefight that lasted 143 rounds and resulted in a tie.[69]

In 1868 Devine visited a boardinghouse on Front Street owned and operated by his friend James Maitland. At some point he caused a disturbance and Maitland ordered Devine to leave, but he refused. A fight ensued. As he retreated out the door, Devine swung his left fist at Maitland. Maitland blocked the blow with a knife, severing Devine's hand from its arm, then pushed his belligerent friend outside and shut the door. Devine begged for the return of his missing appendage. Maitland opened the door and kicked it to him. Devine tried to get it reattached, but when this failed, he replaced it with a hook whose point he kept sharp so he could use it to good effect in a fight. The loss of his hand caused him to drink even heavier than usual, prompting Kelley to fire him.[70]

As a criminal, Devine practiced all types of wrongdoing: assault and battery for a fee, petty larceny, and, finally, attempted murder. This last started out merely as a con targeting August Kamp, a German farmhand who had come into the city to live in a hotel. Devine befriended him, borrowed $20, then repaid his the fellow by trying and failing to shanghai him. Kamp insisted Devine settle his debt. Devine showed contriteness and asked Kamp to accompany him into the city's southern hills to talk things over. There he shot the German in the head with a pistol, leaving the body where it fell. Or so he thought. The fortuitous arrival of a passing shepherd ensured Kamp's survival.[71]

Upon hearing that Kamp still lived, Devine unsuccessfully tried to flee from the city. The German identified his assailant by looking through a rogue's gallery book, and later in a lineup. Devine was charged with first degree murder (despite the fact Kamp had lived), and a jury convicted him, but a higher court ruled the conviction invalid based on a technicality. A few months later a court retried Devine and once more found him guilty. Devine protested his innocence, but the state's supreme court refused to dismiss the case a second time. He was hanged.[72]

Five Bells

Crimps did not just operate in seaports, they also did so on the shores of the Great Lakes. Here they prospered, although they operated a bit differently than their oceanfront brethren. Because the lakes almost unfailingly froze in the cold months, mariners working on them had to winter in boardinghouses. During this season the cost of staying in them naturally went up. The average monthly charge in 1883 for room and board (excluding liquor, sold separately) in Milwaukee, for example, ranged between $35 and $45. Boardinghouse masters allowed their lodgers to stay on credit, knowing captains would gladly pay off their debts come spring to get them on board.[73]

The Great Lakes produced their own notorious waterfronts and boardinghouses. In Buffalo, New York, for example, the most disreputable saloons, gambling houses, brothels, and boardinghouses stood in the Flats, an area of drained swampland along the lakeshore through which went the Erie Canal, an engineering wonder residents mistook for a sewer. Crime ran unchecked here, especially in those places located along Center, Commercial and Ohio streets. Poorly paid lake mariners could hardly afford to stay elsewhere while in the city until 1874 when the Friendly Inn, just one of a chain of boardinghouses in American cities, appeared. Founded to cater to the poor and not just mariners, it offered food and lodging for $4 a week as well as reading rooms filled with temperance literature.[74]

Founders of boardinghouses such as this usually came out of the American evangelical movement intent on bettering society by spreading the Gospel and promoting temperance. Some of its most notable figures became staunch advocates for the rights of seamen and fierce foes of crimps. One such campaigner, Reverend William Taylor, started his career as a Methodist preacher in Baltimore. In the fall of 1848 his bishop directed him to start a mission in California, so he and his family sailed for San Francisco. Upon his arrival on September 21, 1849, he immediately realized he had much work before him. No preachers proselytized here, and its inhabitants had converted the city's only church into a school.[75]

Taylor built a chapel in the heart of Portsmouth Plaza, a den of inequity filled with gambling houses that included the infamous El Dorado and Parker House. His knowledge of, and sympathy for, the life of the seaman came about because of the chaplain's work at the United States Marine Hospital at Rincon Point.[76] He found seamen a useful tool in spreading the Gospel because they visited places all around the world and thus could proclaim the Word in all points of the globe, a precedent he felt Jesus had established by inviting several fishermen to be members of his inner circle of apostles.[77]

Other preachers and religious societies embraced this idea as well. To get the message out, some of them established churches along the waterfronts where sailors lived and caroused. An Episcopal minister, for example, ran the Churchman's Missionary Association for Seamen, a unique building designed by Clement L. Dennington that floated upon the Delaware River along Philadelphia's waterfront, an edifice inspired by the Floating Church of Our Savior in New York City.[78] On the West Coast the San Francisco Port Society established the Mariner's Church of San Francisco at the corner of Drumm and Sacramento streets in 1860. (It did not float.)[79]

On September 25, 1856, Taylor gave his first sermon against the evils of shanghaiing. In it he pointed out that although the word "shanghaiing" had recently entered the English lexicon, the system behind it had existed for a long time, one he deemed nothing more than "vassalage and voluntary serfdom." His suggestions to end it included founding a boardinghouse that did not try to make paupers of its lodgers, the creation of new laws or the strengthening of existing ones to protect sailors, the abolishment of advance wages, and forcing captains to hire the men directly so as to remove the crimps as middlemen. He berated boardinghouse masters who called themselves Christians but did not act like them.[80]

Other evangelicals had already taken up the cause of the sailor long before Taylor set foot in San Francisco. In 1825 Reverend John Truair, a pastor of the Mariner's Church in New York City and editor of *The Mariner's Magazine,* wrote an editorial calling for a national organization to improve the seaman's life. In response, one started up, but it failed that same year. In 1828 a second try resulted in the far more successful American Seamen's Friend Society. Beyond spreading the message of the Gospel to the godless sailor, it established a banking system and a series of honest boardinghouses that came with one catch: lodgers could not swear, play games, dance, or drink alcohol.[81]

The upsurge against imbibing spirits began in America around the 1820s and came out of the Second Great Awakening, a movement started in reaction to the dissolution of state-sponsored churches. Its first meeting occurred in 1801 at Cane Ridge, Kentucky, which attracted 10,000 people and lasted a week. The movement promoted evangelical revivalism and spawned a number of moral reform societies aimed at making America better by eliminating its vices and bringing God to everyone.[82]

"Demon rum" became one of the Awakening's favorite targets because those who became drunk acted below the earthly perfection the evangelicals in the movement strove to achieve. Although the Second Great Awakening died around 1830, the temperance movement it sparked continued to grow. One group, the American Society for the Promotion of Temperance, which later became the American Temperance Society, came up with the idea of signing a pledge (later "The Pledge") to never drink a drop of alcohol again. It originally called for swearing never to imbibe distilled beverages, but in the 1830s the society expanded this to all types of alcohol.[83]

Americans at this time drank staggering amounts regardless of race, age, or social status. Even infants got a share: mothers gave it to their sick babies as medicine.[84] In 1790 Americans consumed an average of five gallons of liquor a year, and by 1830 they drank nearly nine and a half. The consumption of whiskey increased exponentially upon the repeal of America's whiskey tax in 1802 (the one that set off the notorious Whiskey Rebellion), making it so cheap that just about anyone could afford it. By 1825 an average one day's wage could buy two gallons.[85]

Not even the Puritans had abstained. They served wine at their services and other church functions. Boston mourners at the 1678 funeral of a prominent Puritan minister "consumed over fifty gallons of wine, while at the funeral of a minister in Ipswich just a few years later, those in attendance drank two barrels of cider and a barrel of wine." Members of one the earliest temperance groups in America, the Massachusetts Society for the Suppression of Intemperance, drank wine during their meetings. Alcohol touched every aspect of American life, including politics. Candidates who served the most alcohol during a campaign usually won.[86]

Proponents of temperance believed excessive drinking caused poverty and other social ills in general and the ills suffered by sailors in particular, thus bringing this group low because chronic drunkenness allowed others to take advantage of them and treat them poorly. And here advocates had a point— sailors imbibed staggering quantities of alcohol—but, as Richard Dillon pointed out in his book *Shanghaiing Days,* the temperance people had their argument backwards: mariners drank heavily *because* of their poor treatment.[87]

Alcoholism did ruin the lives of many sailors, as happened to Horace Lane, an American merchant mariner who went to sea in the late eighteenth century. He attributed most of the series of his life's miseries to alcohol abuse. By 1820 Lane's drinking problem had become so terrible he left his wife and in 1824 ended up wandering the streets of New York so drunk he suffered from delirium and tremors. He sobered up enough to return to his home around Stillwater, New York, and there moved in with his sister, but his drinking problem did not disappear. To fuel his habit, he turned to burglary and for this served prison sentences in Connecticut and New York.[88] After several years ashore and a failed second marriage, Lane went to New York City and there took a berth on a ship for London. But by now he had become too old to serve as a ship's hand, so he quit this life for good. Methodist reformers

Those who pledged to never again imbibe alcohol signed this 1840s temperance certificate, a lithograph created by Thomas S. Sinclair (Library of Congress Prints and Photographs Division).

helped get him off the bottle through religion, but on the whole he considered most evangelicals hypocrites because, while they called for the aid of the downtrodden, they refused to give them any help other than words of encouragement.[89]

He had a good point. The weekly temperance newspaper *The New-York Organ*, "A Family Journal Devoted to Temperance, Morality, Education, and

General Literature," insulted and degraded those whose lives it wanted to improve. Spewing the same garbage that people still use to this day to justify their selfishness, the article "Short Sermon for the Poor No. 1: 'Time Is Money'" summed this patronizing tone up quite well: "The fault is your own— it is altogether so." It seems doubtful any impoverished person would waste three precious cents for this kind of "help."[90]

British-born actor William H. Smith found a much better way to spread the temperance message. He wrote the play *The Drunkard,* a story in which its villain exacts revenge against its hero by making him an alcoholic. The protagonist heads to New York City and there a reformed drunkard-turned-philanthropist helps get him off of the bottle, prompting the man to pledge he will never drink again. In an era when most plays ran at best a week and popular ones no more than fifty times, *The Drunkard* appeared at the Boston Museum 144 times, then expanded to Brooklyn, Cincinnati and Philadelphia. In 1850 it ran at the 3,000-seat Barnum's American Museum in New York City from July 8 to October 7, and of its 150 shows, 100 ran consecutively. Other plays of this type also appeared in America, but most did not have *The Drunkard*'s success.[91]

Plays might have made converts, but they did nothing to aid those who desired to get off the bottle, especially sailors. Here temperance societies stepped in by setting up boardinghouses in which lodgers could stay sober and out of debt, such as Mizpah Seamen's Rest in New York City. Established by the Seamen's Christian Association on January 14, 1888, and located on the corner of Washington and West Tenth streets, it offered "comfortable, attractive room[s] where seamen [could] find a cordial welcome, plenty of good reading, and conveniences for writing."[92]

Open from eight in the morning until ten in the evening, it held services every night and twice on Sunday. Its missionaries extended their work by going on board steamers of the White Star and State lines on Sundays to hold services. Within about eight months of operation it had hosted "over 1,000 seamen, of whom more than two-thirds have connected themselves with the work. Some 200 had signed the pledge there, and more than 100 have professed conversion." Its success seemingly justified the temperance movement's belief that removing alcohol would better sailors' lives, but they failed to realize the real aid had come from charging a reasonable price for room and board as well as forgoing selling goods and services to them at inflated prices.[93]

A refuge similar to the Mizpah Seamen's Rest appeared in Tacoma, Oregon, in 1897. Founded and operated by Norwegian-born Birgitte Funnemark and her daughter, Christine, as a nondenominational mission, its origin stretched back to 1884 when Birgitte lost her sea captain husband, Albert Abelseth, to a storm in the North Sea, an event prompting her to move to

Tacoma with her children four years later. Her loss gave her much sympathy for the men who toiled in the loneliness of the sea, motivating her to want to do something to give this class of men aid. To that end she saved her money with the aim of opening a place for them.[94]

In 1897 she and Christine converted a two-storey house a few blocks away from the waterfront into the sailor's boardinghouse they called the Seamen's Rest, one funded entirely by donations. A nice place with a canopied front porch and a picket fence, its reading room contained Bibles and other materials in a variety of languages to cater to the international diversity of sailors. The owners held Sunday services complete with organ music and Christine's "soprano voice." Christine boarded incoming ships to offer room and board to those interested. The Rest did so well its proprietresses sold their first house and bought a larger one with eleven rooms on North 11th Street. Although they hosted an average of 500 men each month, the Rest closed after only five years of operation in December 1903 due to Birgitte's decaying health, although she lived until 1919.[95]

America did not have a monopoly on benevolent boardinghouses. In the London slum of Bluegate Fields, located in the northern part of the city's east side, three naval captains set up the Sailor's Home as an alternative place for seamen that did not do everything possible to separate them from their meager pay. The Home charged a reasonable rate for boarding and offered a small beer bar to keep those who insisted on drinking from going out and imbibing the evil concoctions they would find elsewhere. The facility had reading and game rooms with clean, well-kept dormitories for sleeping. Its founders established a savings bank in which lodgers could safely leave their money while at sea. The captains also founded the Destitute Sailors' Asylum around the corner in which penniless sailors who had lost everything could stay. A purely charitable organization, its residents had only to agree to clean the place to be allowed to stay.[96]

While Christian-based boardinghouses created many converts on land, few kept their faith while at sea because shipboard life simply did not offer an environment in which a man could live a chaste life. About this an 1859 article that appeared in the *Atlantic Monthly* opined, "The Bethel, the Home, and the Bible are all right, but they are for the shore, and the sailor's home is on the sea." This anonymous author could not imagine "sailors reading their Bibles aloud of a Sunday afternoon, and entertaining each other with profound theological remarks, couched in hazy nautical language."[97]

Men quite devout on land often lost their faith while at sea. Before becoming a seaman in 1755, John Nicol of Scotland said his prayers daily and read his Bible frequently. This devotion slowly decayed during his twenty-five years at sea, then stopped. While at St. Kitts, an island of the Lesser Antilles in the Caribbean, he became severely ill and swore he would return to God if he survived. As his health improved, his resolve faded.[98]

Moral backsliding at sea happened largely because of peer pressure. Men recently "born again" who came on board and began pointing out the moral failings of others soon found themselves ostracized.[99] This happened to a sailor known only as John B. Born and raised in Ireland, he joined the British Army in 1837 and frequently got liquored up. He stayed in the army until 1850, then returned home to live with his sister, but his alcohol problem persisted. He headed for America and in 1854 joined the U.S. Navy. Not surprisingly, this only increased his intake of alcohol. Chronic rheumatism caused the Navy to place him on the sick list. While on medical leave in Hawaii he visited the Seamen's Friend Society, where he found God and gave up drinking.[100]

Returning to the navy, he began preaching to his fellow enlisted men. Deeming him a fanatic, they told him they would "knock the religion out of" him. One night as he slept, someone cut his hammock. Although the fall caused him significant injury, he continued to treat the others only with kindness. Soon enough they started to speak to him once more. Despite his sincere efforts, he managed to convert only one young sailor. Discharged in New York, he spent a year there "at the Sailor's Home in Cherry-Street," wandered the world for a time, then settled down to work in one of New York's floating churches.[101]

5

Liberty Days

Upon arriving at Gosport, an English city west of Portsmouth, American seaman Jacob Nagle fell in with two friends who invited him to go out to drink milk punch with some lady friends for the day. At its end Nagle asked one of his female companions if he could see her house. The two went there and he slept over, leaving after breakfast. He later learned he had had sex with a woman married to an officer in the Royal Navy, but he did not care because it had meant nothing to him. He had just enjoyed the moment.[1]

Between 1753 and 1795 Nagle made his home in London's East End, a place that offered every pleasure a mariner could want, including some of his favorites, such as opera, plays, alcohol, and especially women. He thought little of his future, instead indulging in his whims. He spent most of his money on women. Once, upon meeting two destitute sisters and their cousin aged between sixteen and nineteen, he and his friends took pity on them by buying them meals and heavy coats. Later they took them out to dinner and a play at Sandown Castle near Deal, then paid for a carriage to take them to Dover. Another time Nagle paid the monthly rent of a young lady he did not know because he could not resist helping a woman with a pretty face.[2]

One Bell

Like Nagle, most sailors failed to save their wages, living for the moment rather than planning for the future. They spent their wages during shore leave—a time they called their "liberty days"—indulging in the vices they had to give up while at sea. Of all these lost pleasures, alcohol loomed largest in their dreams. One witness of this phenomenon commented, "Naturally enough, perhaps, this forced abstinence breeds unholy desires in his soul; the absent liquor becomes tenfold as alluring by reason of its very absence, so when an opportunity comes he takes advantage of it, and drinks copiously." Indeed, once ashore, seamen wanted to make up for lost time.[3]

Alcohol became so associated with seamen that many sailing terms entered the everyday English lexicon as drinking euphemisms. On a ship, "down the hatch" originally meant dropping cargo into the ship's hold, "pickled" a way of preserving food as well as the method chosen to embalm Lord Horatio Nelson's body after his death at the Battle of Trafalgar, and "three sheets to the wind" a way of turning a ship's sails to better catch a breeze.[4] And as much as this writer hates to give validity to any stereotype, the saying "spending like a drunken sailor" had much legitimacy.

Not all mariners drowned their woes with drink. Some chose to use drugs instead. In the late nineteenth and early twentieth centuries opium became their drug of choice. When this became too expensive for the average sailor to afford, many turned to morphine, cocaine, and heroine, at least until the beginning of World War I when their cost became prohibitive.[5] Certainly not all seamen came to shore to get drunk or indulge in other vices. Many attended church while there. Some enjoyed visiting the countryside, getting some exercise, or shopping in foreign markets to buy exotic items, including things for immediate consumption, such as fresh vegetables and fruit, as well as souvenirs that included exotic pets and weapons.[6]

But seamen who came to shore to indulge in the available vices rarely had to go very far inland to find them. Along the shores the Willamette River in Portland, for example, stood a countless number of saloons, dancehalls, and brothels. One of its biggest drinking establishments, a saloon owned by August Erikson, covered an entire block. Within it hung a giant oil painting, *The Slave Market,* containing a scene filled with naked Grecian women. A $5,000 pipe organ provided music. The bar offered free lunches patrons could wash down with five-cent beers or two whiskies for a quarter.[7]

Mariners also enjoyed gambling, an easy vice to indulge in American cities. Those with little money went to "skinning houses" or "low dens," while the wealthy visited a "first-class hell." Gambling halls started to gain popularity in American cities in the 1830s, growing at an exponential rate by mid-century. New York City, for example, had about twelve establishments in 1830 and by 1850 around 6,000, despite the fact the city had officially outlawed them. The New York Association for the Suppression of Gambling estimated that in 1850 the existing houses in which gambling operated exclusively employed 25,000 people, roughly 5 percent of New York's total population of 515,000.[8] A sailor who entered a gambling house had many ways to lose his money. Here he could find everything from dice games to cards to roulette. Or he might go into a pool hall in which he could bet on the outcome of the games played there as well as horse races because of a connection to the track via a telegraph line.[9]

Of the card games available in the nineteenth century, gamblers preferred faro over all others. Originating in England around 1700 where it went by the name "Pharaoh," participants played against the dealer, not each other, and won by matching the cards dealt. Winning involved little skill: the game offered roughly fifty-fifty odds. To tilt this to their favor, unscrupulous dealers marked the cards or used other means of cheating. Legitimate casinos so disliked the odds they started to drop the game altogether, so that by the end of the nineteenth century it had fallen out of favor.[10]

Two Bells

Until the twentieth century, most American and British landsmen considered common seamen undesirable wretches. Because of this unjustified stigma, sailors who came to shore often could not find a "decent" woman to love. A desperate need for companionship coupled with months of unrelieved lust caused many sailors to turn to prostitutes not out of preference but rather for lack of other opportunities. Sailors could find them in nearly every port in the world. In Tahiti, for example, native women sold arriving sailors fruit and themselves. On the island of St. Helena those women who came to shore to wash the clothes of visiting sailors advertised the availability of their bodies by making their cheeks rosy, and in some ports captains allowed women on board for this purpose. Cape Town, South Africa, whose earliest records of a brothel date to 1681, did not try to interfere with the business until 1868.[11]

Although New York City on the whole did not condone the practice, it certainly had much of it, as evidenced by a unique guide written by an anonymous writer using the pseudonym A Butt Ender, slang for a pro-labor Democrat. Published in 1839 under the title *Prostitution Exposed; or A Moral Reform Directory, Laying Bare the Lives, Histories, Residences, Seductions, &c. of the Most Celebrated Courtezans [sic] and Ladies of Pleasure of the City of New-York, Together with a Description of the Crime and Its Effects, as also, of the Houses of Prostitution and Their Keepers, Houses of Assignation, Their Charges and Conveniences, and Other Particulars Interesting to the Public,* it sold in the guise as a tract *against* houses of ill-repute, then slyly gave the addresses, prices, services offered, and the quality and type of women available in them. Out-of-towners probably used this book the most.[12]

Even without such a guide, seamen could readily find prostitutes along the East River as well as the west shore of the Hudson in the saloons and boardinghouses, especially on Water and Cherry streets. Or they could go to the infamous Corlears Hook at the end of Grand Street, a place where respected citizens refused to travel. Known as "the Hook" and inhabited mainly by low-paid dock workers, it contained prostitutes of the lowest sort, ones emaciated by drugs, liquor and disease. The term "hooker" may have derived its name from here.[13]

London had its own infamous low places in which prostitutes worked, such as Shoe Lane and Fleet Street, an area filled with a labyrinth of tight, dark alleyways containing nothing but poverty and other miseries. Here stood some of the city's seediest brothels. Called "bawdy houses" by the locals, this term derived its name from the "bawds" running them—women no longer able to sell themselves who recruited those younger than themselves for that purpose. The remnants of some of these places still exist. Surviving bas-reliefs found in one house called the Cheshire Cheese contain a scene of men and women having sex, and another showing two women pleasuring a single man.[14]

Because London's West End prostitutes sold themselves mainly to the wealthy, sailors generally stuck to the East End where they could find more affordable women in places such as Wapping, Whitechapel (where Jack the Ripper did his killing), Ratcliff Highway, Waterloo Road, Lambent, the Strand, and Covent Garden. Sailors seemed particularly drawn to the brothels on High Street in the Shadwell District because of its loud music. Here a man could find several particularly well-known houses, including the White Swan, the Grapes, and the Paddy.[15]

Most women got into the sex trade out of necessity, desperation, or against their will. A lack of morality or an insatiable sexual appetite had little to do with it. Those forced into it because of economic need often came from broken homes. Revulsion of men or a lack of interest in intercourse did not matter to them: either they worked or starved. Some did not even get paid.[16]

Prostitutes and seamen had a number of things in common. In the Western world, both suffered verbal and physical abuse, stood at the bottom rung of the social ladder, and had little legal recourse to address these issues. Their meager wages made it hard to do more than live from day to day. Their occupational hazards, on the other hand, differed considerably. Most obviously women can become pregnant. The prostitutes in Eau Claire, Wisconsin, had to suffer from indignant mobs burning down their brothels. This became such a problem that the city's newspapers finally took notice and ran stories in 1875 blaming the phenomenon on the failure of law enforcement to close them down.[17]

Most women in the sex trade lived in a state of constant fear from clients, who often took out their frustrations on them. Workingwomen in brothels got into brutal fights with one another that sometimes resulted in maiming or per-

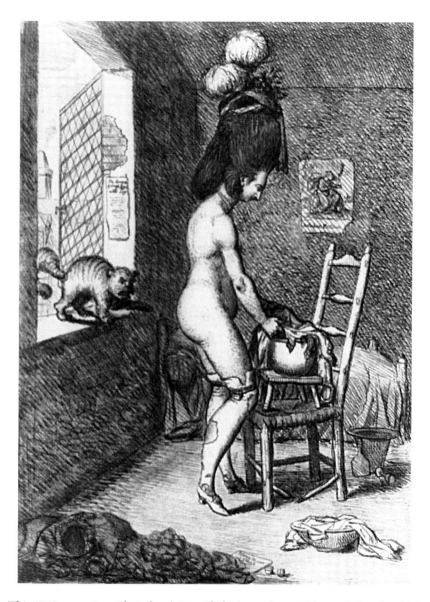

This 1779 engraving, *The Whore's Last Shift,* shows the terrible conditions in which prostitutes lived (Library of Congress Prints and Photographs Division, publisher/creator unknown, February 9, 1779).

manent disfigurement. Guns also presented a danger. In one instance, an exchange of shots in an Eau Claire brothel resulted in the death of one man and the wounding of another in the groin. A workingwoman there got hit in the face, and only later did someone find her wandering aimlessly through the streets.[18]

In New York's Chinatown, Chinese crime syndicates often brought women over from the home country for the specific purpose of making them sex slaves.[19] Some they culled from impoverished families who sold their daughters to them, and others they kidnapped. Yet not all Chinese prostitutes came to America involuntarily. Peasant females from Southern China ranging in age from twelve to sixteen willingly came to escape poverty, signing contracts stipulating a specific period for which they would serve. Such importations became more difficult when the United States enacted the Chinese Exclusion Act of 1882 barring the entry of Chinese into the United States for ten years except for those who came from wealthy families and therefore had the clout to get entry papers as students or professionals. Chinese crime syndicates exploited this loophole by snatching the daughters of the affluent, supplementing demand with white women or those stolen from rival whorehouses.[20]

The London Society for the Protection of Young Females in London issued a report in 1836 detailing the practice of taking girls aged eleven to fifteen from their homes and literally stripping off their clothes and redressing them in gaudy apparel. The girls were then thrown onto the streets, and these costumes advertised what the girls would do if paid. Escaping from the pimps who had procured them rarely happened, and in any case the girls often picked up sexually transmitted diseases in a matter of weeks that would ultimately ravage their bodies. One estimate reckoned that between 1827 and 1836 at least 2,700 such kidnapping cases for this purpose had occurred.[21]

In New York City, the basement saloons in the seedier parts of town employed waitresses who often doubled as prostitutes. They wore costumes meant to advertise their wares and took their clients into the upper rooms to transact business. In some saloons a man could strip a girl for as little as fifty cents. Waitress-prostitutes made an average of $15 to $25 a week, part of this coming from the commission they received for each drink sold. Of this, a percentage went to their pimps. Waitress-prostitutes might drop Spanish fly into the drinks of unresponsive men, in the belief it worked as an aphrodisiac, or drug and rob those disinclined to spend a lot on them.[22]

A hierarchy of prostitutes existed. At the top stood women who worked in bordellos catering to the elite. Next came those who worked common brothels that men of all social stations frequented. At the bottom fell the lowly streetwalker. In San Francisco the courtesans who catered to the city's wealthiest men rarely lasted longer than four months because the work ruined the perfection of their bodies this clientele demanded. Elite bordellos therefore needed to continuously fill vacancies and did so by employing male and female runners much the same way crimps did.[23]

A male bordello runner appeared as a good-looking gentleman who readily caught the attention of naïve young ladies. He frequented ladies' seminaries, church events, hotels, and pleasure resorts only the well-off could afford. Upon choosing his victim, he put forth all his charm to make himself an acceptable escort for the lady in question. Once he had her within his power, he drugged his victim while at a dinner or some event, then took her virginity during her moment of unconsciousness. Now "ruined," he used this fact to blackmail her into service at the bordello he represented.[24]

A female runner naturally could not seduce the young women as such, so she appeared as a respectable matron who would befriend a girl. Gaining her victim's confidence, she lured her into the trap in which a male accomplice would seduce and thus "shame" his victim into working for their bordello. Brothel runners preferred pretty girls who came from villages—"the belles of the towns"—because the farther away they were from San Francisco, the better the chances no one would rescue them from their fate. Of course, not all young women felt enough shame to agree to work for a madame, and when that happened, she was made to do so anyway.[25]

Some London prostitution rings raised kidnapped and destitute girls on farms, then brought them to the city when they reached the right age, keeping them as ignorant as possible. One girl, Ellen, did not even know her last name, nor had anyone taught her to read or write. At the age of eleven a "gentleman" appeared one day and kissed her. Two years later he brought her to his rooms in London, giving her so much wine she could remember nothing else.[26]

Many forced into prostitution lived such miserable lives they often succumbed to alcohol and drug abuse. Those who became pregnant and sought an abortion faced a great risk because a botched attempt usually resulted in death. In addition to pregnancy, prostitutes had to constantly worry about venereal diseases, particularly gonorrhea and syphilis.[27] Historical records indicate gonorrhea, more popularly known as the "clap," "dose," "stain," or "drip," has existed at least as far back as ancient Egypt. For a man, it causes the secretion of "a white-to-yellowish" pus from his penis. In a woman it goes into the uterus and can cause sterility, arthritis, and skin lesions. The cure for gonorrhea did not appear until the 1950s.[28]

Syphilis has even more dire symptoms, at least for the roughly 25 percent who suffer from its third, or tertiary, stage, which can manifest itself over twenty years after infection. It destroys organs, attacks the central nervous and cardiovascular systems, and, more rarely, causes insanity.[29] Before the introduction of the curing drug arsphenamine in 1910, most doctors tried to treat it with mercury, whose poisonous properties could cause, among other problems, bleeding of the gums, ulcerations in the cheeks, gangrene, and even strangulation. This prompted many of those inflicted to try to hide their symptoms rather than subject themselves to the remedy.[30]

The problem of venereal diseases being spread by sex workers did not go unnoticed by the towns and cities in which they occurred. Cape Colony, for one, introduced the first of three Contagious Diseases Acts in 1862 to try to put an end to the trouble. Using a system derived from one employed by the French, the act required prostitutes to register and submit to periodic medical examinations. Those found diseased then underwent treatment, voluntarily if possible, involuntarily if not. Admittedly Cape Colony did *not* implement this policy because of public outcry but rather on the order of Britain's War Office, which wished to get the problem under control because venereal diseases had caused the hospitalization of 13 percent of its military personnel in the area.[31]

In New York City an assortment of evangelicals banded together to create the Female Asylum Society, an antiprostitution organization that attempted to help those in the business get out by setting up places to teach them useful vocations and prevent them from returning to their immoral ways. A lack of financial support caused its failure. In 1831 another group of evangelicals tried it again, this time setting up the Magdalene Society, a reference to the erroneous belief that the Biblical figure Mary Magdalene worked as a prostitute. The Magdalene Society failed mainly because the twenty-six men who ran it would not allow women on the board (although they did ask for female volunteers), plus they squabbled with one another over points of theology.[32]

Evangelical women founded an organization to aid fallen women called the New York Female Benevolent Society, which started operations on December 27, 1832. Its members came exclusively from the Presbyterian faith so as to avoid the interfaith squabbling that had bedeviled the Magdalene Society. It appointed a man to serve as both its spokesman and the one who ran its asylum, the reasoning for this based on the mistaken belief a virtuous woman could not handle the knowledge of what prostitutes did and how they lived. Unlike the societies before it, rather than attack the evils of prostitution, this one promoted its successes of getting them out of the business.[33]

Three Bells

In the 1850s thousands of Chinese came to America to fill the country's demand for laborers. Many of those who arrived did so under contracts in which they agreed to work for a company for a given number of years in exchange for the cost of transportation. As ethnic groups tend to do when in a foreign land, they created their own communities in a variety of cities, and these became known as Chinatowns. Many of those who fulfilled their work contracts stayed on and opened their businesses, at first to cater to their own people, but later expanding to include other ethnic groups, especially the white majority.[34]

One of the largest Chinatowns to develop on the East Coast appeared in New York City. It covered three blocks and contained blacks, Irish, and Italians in addition to ethnic Chinese.[35] Being right next to the city's biggest vice area, the Bowery, Chinese gambling houses attracted many white patrons, but these businesses became victims of their own success. Irish proprietors moved into the area and set up gambling houses that admitted only whites. The New York City Police Department harassed Chinese establishments with constant raids until the Chinese gave them bribes. This became such a problem they banded together to form the Fan Tan Syndicate in 1891 for mutual protection against such harassment. The syndicate's success caught the attention of the Hop Sing Tong, a Chinese criminal gang, who insisted on taking a cut of the action as well as demanding protection money.[36]

Chinese tongs operated primarily in America's Chinatowns, often dividing a city's territories up and using men armed with guns (the *bow how doy*) as enforcers who also intimidated or eliminated potential witnesses against their gang. America's first two tongs, the Hip Song and Kwang Dock, formed in 1854 along the West Coast for mutual protection against whites and their mob violence, then got involved with Chinese-run vice operations. The Hip Song Tong expanded all the way to the East Coast. Local politicians and the police force in San Francisco and other cities with Chinatowns along the West Coast had little interest in shutting down these vice operations because the tongs paid them to look the other way. Chinese business owners living in San Francisco also hired white guards to protect them from white hoodlums and other troublemakers, especially in the gambling halls where riots, muggings, and fights among patrons of all ethnicities frequently occurred.[37]

San Francisco's Chinatown attracted sailors seeking liquor, drugs, and bordellos filled with women from China. Here men could get Chinese prostitutes to do peculiar—and unmentionable—things to which no white woman in the business would consent. A rumor that Chinese women had vertical rather than horizontal vaginas allowed them to charge the curious ten cents a peek.[38] When San Francisco's Great Earthquake and Fire occurred on April 18, 1906, it destroyed this district. Upon the city's rebuilding, most of its vice operations never reopened.[39]

The quake failed to shake the life out of an adjoining vice district known as the Barbary Coast. Although its borders grew and shrunk, it generally encompassed "both sides of Broadway and Pacific [s]treets, and the cross streets between them, from Stockton [S]treet to the water front [as well as] ... nearly

A 1909 view of New York City's Chinatown (Library of Congress Prints and Photographs Division, publisher/creator unknown, 1909).

the whole length of Dupont [S]treet [which no longer exists], running south from Broadway, and many of its intersecting by-ways." The Barbary Coast, whose name probably refers to the pirate haven along part of the Mediterranean's African shore, began as a place of refuge for Latina harlots and thieves living on Telegraph Hill along Pacific and Broadway streets, although by 1897 they had disappeared from there. Criminals of all sorts and ethnicities soon followed, making the entire area a refuge because the police dared not enter it, at least in its earliest days.[40] Saloons made up about every other building along its streets, some having colorful names such as the Roaring Gimlet, the Cock of the Walk, the Bull's Run, Every Man Is Welcome, and Star of the Union.[41] Along its streets stood a number of "deadfalls," small places in which one could get a drink. Its dancehalls usually contained a melodeon, a reed organ capable of putting out enough sound to overcome the noise of those within and attract those without. Concert saloons staged sexually risqué shows that sailors came to see in droves.[42]

A journalist writing at the turn of the twentieth century described one concert saloon as "small and dingy" with a low, black ceiling and an entrance consisting of nothing more than latticed doors through which one could see a faint red lantern glowing outside. Scattered sand covered its floors and the chimneys of the oil lamps lighting it had blackened with extensive use. The

A view of San Francisco's Chinatown (Library of Congress Prints and Photographs Division, Keystone View Company, 1929).

place was filled with tobacco smoke, and some tables had green tops with tacks for use by gamblers. One end of the room remained clear to allow people to dance, with only a violinist and pianist providing the music. At the other end of the room stood the bar, and behind this hung a mirror on which someone had drawn decorations using soap.[43]

Here, too, contrary to the social norms of the time, men and women drank together.[44] Throughout the nineteenth and early twentieth centuries, saloons that served middle- and upper-class Americans did not allow women to occupy the same room as the men, forcing the former to buy liquor out of side doors or do their drinking in separate rooms. Few women broke this taboo until Prohibition, a fact exemplified by the famous Lucky Strike ad in which a young lady holds up a cocktail in a manner similar to the Statue of Liberty.[45]

Gambling houses prospered, too, some hidden from prying eyes. A nineteenth century travel writer named Colonel Albert S. Evans visited one such place. At first appearance it looked like a small deadfall with the promise of little but drinking. Along its far wall hung a sign on a green door that said, "Club Room—Now Open." A "well-dressed, gentlemanly man" guarded it, allowing only those he deemed acceptable through. Evans and his companions told him they had come from New York and just wanted to check it out. He allowed them to pass.[46] They went down a flight of stairs and into a hallway that Evans described as a smoke-filled "wide, low hall, furnished with long tables covered with glazed cloth, lighted brilliantly with gas, and crowded with men who gathered in groups around the different tables." Its foul-smelling air felt close. Dealers and their assistants "dressed in long black robes, which completely hide every article of everyday clothing which they have on, with wire masks which conceal their features, though partially transparent, and slouched hats, which hide every trace of hair, making subsequent identification absolutely impossible." They wore these costumes "to prevent policemen ... from being able to identify ... and prosecute them." Nothing but signs containing the club's rules decorated the walls. The room existed only for the function of gambling and nothing else.[47]

Some of the most disreputable establishments in the Barbary Coast stood along Pacific Street. One example was Buffalo Bill's Den, which closed in 1893. Another was run by Hattie Cavanaugh, who, despite having had her license revoked, kept operating by transferring ownership to someone else. Other saloons included the Cowboy's Rest and The Whale, the latter of which lost its license in 1893 but stayed in business anyway, possibly because its owner had bribed a politician or two.[48] Rough customers patronized it. In 1890 a fellow named Frank Randall got into a fight with its barkeep, James Griffith. During the altercation Randall hit Griffith with a cane. Griffith responded by shooting Randall in the thigh, so police charged him with attempted murder.[49]

In 1900 a reporter from the San Francisco newspaper *The Call*, Seymour Briscoe, explored the Coast's saloons by going undercover as a barkeep. He quickly learned this position required more skill at bouncing rowdy customers than mixing good drinks. He met a range of colorful characters who frequented Barbary Coast bars, including Portuguese Joe, a former seamen whose years of hard living had ruined his face, and Comstock Pete, a stock broker once worth $100,000 and now destitute. Briscoe also picked up a bit of the Coast's slang. One man, for example, came up to him and asked, "Say, ain't you de mark that used to sling for de Palm Leaf on Fourth [S]treet?" Briscoe understood this meant, "Weren't you the barkeep at the Palm Leaf?"[50]

Briscoe found that of all the drinks patrons imbibed, none got them drunk faster than absinth.[51] Once a favorite of the French, who outlawed it in 1915, this drink originated "in French-speaking Switzerland in the late eighteenth century." Characterized by its green color and bitter taste, it derived the former from lemon balm, an herb in the mint family, and the latter from wormwood, a shrub whose scientific name, *A. absinthium,* gave the drink its name. A variety of recipes existed, but all involved the same process. Distillers obtained the drink's base alcohol content by fermenting grapes, beets or grain, the last two making a lesser quality liqueur. Once distilled, a maker added the color and flavor, then stored it in a barrel for aging.[52]

Briscoe wrote his story about the Barbary Coast at a time when it had become an attraction for slum tourists, who marveled at halls in which blacks and whites danced together, saloons in which men and women drank together, and the spectacle of drunken sailors.[53] Slum tourism, or "slumming," began in America during its antebellum period. The wealthy paid guides to take them to places such as New York City's notorious Five Points. Slummers made these trips in large part because it helped to reinforce their stereotypes of the poor and their feelings of superiority over them. Slumming guidebooks for self-guided tours also appeared. The practice continued until at least the 1920s, where a slum tour in Chicago gave customers a glossary filled with "proletariat slang."[54]

In 1897 Chinatown started to expand into the Barbary Coast, driving out the whites living there. Demolition destroyed some of the Coast's more infamous establishments, while others took on new functions. A dive known as Hell's Kitchen, for example, became a Chinese hospital. These changes caused a considerable drop in the crime rate.[55] The Great Earthquake of 1906 further devastated the Coast by causing much of it to go up in flames, including many establishments owned by Jerome Bassity, its biggest saloon and brothel operator.[56]

Bassity decided to rebuild despite an ongoing grand jury investigation against him, which he did not think would indict him. (It did not.) His first new brothel, built on Commercial Street in partnership with a madam named Marcelle, housed 100 prostitutes. On its opening night of December 17, 1906, it offered all available pleasures for free. Many of the Coast's other vice operations also rebuilt, going full bore by 1907. The Coast's time as a tenderloin district began its final end in 1911 with the election of a new mayor, James Rolph, Jr., who had won his office with an anti-vice platform. Rolph waged a relentless war against the Coast's vice operations with the aid of city ordinances and new state laws, driving all the operations out within six years.[57]

Four Bells

A large number of sailors took their liberty days in New York City. The number visiting increased from about 22,000 in 1835 to 66,000 in 1860.[58] Sailors here often headed for the seediest part of town, the Bowery, because it offered every vice they could possibly want at prices they could afford. Originally a seventeenth century path that went from the town of New Amsterdam to Manhattan Island's outlying farms, the Bowery's name derived from the Dutch word *boerderij,* which means "farm" or "county seat." When the urban area of New Amsterdam, renamed New York by the English, encroached upon

This 1900 photograph by B.L. Singley (?) shows the Bowery (Library of Congress Prints and Photographs Division, Keystone View Company, March 5, 1900).

and transformed it into a street proper, it became a residential area in which mainly Quakers lived. Over the years they left and it degenerated into a vice-ridden slum.[59]

The street stretched for about a mile from Chatham Square to Cooper Union. In the Bowery's slum days it contained a surplus of recently arrived immigrants. Poverty sparked some of its inhabitants to form a few of history's most infamous American gangs, including the Dead Rabbits, Plug Uglies, and Shirt Tails. The New York City draft riots during the Civil War started here. Of all the streets in New York, only this one lacked a single church, and for much of the nineteenth and twentieth centuries the elevated trains hanging overhead cast it in dark shadows.[60]

The street's fourteen blocks offered tattoo parlors, music halls, restaurants, oyster houses, liquor shops, and a large number of overcrowded and smoke-filled drinking establishments. A reporter writing in *The Century* magazine in 1891 counted no less than eighty-two ground floor establishments that sold alcohol.[61] In the Bowery's earliest days, its dives served alcohol not in glasses but via a tube through which patrons sucked in as much as they could without taking a breath. Needless to say, many of them developed impressive lung capacities.[62]

The Bowery also hosted six novelty museums. In one of these, patrons could enter a bare room in which a phrenologist would examine their heads so as to present them with a chart of the findings based on the pseudoscience of phrenology. Invented in Vienna by Franz Joseph-Gall, phrenology could purportedly determine a person's characteristics and mental capacity by measurement of the features of the head, such as bumps on the skull and the shape of the eyes. Those who stepped into the museum's room for their examination heard the sound of a click and the falling of a partition before their eyes that read, "Professor Blinkum's charge is $2." Poor tourists such as the sailor could ill afford to pay such an exorbitant fee, but toughs stood by to work over those who refused.[63]

Like many slums in American cities of the nineteenth century, the Bowery produced a range of political bosses, the most dominant throughout the later part of the century being Timothy "Big Tim" Sullivan. Like most of those raised in a run-down neighborhood, he went to work at an early age, first as a newsboy, then as extra help in several print shops. His nickname derived from his height of six feet and weight of 200 pounds. He started out as a Bowery businessman, his earliest ventures including six saloons, fight promoting, and a racetrack. He later expanded into pool halls, saloons, gambling houses, and brothels. He became known as the "king of the underworld," a useful thing to be because it allowed him to "own" the police and avoid being arrested when he got into barroom fights.[64]

Sullivan's involvement with New York's Democratic political machine, Tammany Hall, began in earnest in 1886 when he won the first of seven terms in the New York State Assembly as a representative of the Five Points District. He switched to the state senate, then ran for and won a congressional seat in 1902 and 1904. Chief detective Thomas F. Byrnes of the New York City Police Department accused him of enabling the area's criminals, but he successfully defended himself in the Assembly by outlining his rags-to-riches career and disputing Byrnes' assertions of guilt by association. In 1900 a charge that he had a major interest in the expanding trade of prostitution in the Lower East Side also went nowhere.[65]

Sullivan used nepotism extensively to ensure his allies stayed loyal. His cousin "Little Tim" Sullivan, for example, became a lawyer and powerful politician in his own right. Sullivan, like most bosses of his era, took care of those he represented in some very overt ways. He made sure criminals received pardons, constituents called to jury duty got out of it, and those in need of building and business permits received them with minimal hassle.[66]

To ensure even the poorest did not go hungry, "Big Tim" Sullivan, along with several prominent politicians and policemen, established the Timothy D. Sullivan Association. On Christmas Day 1906, its annual handout served 3,000 people and gave away "5,000 pounds of poultry, 230 gallons of potato salad, 1,500 mince pies, each man having a half of a pie, 200 big bunches of celery, 2,000 loaves of bread, 40 cans of hot coffee and 40 kegs of beer. As each man went out of the door he received a briar pipe and a package of tobacco, together with a card which ... [would] entitle him to a present from ... [Sullivan] on his return to the city on February 6."[67]

In 1912 "Big Tim" Sullivan again ran for and won a seat in Congress, but he never took it. He had a peculiar mental breakdown that involved severe depression, paranoia, and hallucinations. In 1913 a court declared him a lunatic. Some accounts hinted he had developed the third stage of syphilis, the one that can cause insanity. He moved into his brother Patrick's country estate in Eastchester, from which he periodically ran away. His final disappearance lasted for two weeks, ending when someone recognized his thus-far unidentified body in the Fordham Morgue on September 13, 1913. A train in New Haven had killed him. His brother rescued his body just before it went into a grave in the potter's field.[68]

Sullivan left a large business legacy behind, including a lucrative theater franchise. In 1898 he renovated a church on Dewey Street and converted it into a successful theater. In 1904 he invested $5,000 in a venture by Seattle theater manager John W. Considine to buy four theaters in the Pacific Northwest. By 1907 the two owned about forty houses across the country that showed movies and hosted acts such as Will Rogers and Charlie Chaplin. Sullivan's share of the take amounted to about $20,000 a month.[69]

These theaters primarily handled acts that worked in vaudeville, itself born out of the Bowery's concert saloons, which showed a variety of spectacles including the cancan, boxing, wrestling, fights between rats and dogs, and, in later years, blackface minstrel shows and similar acts that exploited racial stereotypes for laughs, complemented by a variety of music acts—all the stuff that would make vaudeville such a success. As early as the 1830s, the lower classes came here to see shows in part because nothing like them appeared on Broadway. These earliest theaters had side businesses in their upper rooms that included prostitution and punch rooms.[70]

Sailors loved the theater. Horace Lane, whom we met in the previous chapter, considered it a part of his downward spiral into penury and crime: "The most bewitching, soul-enchanting of all the fascinating inducements that cleared the way to my sorrow, was the theatre. I would have sold two meals each day, and gone hungry, to procure money to get into this den of arch-mockery. I sold all my best clothes, and every thing that would fetch a shilling, to keep up this silly nightly" indulgence.[71]

6

Shanghaied!

Broughton Brandenburg, lately arrived in London and on his way to a shipping office, found himself stopped by an amiable Irishman who asked if he would split a sixpence drink with him at a nearby pub. Brandenburg agreed. Within, a Scotswoman barkeep asked if he had any money. Lying, he answered that he had just spent his last sixpence. She showed him two shillings and said her brother could get him a berth on a gentleman's yacht if he wanted it. Replying that he did, she handed him one of the coins and escorted him and the Irishman to a boardinghouse located "near the East India docks" two blocks away.[1]

Brandenburg did not have a favorable impression of its proprietor, describing him as "a one-eyed old villain with great arms on him like an ourangoutang [sic]." Given a bed and credit, Brandenburg noticed the landlord treated those with money far better than those without. Two days into Brandenburg's stay, the owner rounded up the lodgers in his debt, Brandenburg included, and said he had found them berths on a ship to which he would take them in several hours. Brandenburg, no fool, wanted to know the type of work and the ship's name. The landlord, who by now Brandenburg had identified as a crimp, gave no name but did claim this vessel would sail for Liverpool. Brandenburg pretended he believed that.[2]

The one-eyed crimp plied the men with drinks, but Brandenburg clandestinely dumped his, faking inebriation to mask his deception. At midnight the crimp led the now pliant lodgers to the docks. Brandenburg fell behind, then asked a dock watchman for the destination of the ship on which the crimp wanted him to sail. It would go to Australia, a place Brandenburg had no intention of visiting just then. He walked no farther. Expecting trouble, he picked up an iron rod lying on the dock for self-defense.[3]

The crimp returned. Brandenburg dropped his fake sailor's brogue and asked what he owed for his two-day stay as he planned to pay his host fair compensation. The crimp demanded a staggering £2 10*s,* the equivalent of about $12. Brandenburg balked, telling him to take five shillings else he would turn him into the authorities for an attempted shanghaiing. The crimp turned purple with rage but he took the money anyway.[4]

Brandenburg did not fit into the usual mold of a man sailing at the turn of the twentieth century. Well educated, he had gone to sea as a journalist with the intention of writing a series of articles about life at sea. He already knew of the menace of crimps and, forewarned, never faced any real danger of being shanghaied.[5] Those men not so well informed suffered great deprivations, sometimes sailing the world for many years before returning home and often getting into types of trouble they would have never imagined experiencing.

One Bell

Edward Miller, a violinist from Michigan who came to San Francisco to play in an orchestra, and Lester B. Willett, "a decorator and designer" from Chicago, met for the first time on February 22, 1907, when they awoke together in a cramped room filled with bunks. Its swaying indicated they sailed upon the sea, but neither knew how they had gotten there. Both recalled seeking entertainment along San Francisco's waterfront the night before, but beyond that, nothing. Reaching the main deck, the first mate informed them that they sailed upon the British ship *Glendower,* bound for Sydney, and they had to work as hands whether they liked it or not. Neither man knew a thing about sailing, and Miller found the work particularly onerous as he had never before done manual labor.[6]

The two decided they wanted to return to San Francisco, but upon arriving in Sydney they learned the *Glendower* would next head to England. She moored beside a steamer planning to sail to Valparaiso, Chile, a destination much closer to their objective of reaching San Francisco. They deserted to the steamer and, once on board, a sympathetic crewman helped them stow away. Caught, they agreed to pay for their passage by shoveling coal into the furnace. At Valparaiso they decided to remain aboard because their vessel's itinerary would take her north to trade along the coast and thus closer to San Francisco. They received their first shore leave at the nitrate port of Antofagasta, a northern Chilean town built on a flat shelf between the ocean and inland hills that one guidebook described as a "decidedly lacklustre desert city."[7]

As Willett and Miller wandered about, a storm swept in from the sea that forced their ship to leave without them. They figured they could find a berth on another, but much to their dismay soon learned seagoing vessels came into the harbor only every few months because of its bad anchorage. With just a few shillings between them, they could not afford an extended stay. "One day Willett saw a map of South America in a store on the main street. He noticed that the continent was comparatively narrow in the latitude of Antofagasta and that almost directly across on the Atlantic side" stood Buenos Aires, a busy port where he figured he and his companion could readily find a ship heading home.[8]

Only it turned out this city stood 1,000 miles away to the southeast—the map had had it seriously wrong—and no regular route or system of overland transportation existed to get them there. With nothing to lose and no other options, they decided to walk.[9] The first part of their journey involved crossing the forbidding Atacama Desert, a place so dry it contained areas where no rain has fallen since records began. Primarily a flat plain barren of much save for gravel and the odd hill or sand dune, its only oases existed where it met the foothills of the Andes.[10] Here ranchers raised livestock in the "high altitudes ... and in the valleys of rivers fed by the melting of high mountain snows."[11] Ranchers transported the Americans across the desert to the foothills of the Andes Mountains in ox-driven carts, allowing the two to make 100 miles in ten days.[12]

Here desert gave way to a less dry and more productive landscape filled with aromatic ñipa, bright flowers, and trees that bore fruits and nuts. The Americans saw nothing blossoming because they passed through in August, winter in the southern hemisphere. They followed an old trail across the mountains proper, which took them above the snow line for about half the trek. At these high altitudes their meager clothes offered no protection against the intense cold, snow, and high winds that could push a traveler off the side of a cliff. Altitude sickness, called the *puna* by the locals, caused nose bleeds, bleeding in the lungs, and shortness of breath. At times they descended into valleys where they had to ford rivers, a precarious thing to do, as these waterways swelled dangerously at certain times of the year.[13]

Between foraging and help from the local mountain people—Quechua-speaking natives—the Americans managed to avoid starvation, although this sometimes meant eating raw corn. As they approached the Argentinean side of the mountains, the landscape turned into red granite with an arid climate that supported cacti and thorny bushes. The mountain path they had thus far used took them to the Argentinean town of Mendoza, a comparative oasis because it had wide tree-lined streets and a well-stocked general store.[14] It served as the terminus of the Buenos Aires Ferrocarril Oeste, a railway owned at this time by the British.[15]

Some of its workers kindly gave "each of the Americans a pair of shoes and a blanket" as well as a ride out of the mountains into the Argentinean Pampas, a place as legendary as America's Wild West. It consists of flat, fertile plains barely a few hundred feet above sea level that extend roughly 400 miles west of Buenos Aires. In the nineteenth century the area drew in immigrant settlers from around the world and spawned the famous Argentinean cowboy, the gaucho, whose cultural roots went as far back as the seventeenth century.[16] Willett and Miller traveled across the Pampas via ox cart, reaching Buenos Aires in September. They went straight to the American consulate for help. The consul told them that the ship *Horatius* would leave for New York in two days. Without money to pay for their passage, the two agreed to sign on as firemen.[17]

Two Bells

Alfred E. Clark left his Oregon farm and headed to Portland to study for the ministry in 1888. By January 1891 he had become so disillusioned with the prospect of being a man of God, he left the seminary. For the next year he managed a couple of farms, a life he liked no better. He quit farming and headed back to Portland to experience the sins it could offer. On his first night there, a man suggested he stay at a boardinghouse for sailors on Second and Glison streets, a run-down warehouse that "had everything in it except bats flying around. Downstairs there was a big room with two long tables where mess was served" in the same manner as one would find in the forecastle. It had a kitchen and washroom—unusual features in a boardinghouse—and sold no liquor, something lodgers could purchase just around the corner.[18]

One of Portland's most notorious crimps, Lawrence "Larry" Mikola Sullivan, owned and ran it. Born in St. Louis around 1863, Sullivan moved to nearby Astoria as a youth. Thereafter he went to Portland, where he enjoyed a successful bare-knuckled prizefighting career. Upon his retirement from that business, he got into politics. A good-looking man, he did well as a ward boss, acting as a mediator between the city's politicians and those who owned vice operations. He made money easily but spent it just as quickly. He could arrange for votes for a candidate at a moment's notice. Once, for example, he hired the entire crew of a Dutch ship—none of whom could speak a bit of English— to vote for his candidate. Despite spending $2 per crewman, it did him little good. His man still lost.[19]

A day after Clark arrived at Sullivan's boardinghouse, he invited all his lodgers to come with him on a pleasure cruise to Astoria aboard the steamboat *Iralda,* which he had just chartered for that purpose. Clark jumped at the chance. Sullivan brought women on board before departing, then, once under way, largely disappeared. A fellow named Mr. Smith served as the host. The party-goers drank in excess, danced, and enjoyed a large lunch that included oysters, pork, crab, and fried salmon.[20]

Upon reaching Astoria, Smith offered his guests a chance to see the city itself for an hour and had those interested in this venture put their names on the passenger list to ensure no one got left behind. None of them bothered to take a closer look at this document, Clark included. After seeing the city, someone asked the party-goers if they would like to take a tour of the deep-sea ship *T.F. Oakes,* a steel-hulled vessel with a new-fangled steam winch (this ship was the same one whose crew would suffer from terrible scurvy five years later). Those who wished to visit boarded rowboats to get to her.[21]

Clark recalled that after a brief tour, "four large men who were dressed in policemen's uniforms came out one of the cabin doors. They all carried a .45 revolver in each hand. One of them told us to be good and we wouldn't get hurt. Almost at the same time the captain of the Oakes, two mates and the bos'n [boatswain] came out the other cabin door. The mates and the bos'n carried big steel handcuffs with them," which they slapped on the visitors' wrists. The ship's master, Captain Reed, informed them they would set sail for Le Havre, a French port with the famous harbor known as the Havre-de-Grâce.[22]

Some of the prisoners pointed out they had not signed articles as required by law. The captain replied, "Oh, yes, you did.... I've got all your names signed to ship's articles right here in my pocket. You signed them before you left the Iralda." He produced the so-called "passenger list" upon which they had placed their signatures. The guards took the handcuffed men below into a dark hold where they stayed until the next morning. At dawn they returned to the main deck. Now on the open sea, the captain ordered them released from their bonds since they could no longer desert. Clark received his first command: "Loose the main royal." It had come from the first mate, Black Johnson, whose name derived from both his skin color and disposition. As a landsman, Clark had no idea what the order meant (Johnson had told him to climb aloft and unfurl the topmost sail on the mainmast), but fortunately a seasoned hand named Jock Morgan took pity on Clark and taught him how to do his duties.[23]

Clark learned to sail pretty well, although he did not like the food, which tasted awful and failed to fill his belly for the entire 120-day voyage. He got on well with the sailmaker, who kindly fashioned him a pair of canvas trousers. At one point Clark got into a fistfight with Black Johnson. Having had some boxing lessons, he held his own until someone knocked him out by hitting him with a belaying pin from behind. Not long after this incident, Johnson disappeared during a nasty storm. Years later Clark learned Johnson had fallen overboard but managed to catch the rail. He called for help and the one who answered whacked his hands to ensure he fell into the churning water below.[24]

Reaching Le Havre in February 1892, Clark and his fellow Americans went to the U.S. consulate to receive their discharge papers and pay. Here he learned that Sullivan had signed him up as an able-bodied seaman and had taken his $60 advance to cover the cost of the riverboat excursion. Because Clark had never before set foot on a ship, the captain had downgraded him to an ordinary seaman and for this he received only $15 a month rather than the $30 he would have gotten as an able-bodied seaman. He therefore earned $60 in regular wages for the two-month voyage to Le Havre and at its end it left him with nothing since Sullivan had taken this. Clark liked sailing but swore he would not do so unless paid. After a four-week stay in France, he took a berth on the forty-year-old ship *St. David* under the command of Captain Frost. The ship, bound for Philadelphia, got blown seriously off course by a storm and ended up in the Sargasso Sea.[25]

This body of water has some peculiar properties. The confluence of northern and southern trade winds cause it to rise more than a foot higher than the rest of the Atlantic. A thick seaweed called sargassum floats across its surface, giving it its name.[26] The wind conditions also whip up numerous waterspouts. Clark reported he saw as many as fifteen to twenty at once, which the *St. David* deftly evaded, although these tornados on the water pose little danger to larger vessels. Clark had heard firing a cannon into one dispersed it, but since the *St. David* lacked such artillery, he never learned if it worked or not. (Marq de Villiers addressed this in his book *Windswept: The Story of Wind and Weather:* "Contrary to legend, firing a cannonball into a waterspout will have no effect whatever, except to wet the cannonball on its way through.")[27]

As the voyage dragged on, it became apparent Captain Frost had gone mad. One day while Clark was at the wheel, he watched him come on deck and yell at several men aloft. One replied with something smart. Frost dashed back into his cabin, returned with a rifle, and started shooting at the men. Horrified, Clark let go of the wheel and tried to intervene, but he was too late. A man named Able Jones fell to his death. The crewmen overpowered Frost and threw him into irons, then the first mate took command. They later gave Frost his freedom but all kept a close watch on him.[28]

Despite the fact the crew had done the right thing, overpowering and relieving a captain of duty constituted an act of mutiny. Upon docking in

Philadelphia, local authorities placed the crew under guard with plans to move them into a jail for holding until trial. Though certain of exoneration, Clark did not like the thought of spending time incarcerated, so he bribed one of the guards on board with $2 to ignore him as he jumped overboard and swam to an oil tanker bound for England.[29] He could not have picked a more dangerous type of ship on which to serve. At this time vessels transporting large quantities of petroleum lacked modern safety features such as double hulls and well-spaced tanks to ensure stability. Empty oil tanks had the added danger of spontaneously exploding because of a buildup of gasses within.[30]

Clark suffered from a rough ride but fortunately experienced no detonations. In England he found a berth on the *Lancaster Lass* of Glasgow, a vessel bound for Sydney on which superstitious seamen refused to sail because all the rats had left her, supposedly a precursor of her impending loss at sea. The *Lancaster* made it to Australia as planned, then sailed to Rio de Janeiro only to face a quarantine due to an outbreak of smallpox and typhoid fever.[31]

This Brazilian port has a well-protected harbor enclosed by high rocks. Its numerous side bays give it a total surface area of about fifty miles, one dotted by a number of islands, some of which had fortresses upon them in Clark's time.[32] Tired of serving on the *Lancaster,* Clark decided to jump ship, quarantine notwithstanding. He planned to swim to shore but gave up that idea after seeing a squid and ray get into an epic battle as well as witnessing the following: "A big steer [being hauled onto a cattle boat] struggled out of the sling and fell into the water. He started to swim, but he had only got under way when the sharks hit him and he was torn to pieces."[33]

The recent outbreak of communicable diseases gave Clark an idea. Having heard swallowing tobacco simulated the symptoms of cholera—an ailment that causes intense diarrhea and vomiting—he tried this and it worked. A physician travelling from ship to ship to treat the sick misdiagnosed him as Clark had hoped, sending him ashore to a hospital. There he escaped while still wearing his hospital garments. He happened upon a fellow American who gave him some civilian clothes and told him he could find shelter at a boardinghouse run by another American, Mike Russell. Clark stayed there for the next two weeks. Upon learning that the Brazilian navy had revolted against the country's president, he decided to join the rebels. Russell found him a place on board their flagship, the *Aquidaban,* on which the revolutionary congress gathered for its meetings.[34]

The rebellion had broken out over unresolved issues dating back to the collapse of the Brazilian monarchy a few years earlier, a process that started

Bay of Rio de Janeiro with Sugar Loaf Mountain in the background (Library of Congress Prints and Photographs Division, publisher/creator unknown, ca. 1909–1919).

during the reign of Brazil's last sovereign, Emperor Pedro II, because of his quarrels with the two most powerful forces in the country, the Roman Catholic Church and the slaveholding elite. His break with the church began when he joined the Freemasons—something the church forbade its flock from doing—and solidified this the moment he had two bishops arrested for opposing his decision. The slave owners turned against him upon learning of his plan to emancipate the country's entire slave population, which he did in May 1888. Without the support of these two political forces, Pedro lost his grip on power and abdicated on November 15, 1889.[35]

The Brazilian army, along with the tepid support of the navy, filled the power vacuum and established a republic. Its first president lasted until 1890 when his vice president, Floriano Peixota, took over. Peixota alienated the navy by replacing many of Brazil's state governors with army officers.[36]

One of the navy's highest-ranking officers, Admiral Jose Custódio de Mello, disliked the republic in general and President Peixota in particular. He had never lost his admiration of the monarchy, so in 1892 he sailed to Chile to visit the emperor's exiled grandson, Dom Augustino. There he threw him several expensive balls and dinners on board the Brazilian warship *Almirantic* at a cost of $2,500. A year later the Peixota-appointed minister of the marine,

Admiral Ladario, refused to reimburse de Mello for this, souring Ladario's relation with the entire Brazilian navy. The public, which supported de Mello, raised reimbursement for him.[37]

His patience broke when the senate failed to allow one of his fellow naval officers, Admiral Wandenkolk, to have a civilian trial for his treasonous act of rebellion the year before. "On the night of [September 5, 1893] ... de Mello managed to have the President, the members of the Cabinet and the commanding officers of the fleet in the bay to attend the performance given by the Italian Opera Company in the Lyric Theatro [in Rio]. The Admiral quietly withdrew about 11 o'clock and, as had been previously arranged, an attack was presently made at different points on the railway." The severing of telegraph and telephone lines ensured a blackout. Arranged disturbances in the outer parts of the city drew the police there. Naval men loyal to de Mello took command of all the war vessels in Rio's harbor. The next day de Mello demanded President Peixota's resignation, threatening to bombard Rio if he did not comply. He also recruited a land force.[38]

The Brazilian navy blockaded three ports: Santos, Santa Catharina, and Rio.[39] Since Brazil's government collected most of its revenues through customs, de Mello had instituted the blockade to cut off this source, hoping it would bankrupt Peixota into submission.[40] Having made good on his threat to bombard Rio if the president did not surrender, de Mello ordered a second attack in late September, simultaneously issuing a proclamation stating he had started the rebellion to force the president to step down because of his corruption and move towards becoming a dictator. In early October, de Mello ordered the bombardment of Rio's customs house and navy yard.[41]

His strategy might have worked had it not significantly affected the commerce of powerful foreign nations, especially those involved in the lucrative coffee trade. The U.S. became interested after it lost contact with its minister to Brazil, Thomas S. Thompson, who maintained strict neutrality and refused to speak with President Peixota. Secretary of the Navy Hilary A. Herbert sent two ships, the *Newark* and *Charleston,* to Rio to monitor the situation.[42]

The rebels held several key islands and fortresses in Rio's harbor that periodically fought it out with government held ones; but by the end of December these skirmishes had died down, possibly because both sides had run out of ammunition. On December 21 an especially notorious attack broke out when rebel launches came along the shore and started firing to destroy whatever they could hit, bystanders included. One report estimated sixteen people died.[43]

Secretary Herbert announced he might send two more ships to the city "to prevent ... interference with commerce and destruction of American interests," a decision influenced by the pleas of important American exporters who demanded protection and the opening up of trade in Rio. Herbert made good on his promise. He gave the command to an aggressive officer, Rear Admiral Benham, who warned the rebels he would ensure Americans could bring their goods ashore. Not long after that, a Brazilian ship fired a blank at an American cargo vessel under the protection of the USS *Detroit,* which returned fire with a live shot. The American commander warned he would aim the next one to sink. No more attacks against U.S. merchant ships occurred. The rebellion crumbled when European nations adopted this policy as well. On April 16, 1894, de Mello and 1,500 of his land troops fled to Uruguay to surrender to its government.[44]

After this, Brazilian authorities took Clark and the rest of the *Aquidaban*'s crew to a compound onshore. Every morning authorities chose ten men at random for a court-martial, which unfailingly found them guilty and ordered their execution by firing squad. Clark had to dig the graves of these unfortunate souls on several occasions. When the U.S. consul, O.F. Williams (coincidentally the same man who had given Clark his discharge papers in Le Havre), met with him and demanded to know why he should not let the Brazilians execute him for treason, Clark replied the rebels had shanghaied him and he had never willingly fought for them. Mike Russell, who had accompanied Williams, backed this story, then testified on Clark's behalf at his court-martial, earning him exoneration.[45]

Clark returned to the *Lancaster.* About a week out to sea he caught smallpox, the now extinct yet deadly disease that caused aches, pains, and pustules that often left the face scarred. Clark became so delirious he tried to jump off the ship. To prevent a recurrence of this, someone tied him to his bed. About six weeks out, a storm crippled the *Lancaster,* so she limped into Buenos Aires. Here Clark and a friend named Ben Farnsworth jumped ship, a prudent move because the *Lancaster* sank shortly thereafter—maybe the rats had known something after all.[46]

Clark and his friend made their way into Argentina's interior, visited a ranch, and crossed the Andes to Valparaiso, where they separated. Clark briefly worked in a shop that made parts for locomotives, then took a berth as the boatswain on an old square-rigged ship named the *Penobscot.* He continued to sail until the outbreak of the Spanish-American War in 1898, at which point he joined the First Colorado United States Volunteers and served in the Philippines. Upon his return home, he settled down in Portland and never traveled so extensively again.[47]

Three Bells

In May 1889 the crusading New York newspaper *The World* learned that someone in the city had kidnapped a significant number of newly arrived immigrants and shipped them as slaves to the cities of Progreso and Merida in the Yucatán Peninsula. The paper sent reporter Isaac D. White there to investigate, a fellow who did not receive a byline at the time because the *The World,* with rare exceptions, refused to give such credit.[48] This paper, the central source for the account, started in 1860 as the *The New York World* under the ownership of a Philadelphia journalist named Alexander Cummings. Its religious flavor and cost of one cent did nothing to make it popular, so a year later Cummings sold it to a group of Democratic financiers who transformed it into an organ for their political party. It did well until about 1876, then fell on hard times. The owner of a railroad bought it that same year, then sold it in 1879 to Jay Gould, the notoriously corrupt financier. Gould, a Republican, did not really want a Democratic paper, and under his ownership it lost about $40,000 a year.[49] An obscure journalist and newspaper owner from St. Louis named Joseph Pulitzer—a naturalized citizen originally from Hungary—wanted to buy the ailing paper, but he faced two obstacles. He lacked sufficient funds, and Gould disliked him because Pulitzer had written unfavorable things about him. Fortunately Gould never let a grudge get in the way of money. Not only did he agree to sell, he financed the $346,000 loan Pulitzer needed to purchase his prize.[50]

Pulitzer shortened the paper's title to *The World* and began tinkering with headlines to make them catchier. Planning to publish a periodical for the masses, he determined it would include clear prose with accurate facts. He hired only the best journalists and set it up as a crusading force against the ills of society, such as monopolies and corrupt officials. The paper's mandate included defending the rights of the working person, the poor, and immigrants. Pulitzer encouraged his journalists to pursue their stories aggressively and to produce articles evoking a high emotional response.[51]

During Pulitzer's early years at *The World,* he ran it as a hands-on dictator. Under his direction it became New York's best-selling paper. Other interests began to pull him away from day to day operations, so by the time William Randolph Hearst's *New York Journal* started to outsell the *The World* in the 1890s, Pulitzer's lieutenants had to deal with this challenge without his input. They panicked. Rather than bolster what had made the paper great, they mimicked the style of yellow journalism found in Hearst's paper. This type of reporting lasted until Pulitzer called his entire staff to a meeting two years later and laid down the law: he would allow only accurate articles, although ones with "color."[52]

The events that concern us here occurred a decade before the infamous contest between Pulitzer and Hearst forever and unfairly soiled *The World's* reputation. Shortly after starting his investigation, White quickly ferreted out the man responsible for the shanghaiing: John "Liverpool Jack" Fitzpatrick, a crimp who ran an employment agency on Greenwich Street. One newspaper article described him as "a blustering bully, twice the size of ordinary men and a great many times as insolent and overbearing. He was the terror of Greenwich street. Nobody thought of opposing his wishes; policemen whose beats entered or bordered his builiwick [*sic*] seemed rather to cultivate his good graces than to admonish him to keep the peace." Fitzpatrick like to prey upon immigrants newly arrived in the city and to that end named his so-called employment agency Little Castle Garden, an appellation meaningless to the modern reader but quite significant to arriving immigrants.[53]

For the first fifty-five years of the nineteenth century, new immigrants arriving in New York City usually stayed in rundown boardinghouses where crimps and other con artists preyed upon them without restraint. The New York State Commissioners of Emigration decided to remedy this by creating a safe place to process them. For this the commissioners chose Castle Garden, at the time the resort Castle Clinton, "a circular fort ... [that stood] on an artificial island built with rocks, about 200 feet out in the water." Connected to Battery Park by a bridge, it offered an excellent wharf to unload people en masse.[54] It opened for this new purpose on August 1, 1855, with the mandate of weeding out undesirables and protecting incoming immigrants from the criminals who preyed on them the moment they began their journey to America. Irish heading to America in the 1840s, for example, usually gave up all their money to the person who arranged for their transport on a ferry to Liverpool, their main departure point. Those who managed to hold onto to some of their savings lost it in that city to a variety of characters, including boardinghouse runners and booking agents.[55]

The more immigrant passengers a ship could transport in a single voyage, the higher the profits. To that end shipping companies stuffed as many people on board as possible by putting them in berths that sometimes had no more than five and one-half feet in area and contained three stacked bunks, leaving each occupant no more than twenty-five inches of space in which to sleep. Seasickness occurred, as it always did, causing those at the bottom to feel that which came from the top. During heavy seas a person on the top bunk sometimes fell out. If disease struck, the cramped quarters ensured a major epidemic as no place existed to treat the sick. An outbreak of smallpox, for example, might have a mortality rate as high as 90 percent.[56]

Purchasing a ticket did not guarantee meals despite the fact that in 1842 the British Parliament had passed a law guaranteeing all passengers a minimum of food; the law was strengthened in 1848. Many captains just ignored it. Some brought the required amount of food on board, then sent most of it back to shore on a tender where they sold it and pocketed the profit. Even as late as 1902, passengers still had to pay extra for food on some lines. Nor did they always get good potable water. Many ships gathered it from briny rivers using barrels once filled with wine or tobacco.[57]

Crews preyed upon their immigrant passengers as well, often stealing their luggage and taking advantage of women.[58] While sailing on the *Cambria* from Liverpool to Castle Garden, Mary J. Brent agreed to have sex with the second mate because he promised to marry her. Upon reaching Castle Garden, he refused. Brent asked Castle Garden's authorities to compel him to do so, but they lacked the power. They could have had him arrested for seduction, but she declined to press charges.[59]

The State of New York passed a law making it illegal for anyone except authorized people to sell incoming immigrants tickets to boats, trains and ships, then it expanded this ban to include boardinghouse keepers and employment agents. By 1867 policemen stood guard.[60] Despite these restrictions, runners found Castle Garden an irresistible target, even after their banishment. One May morning in 1856 a steamboat containing "a party of runners, under the direction of Councilman Jacob L. Smith," boarded the immigrant ship *Saint Nicolas* as she sailed toward Castle Garden.[61] Smith had obtained a document giving him the authority to commandeer the vessel. The document had been issued by acting mayor Isaac O. Barker, who later claimed he thought he had only signed a pass to let Smith on board, not seize the ship.[62]

The runners disembarked at Castle Garden, where they "coaxed and bullied all of the passengers that they could into buying tickets to the West by the Pennsylvania Central Railroad." They harassed anyone coming through the gate, stole the passengers' luggage, transported it to a pier along the Hudson River, then held it there for ransom. Garden authorities tried to remove the runners, but they got out their knives and fought back. The Committee of Emigration, in cooperation with the German Society, did manage to recover most of the stolen luggage.[63]

Because he ran an employment bureau, neither Fitzpatrick nor his runners could legally step foot in the Garden, which explained why he had named his agency Little Castle Garden. He figured, not incorrectly, immigrants would come there in the belief the real Castle Garden either sanctioned or ran it. Fitzpatrick often confiscated baggage and placed it in "storage," forcing victims of this scam to pay a fee to get it back. One immigrant, incensed by this shakedown, went back to Castle Garden and told its authorities he and about thirty others had to pay $2 apiece to get their possessions back. The Garden sent a police officer named Baumgartner to arrest the crimp, but Fitzpatrick beat him into submission.[64]

For his Mexican scam, Fitzpatrick and his runners actively worked the docks to find victims. Either he or a runner promised whomever would listen jobs in a "beautiful place in the tropics, where they were to work in the cool of the morning and evening, and spend their leisure hours beneath shady palms and coconut trees." He guaranteed high wages, free rooms, and a $12 a month fee for meals (these details changed when it was convenient). "One lot of men who signed their names on a blank sheet of paper subsequently found that there was a contract in Spanish on the other side binding them to work for a year. Others" thought they had signed "the shipping list of the vessel they sailed in." Fitzpatrick assured them they would receive jobs on a railroad, but of the 150 men he shipped to Progreso, only thirty-two worked on it.[65]

Although Fitzpatrick preyed mainly on immigrants, he did not miss an opportunity to bamboozle native New Yorkers. On the evening of June 9, 1889, one of his runners working the docks approached two American friends, James Smith and John Moran, and told them about high-paying work in Mexico. The two agreed to discuss it further with Fitzpatrick himself, but upon reaching Little Castle Garden, they learned he had gone to visit the ship *City of Washington*. The runner said he would take them there if they wished. They did, but before reaching their destination, the runner got them liquored up.[66]

Fitzpatrick personally blocked the *City of Washington*'s gangplank. As each man passed to climb it, Fitzpatrick promised him a job in Mexico that paid $3 or $4 a day with the cost of board included. Moran had so much whiskey in him he would believe anything. Smith remained skeptical, but it sounded like a good deal, so the two boarded, adding to a number of others already there. As the departure time of eight in the evening approached, some of them attempted to get off, but Fitzpatrick threatened to beat those who tried to pass him.[67]

The ship took them all to Progreso, a small settlement built on a beach that served as the port for Mérida, the capital of the Yucatán Peninsula located twenty-five miles to the south. The peninsula itself had no resemblance to tropical paradise promised by Fitzpatrick.[68] Instead of a beautiful paradise, its flat, monotonous plains produced palm and coconut trees capable of living in the hot, dry environment where the chief cash crop, henequen, required no water.[69]

Those immigrants and Americans who worked there did so at slave wages with men guarding them to ensure they did not escape. Smith refused to labor under these conditions; his friend Moran started to have a mental breakdown. The two made their way to Mérida to visit the American consulate. The consul said he would look into the matter but refused to give them aid. Low on funds, Smith agreed to the terms of his contract, but after a week in hot conditions without sufficient food, water, and rest, he quit and returned to the consulate. This time he told the consul he planned to escape and, once in America, he would tell anyone in the U.S. government who would listen that the consul had refused to help Americans in need. This motivated the official to give Smith a document of release from his contract. Smith spent the last of his money securing passage on a ship back home. He had to leave Moran behind because Moran had come down with a terrible fever and could not endure the trip.[70]

White arrived in Progreso a month after his newspaper learned of Fitzpatrick's slave racket. "I was not long in finding an American face and the face seemed to discover in me a New Yorker. I asked its owner if he'd been sent down by Fitzpatrick and he said he had. Then I made known to him my errand. The way he grabbed my hand and shook it almost brought tears to my eyes." This fellow told White that he and several other Americans had sent *The World* a letter three weeks earlier with the hope the paper would send someone to investigate. White rounded up twenty more of Fitzpatrick's victims and took them to a restaurant at which he bought them meals. He learned some of the specifics as to how Fitzpatrick had tricked them into coming to Mexico as well as the details of their working conditions.[71]

Most spent their time transferring freight from ships to awaiting train cars or into warehouses, reloading the vessels with bales of hemp. They toiled all day in the hot sun save for an hour or two in the afternoon. Their low wages barely covered expenses. To save on money, some of them got together and rented vermin-infested huts with one room, while others slept on the merchandise found in the warehouses in which they worked. Their food, hardly adequate to fill their bellies, tasted terrible, and none of them could speak Spanish.[72]

Because they had all signed a contract for one year of work, the Progreso police tracked down and returned those who tried to escape on the grounds they had broken the contract. (Smith had apparently avoided this fate because he had once served in the U.S. Army and had a disposition so tough no one wanted a confrontation with him.) In despair, one man tried to commit suicide and two others wound up in an insane asylum. The Americans found they not only had to pay for their voyage from New York, they would also have to purchase tickets to get back home, something their low incomes made impossible.

They told White they would gladly fight for their freedom under his leadership, but he quickly quelled that idea. He rented some rooms at a nearby American-owned and run boardinghouse into which he brought them in twos and threes so as to avoid attracting attention. He took their full statements there.[73]

He learned that two men owned the operations for which the Americans slaved away: Daniel Mena in Merida and Don Alfonso Escalante in Progreso.[74] When Mena's American workers had demanded higher wages, he threw them in jail on the grounds they still owed him money for their passage from New York, their refusal to work equating a refusal to remunerate their debt to him. A few days later soldiers fixed bayonets onto their rifles and surrounded them in the jail yard for about six hours for purposes of intimidation. Mena would not give them a raise, but he did promise overtime after 7:00 p.m. if they agreed to come back to work. As noncompliance meant continued incarceration, all agreed. The next day Mena brought in soldiers to ensure the workers did not strike again.[75]

Both Mena and Escalante regularly sent the police to round up employees who stayed home due to illness. One victim recalled spending four days in jail with no food for this reason. Another, Walter Graham, said he had sat down on the dock because he felt sick. The foreman asked if he would work. He answered he would not, so the foreman had the police lock him up. For reasons not made entirely clear, they released him a few hours later only to track him down to his boardinghouse and drag him back. During the return trip they gave him a beating so severe it left his shoulder dislocated. He returned to work for half pay as a warehouse watchman. Those so sick they became hospitalized did not fare any better. White found five of Fitzpatrick's victims in Progreso's Hospital de Caridad in which he discovered one of them, Adolf Metzel, covered in vermin and filth, probably because he had not had a bath or change of clothes in eighteen days. He had lain there for nearly a month, paying for his own water until White came to town.[76]

White arranged for a meeting with Mena and Escalante, but only the latter showed up. Escalante denied having treated his American workers poorly or having them arrested for refusing to work, although he admitted he had done this to a few for drunkenness, nor had he prevented them from leaving the country. They could go whenever they liked. White immediately put this to the test. He chose nine of Escalante's workers and paid for their passage back to New York. An enraged Escalante accused White of fomenting a rebellion and had him arrested. White arranged for an Englishman working at a local telephone company to send a telegram to the American consulate in

Mérida and another to the *The World*'s offices. An hour later he stood before both the American consul and Progreso's chief magistrate. The latter freed him with the caveat he might face detainment in the future. To avoid this, White left for New York on the *Mount Edgecombe,* the first available ship. Of the 150 men shanghaied by Fitzpatrick, forty managed to find their way home right after White broke the story. The others could return as soon as they could afford to do so.[77]

Back in New York, White turned his evidence over to the police. They duly brought in Fitzpatrick. He threatened to harm White and anyone else who dared to testify against him.[78] Authorities imprisoned Fitzpatrick in the Halls of Justice, a New York prison that opened in 1838 but no longer exists. Built on a drained lake and better known as the Tombs, its architect based his design on the illustrations of an Egyptian mausoleum found in a popular book of the day, *Steven's Travels,* giving this jail its better known nickname.[79] It had sparse cells for which occupants had to arrange their own furnishings if they could afford it. Flooding and dampness plagued the lower cells, and the six best ones housed wealthy offenders.[80]

Although Fitzpatrick did not stay long, city officials refused to renew his license to operate Little Castle Garden, putting him temporarily out of business. He reopened under another person's name. The police arrested Fitzpatrick again, this time for holding immigrants' luggage ransom, and threw him back into the Tombs for several more weeks. The mother of John Moran, the man left with a high fever in Mexico, demanded Fitzpatrick remain in custody until her son returned home.[81]

The State of New York charged Fitzpatrick with kidnapping. He pled not guilty.[82] New York's assistant district attorney figured the evidence *The World* had provided would easily result in a conviction, but Fitzpatrick had no intention of letting that happen. He retained the law firm of Howe & Hummel, which employed a strategy to delay the trial for as long as possible to give its client the time he needed to intimidate witnesses.[83]

Fitzpatrick's toughs found two of them in the Bowery and would have beaten them senseless had a policeman not fortuitously appeared.[84] While staying in a lodging house, another witness, Edward Blake, found himself confronted by Owen Carroll, one of Fitzpatrick's top lieutenants. Carroll suggested Blake might want to head out West, insinuating he had better leave town or else. The thug also tried to get him to give up the names of his fellow witnesses. Blake and three others complained about this to the attorney general, who placed them into protective custody at the House of Detention.[85]

Before the trial started in September, Moran made his way home, then testified against the accused when this deliberation began. The trial lasted from late September into the first couple days of October. A jury took all of eight minutes to convict Fitzpatrick. The judge sentenced him to nine years in Ossining, better known as Sing Sing, a brutal place in which guards regularly employed whipping as a means of punishment. This and other New York State prisons also forbade inmates from speaking to one another.[86]

7

Impressment

Shanghaied by a Navy

On the evening of September 14, 1810, Lieutenant Donadieu of the Royal Navy led a gang of men into London to find a few hands for a man-of-war. Hearing the music of a fiddle coming from the King and Queen public house on Old Gravel Lane, he sent a midshipman and two others in to find suitable candidates for naval service. Armed with a warrant, Donadieu's midshipmen seized two men and returned with them to the street. The King and Queen's proprietor, George Martin Bluchart, did not take kindly to this kind of conscription in his establishment, so he gathered together a mob with the intent of freeing the two men, and thanks to his efforts one got away.[1]

Authorities arrested Bluchart for defying a warrant. His solicitor, Mr. Allen, argued that since Lieutenant Donadieu had not personally stepped into the public house, his warrant had not applied, which in any case contained the wrong type of royal seal on it, making it worthless. The court overruled this latter objection and proceeded to find Bluchart guilty, sentencing him to two months' imprisonment. Here we have an example of impressment, the naval equivalent of shanghaiing.[2]

One Bell

Impressment had the full legal backing of whatever government sponsored it, Britain being one of its most notorious practitioners. Its Royal Navy targeted mainly the poor, grabbing them off the streets without discrimination against any particular race; so long as a man could work, he would do. Pressed men had no defined term of service, so those taken might have to stay in for the rest of their working lives.[3] Impressment differed from the kind of general draft used by Britain and the United States in the twentieth century because

122

this type employed a lottery system designed to avoid discrimination by race or class and gave those conscripted a defined period of service.

As far back as the Saxon kingdoms, the English had used impressment as a means of naval recruitment when volunteers became scarce, a chronic problem because officers often treated enlisted men with brutality. On a ship of the Royal Navy (RN), punishments for even the most minor offense included flogging, reduction of rations, and creative reprimands such as scraping a man's tongue with an iron hoop for using profanity. Pressed men serving in the RN during a war faced the additional danger of frequent combat.[4] They rarely drew their pay, sometimes going years at a time without receiving so much as a halfpenny. The RN did this because it incorrectly believed a man owed wages would not desert, and to this end it frequently transferred enlisted men from ship to ship to keep their names off the books and thus prevent them from obtaining their earned pay.[5]

In 1728 James Oglethorpe published *The Sailor's Advocate,* a pamphlet outlining his argument as to why impressment harmed Britain's merchant marine. Although merchant ships depended on the RN to make trade safe almost anywhere in the world, it in turn needed the merchant marine because the money that overseas commerce generated paid for its ships, arms, and wages. Moreover, impressment impinged upon the liberties of British subjects, as outlined in a number of court cases as well as several significant documents, including the Magna Charta and the Petition of Right, the latter of which laid out a process to sue the Crown. Press-gangs picked on the poor because that class could not afford to sue for its freedom, and even if it could, the RN would gladly pay a fine and keep its pressed men.[6]

Oglethorpe believed a man who lost his liberty soon lost his courage: "Oppression certainly debases the mind: and what can be a greater oppression than forcing men as prisoners on board a man of war without necessaries, without allowing them time to order their affairs, or to take leave of their families?" Because of desertions, the RN had to deny pressed men shore leave, and this, so far as Oglethorpe could see, adversely affected their health, as did the food, which he believed promoted disease because of a corruption of the blood (more probably malnutrition). Impressing merchant crews caused commercial ships financial ruin, forcing them "to lie in their ports" while their perishable cargoes rotted away.[7]

As long as the RN pressed the uneducated it could get away with this system of recruitment, but in 1795 Parliament passed two acts establishing a quota system in which each of Britain's counties had to enlist a percentage of its eligible male population for military service, a process netting about 15,000 men by 1797. Many of these conscripts possessed basic educations and therefore could read popular works of the day such as Thomas Paine's recently published *Declaration of the Rights of Man and of the Citizen,* a tract in which he argued every free person, no matter his class, had inherent liberties.[8]

From April to June 1797, these better-educated enlistees coordinated a mostly nonviolent mutiny at Nore, located in the Thames Estuary, and Spithead, a channel between the Isle of Wight and mainland England. They demanded the wages owed to them—many had not received any in years—better food with vegetables plus "fresh beef," and shore leave for all. They also wanted a guarantee that wounded seamen would obtain sufficient medical care and contingency wages. The mutiny prompted Parliament to pass the first naval reforms since 1652.[9]

Two Bells

Colonial Americans for the most part opposed impressment on economic grounds since it decimated the effectiveness of their merchant marine.[10] Parliament, itself concerned about the adverse effect on American trade, forbade the practice there with the passing of a 1708 act called the Sixth of Anne. This problematic piece of legislation had no defined expiration and thus allowed the RN ignore it throughout the eighteenth century when convenient.[11]

In the American colonies, the moment a press-gang came to shore, professional seamen went into hiding, leaving the gang to prey on everyone from slaves to servants to fishermen to legislators. It affected the population of colonial towns and cities more profoundly than those in Britain because of the smaller number of people living in them. Press-gangs could and did devastate the community's productive male population, which in turn seriously harmed commerce. A 1757 sweep of New York City, for example, ensnared 800 men, one-quarter of the total male population.[12]

Press-gangs preferred taking able-bodied seamen because of their valuable experience aloft. During times of war, AB seamen commanded much higher wages than usual on merchant ships, so few wanted to serve in the RN.[13] AB seamen in the American colonies who went into hiding from press-gangs often found merchant ship owners willing to shelter them despite the fact doing so violated the law. Yet it really presented little risk, as most colonial juries refused to convict those who offered it.[14]

Thomas Paine's first great tract, *Common Sense,* cited impressment as one of the reasons the colonies had rebelled.[15] True enough, but this was hypocritical: the Continental Navy also practiced impressment, leading to a notorious incident in Baltimore in 1777. Upon the launch of the newly constructed *Vir-*

ginia—one of the thirteen frigates authorized by the Continental Congress two years earlier—her master, Captain James Nicholson, decided he needed thirty more hands before setting sail. He sent a press-gang into the city to obtain suitable candidates. When word of this reached Maryland's governor, Thomas Johnson, he ordered Nicholson to free the pressed men. Nicholson refused on the ground that his authority came from the Continental Congress and therefore superseded the governor's.[16]

Johnson disagreed. He sent a formal complaint to Congress' president, John Hancock, creating a controversy because this forced that body to deal with the sticky question of defining the extent of its authority over the colonies. After much wrangling, it decided those pressed men who willingly signed the *Virginia*'s articles would stay, while those who refused could leave. Thirteen men departed. Despite Governor Johnson's triumph, colonies continued to employ impressment throughout the war, and even the chastised Nicholson used it a few more times.[17]

Ben Franklin thought the colonies themselves ought to control impressment, one of the ideas he put forth to the Albany Congress, a committee created by the British Board of Trade in 1757 with the charge of creating a plan to repair trade relations with the Iroquois. The Albany Plan, as it became known, proposed the creation of a grand council consisting of delegates from all colonies who would control colonial defense (including impressment), trade relations with the Native Americans, and western land policies, settle differences among them, and raise taxes to pay for a colonial military overseen by a president-general appointed by the Crown. The delegates rejected the plan.[18]

The pressure impressment caused American colonials often motivated them to riot against it. Sometimes they formed mobs that attacked officers and held the officers hostage in exchange for the release of recently pressed men. Some tried to board or burn naval ships, while others successfully seized the boats on which the pressgangs had come to shore, brought them into the center of town, and burned them in effigy. This last type of retaliation occurred in June 1765 at Newport, Rhode Island, as a response to five weeks of continuous impressment.[19] During a later riot in that same city, citizens defended a deserter from a naval detail sent to retrieve him, then rushed to nearby Fort George to help its garrison fire upon a ship of the RN.[20]

Possibly the worst impressment riot in the American colonies occurred in Boston in 1747 when its inhabitants refused to stand aside as yet more pressgangs dug into its already devastated male population, picked clean by years of two back-to-back wars.[21] The first of these had started because of an incident in the West Indies between Britain and Spain, the latter of which controlled the area with an iron hand and allowed the British to trade there for only a short, predetermined time of the year. The Spanish navy caught a British ship in its waters out of season and sent over a boarding party to investigate. An altercation broke out in which Captain Robert Jenkins lost an ear. Supposedly having preserved the ear, he showed it to Parliament, and this whipped up public sentiment for what became known as the War of Jenkins' Ear, declared in October 1739.[22]

This struggle merged into the War of the Austrian Succession, or King George's War, in 1746, which had begun when the Austrian emperor died in 1740 without a male heir and left his domains to his daughter Maria Theresa. The newly crowned King Frederick II of Prussia used this as an excuse to invade the empress's prosperous province of Silesia. Foreign powers with interests in the conflict's outcome entered on one side or another, expanding it beyond its original scope. It did not end until 1748.[23]

The aforementioned 1747 Boston riot occurred not from purposeful malice but rather pure happenstance. In the summer of that year a message reached the British naval station in Louisbourg, Nova Scotia, informing its commander, Admiral Charles Knowles, that he had received a promotion to rear admiral and would take over as commander-in-chief of the Jamaica fleet. He ordered his squadron south, but not long into this journey a massive storm overtook it that caused extensive damage and the loss of quite a few men. The squadron limped into Boston for repairs. By the time it had readied for sail in mid–November, desertions and losses to the storm had reduced its crews to unacceptable levels. Knowles sent press-gangs into the city on the night of November 16 with the purpose of finding deserters and additional men, the gangs taking a total of fifty seamen and landsmen.[24]

What became known as the Knowles Riot began the next morning when a mob consisting of servants, blacks, and mariners gathered on King's Street to throw bricks and stones at the general court's house. Governor William Shirley fled to a nearby fort, Castle William Island, from which he directed the militia to quell the riot, but it refused.[25] The mob, consisting of several thousand people, kidnapped at least ten naval officers, attacked the sheriff, threw one of his deputies into a stock, and burned a barge it erroneously believed belonged to the press-gang. It demanded the return of the pressed men as well as a pardon for a man convicted for murder during an earlier impressment riot. The riot lasted for three days and in the end all but twenty pressed men went free.[26]

Throughout the rest of his career, Knowles left a trail of controversy. A year after the riot bearing his name broke out, he commanded a squadron in an unsuccessful attack against the Spanish. Afterward he accused his captains of a lack of aggressiveness. They countered by charging him with delaying the attack and falsifying his report to the Admiralty. Four of the captains as well as Knowles himself faced courts-martial over this. One proceeding found Knowles guilty and issued a reprimand. Each of his captains on trial (for cowardice) challenged Knowles to a duel. He fought the lot, one at a time, and killed the one who had served as the chief witness against him. Neither the reprimand nor the duel kept him from winning a seat in Parliament, nor did it impede his appointment as governor of Jamaica in 1752. Here he annoyed the local elite by moving the capital from Spanish Town to Kingston. Although he resigned over the matter, the Crown supported him. He died on December 9, 1777.[27]

Bostonians did not forget the sting of Knowles' press-gangs. Their ire increased with the passing of the Stamp Act in 1766 (repealed the next year) and the Townsend Revenue Act of 1767, the latter of which imposed duties on certain goods and "established a board of customs in Boston" for the first time. In response to threats to officials, the British government sent the HMS *Romney* into Boston Harbor as a means of intimidation and to aid the city's customs commissioners. On May 9, 1768, the ninety-ton merchant sloop *Liberty,* owned by the notorious smuggler John Hancock, sailed in with a cargo of wine from France and docked at Long Wharf. The *Liberty*'s captain, Nathaniel Barnard, declared he had twenty-five casks of wine on board, but inspectors found 127.[28]

For this act of smuggling the customs commissioners asked the captain of the *Romney* to send a detachment of men to seize the vessel. On June 10 several boats under the command of John Calendar came ashore to execute the request. A crowd had seen the boats coming and, presuming they belonged to a press-gang, formed a mob. When the seamen and marines reached the wharf, the mob started pelting them with stones. Under orders not to fire at civilians, the navy men took their lumps, then the *Liberty.* The angry Bostonians turned on the commissioners themselves, forcing them to flee for their lives first to the *Romney,* then to Castle William Island.[29] Called the Liberty Riots, this act of civil disobedience prompted the RN to order that from then on its ships in the American colonies would no longer impress men onshore. They would instead lie in wait in port and intercept ships as they came into the harbor.[30]

Three Bells

Until the mid-nineteenth century when it became internationally outlawed, Western governments at war relied heavily on privateering as a means of attacking the enemy's merchant marine. This sort of warfare allowed these "private ships of war" to attack enemy vessels with the permission of a ruling government, which issued documents called letters of marque as official authorization. Those without one committed acts of piracy. The funding for privateer ships came from civilian investors hoping to sell captured vessels and their cargoes for a profit. Although used mainly by European maritime nations, that continent's countries did not have a monopoly on the practice. Article 1, section 8, of the U.S. Constitution granted Congress the ability to issue its own letters of marque, something it did to great effect in America's two wars against Great Britain. During the War of 1812, for example, American privateers captured or sank about 2,500 enemy merchant ships and caused the British economy an estimated $40 million in losses.[31]

Serving on a privateer had far more appeal than enlisting in the RN. Those who sailed on privateers worked shorter voyages, received better food, and faced less discipline. But like most things, it had a downside. The men received no pay, instead agreeing to take a percentage of the prize money by signing articles that listed the ship's rules and outlined in detail the division

This lithograph, first printed around 1830, shows the American privateer *General Armstrong* attacking a British vessel during the War of 1812 (Library of Congress Prints and Photographs Division, N. Currier, ca. 1830).

of shares. The articles also stipulated punishments for disobedience, such as the loss of one's earnings for showing cowardice or stealing.[32]

Half the profits from the prizes went to the financiers and the other half to the crew. The amount received depended on one's rank and duty. A carpenter, for example, made more than a landsman but less than a boatswain. Few voyages paid off big, if at all. Enlisted men, who received just a few shares, came home with an average of £11, although some earned a bonus for things such as suffering a wound in the line of duty or being the first man to sight a prize.[33] Chronic failure to find legitimate prizes sometimes had the unintended consequence of motivating crews to turn to piracy to make the cruise profitable.[34]

Because British privateers had to compete with both the merchant marine and the RN for experienced seamen, they took nearly anyone who volunteered, and advertised to attract them. Two such ads appeared in the March 3, 1757, issue of London's *Public Advertiser*. The first reported that the *St. George* needed a few seamen and warned she had nearly filled her crew, so those interested had better hurry up. The second gave the particulars of the size and armament of the *Middleton,* then went on to say, "All Gentlemen Sailors, able-bodied Landsmen, or Boys, that are willing to try their Fortunes in this fine sailing Ship, may repair on Board of her directly, or to the King's Head in East Lane, where proper Persons will attend to receive them. Seven Guineas [a gold coin] advance Money and seven Shares to good Seamen; and three Guineas and five Shares to Landsmen; and two Guineas and three Shares to Boys. Wanted immediately, a Surgeon's Mate for the above Ship, let him apply to Mess. Le Gros and Le Cras, Merchants, in Bishopsgate-street, near Cornhill."[35]

In its colonial days, New York City served as a major launching point of privateers, with the result of draining much of the manpower available to the RN. In 1759 alone, forty-eight privateers sailed from there with a total of 5,670 men on board, bringing back £200,000 worth of prizes between 1760 and 1763. Losing men to privateers in New York became a particularly troublesome problem for the RN during the French and Indian War. To attract men, it offered volunteers an impressive £6 per month plus immunity upon completion of their service from impressment for the duration of the conflict. This failed to work. One captain, John Hale of the HMS *Winchester,* tried to entice his many deserters to return by promising them no punishment, but to no effect. He decided to instead start seizing men from incoming privateers.[36]

On August 18, 1760, he fired a shot at the inward bound twenty-two-gun privateer *Sampson* under the command of Osborn Greatrakes, convincing her to heave to. He sent out a barge with a boarding party of men headed by his third lieutenant, a fellow named Frodsham. Upon reaching the *Sampson*'s bow, Frodsham hailed her. The crew replied with musket fire. He ordered them to stop shooting, then told his men to row back to the *Winchester.* The *Sampson's* crew continued to shoot at them, killing four despite the fact no one had returned fire. The rebellious crew headed to the wharf but stayed far enough away from it to avoid molestation from the docks.[37]

Captain Hale and two lieutenants went ashore and obtained from New York's lord mayor a warrant against the *Sampson's* crew. The next morning Hale brought his ship in to assist the city's magistrates in seizing it. Upon seeing the *Winchester* coming, the crewmen boarded boats and rowed to points of land outside of the town. In response, New York's royal governor issued a proclamation to have them arrested.[38] Magistrates boarded the *Sampson*, on which they found some passengers, the captain, and his first mate. They placed the two officers under arrest. Greatrakes reported he had begged his men to submit to the *Winchester,* but they had mutinied and locked him, his mate, and several others in his cabin. After a jury acquitted them, Greatrakes and his mate returned to their ship and sailed away. Authorities caught only three of the mutineers, all of whom had to serve on the HMS *Dove.*[39]

Four Bells

In 1822, after two years in the West Indies, an English navigator named Aaron Smith decided to leave Kingston due to poor health and a desire to see his family at home. To that end he asked a friend, Captain Talbot, to obtain for him a berth on an outgoing ship bound for England. Talbot secured him the first officer's position on the brig *Zephyr,* a vessel commanded by a Captain Lumsden. She left at the end of June. A day after rounding the southwest point of Cuba, Smith sighted a suspicious looking schooner. Going aloft with his telescope, he identified her as a pirate. He and the officer of the watch informed Lumsden of the find, but the captain decided to take no evasive action because he did not believe pirates would attack a ship flying British colors.[40]

The pirates disagreed. By the time Lumsden realized this, the *Zephyr* could not escape. Once within hailing distance, the pirates ordered her captain to their ship for a meeting. Lumsden refused. Musket fire came his way. He trembled in fear but did not lower his stern boat as commanded. Smith recalled, "A boat from the pirate [ship] now boarded the Zephyr, containing nine or ten men, of a most ferocious aspect, armed with muskets, knives, and cutlasses, who immediately took charge of the brig, and ordered Captain Cowper [a passenger], Mr. Lumsden, the ship's carpenter, and myself, to go on board the pirate [ship], hastening our departure by repeated blows with the flat part of their cutlasses over our backs, and threatening to shoot us."[41]

The pirate captain, whom neither Smith nor the later newspaper coverage named, had a Spanish father and an Indian mother from the Yucatán Peninsula. About thirty-two years of age, he could speak broken English, probably because he had once served in the Royal Navy as an enlisted man. In ill health, he wanted a navigator for his ship. Although pirates had no trouble recruiting disgruntled sailors with basic seamanship skills, they rarely attracted specialists such as coopers, carpenters, and navigators. These they had to press into service. To avoid being forced into this, Smith falsely claimed he had a wife and children because he knew pirates did not like to recruit married men. The pirate captain decided to press Lumsden instead, who begged Smith to take his place because he really did have a wife. Smith, although disgusted by Lumsden's whining, acceded to his wish and told the pirate captain he would serve as his navigator.[42]

After a thorough plundering of the *Zephyr,* the pirate captain let her go upon receiving Lumsden's promise that he would not sail to Havana and report the incident, warning him if he broke his word, the pirate captain would hunt down and kill him. Despite this threat, Lumsden did just that. He also put in a claim of losses worth double what the pirates had stolen. The pirate captain, infuriated that Lumsden had both lied to and told lies about him, sent several of his men to assassinate this scurrilous English master, but to no avail. One of them returned to report Lumsden had already sailed away.[43]

The pirate captain had a terrible temper and a hunger for vengeance. After capturing a man who he believed had plotted to assassinate him and his crew, he had this fellow stripped naked, stretched out, and tied up near a swamp under the blazing tropical sun of July. He made Smith watch to demonstrate what he did to those who defied him. The prisoner could not or would not tell the pirate captain what he wanted to hear, so the captain had a pig iron collar placed around the prisoner's neck and told his men to throw the poor fellow into the ocean. He drowned.[44]

Despite witnessing this, Smith refused to assist in the capture of a ship. The pirate captain ordered him blindfolded and tied up, then had muskets discharged to simulate a firing squad to give his reluctant navigator a terrible fright. Smith continued to decline, so the captain ripped open some musket cartridges, poured the gunpowder beneath Smith's feet, and lit it. This caused an intense fire that scarred Smith's legs permanently and left him bedridden for weeks. He started to collaborate upon recovery.[45]

In early August 1822 the pirates chased down and captured the *Industry,* a British merchant brig under the command of Captain Cooke, whose version of events of what happened next went like this. Smith, "armed with one or two brace of pistols and a sword," led a boarding party of seven. He asked if Cooke had any passengers. Cooke replied he had one, so Smith ordered him and the passenger to come to the pirate vessel. Cooke balked, so Smith fired a pistol at him, purposely missing because he only wanted to show he meant business.[46]

Smith's account of the encounter differs considerably. He wrote, "When we reached her, we were met by the captain [Cooke] of the brig at the gangway, who asked us who and what we were; to which I was obliged to give an evasive answer, by saying, that the corsair [the pirate's ship] was a privateer." Smith brought Cooke back to the pirate's schooner. Once on board, he sensed trouble from the pirate captain, upset by Cooke's defiance. "From the fury in which I saw the pirate, I anticipated the most serious consequences to the poor fellow; and, in order to save him, if possible, claimed relationship, and told him he was my cousin, and that, therefore, for my sake, and in consideration of the services that I had done for him, he would not maltreat Captain Cooke. For once I prevailed over his brutal disposition."[47] With the *Industry* still in their power, the pirates took another merchant ship, the *Victoria,* on August 7. Smith again led the boarding party. At his trial, he did not deny this, explaining he had done so under duress. The pirates plundered this newest prize, then allowed the prisoners from both captured vessels to leave on the *Industry*.[48] Smith claimed credit for arranging all of this, and bemoaned the fact that Captain Cooke not only failed to thank him, he also later leveled false accusations against him.[49]

The pirate captain erroneously believed Smith had knowledge of first aid, so he forced him act as a surgeon from time to time. This skill, such as it went, would provide Smith with his salvation. Near the end of 1823 the captain came down with a nasty fever. He promised Smith his freedom if he cured him. Although Smith doubted the captain's word, he thought the situation might aid him in effecting an escape. He commanded the captain to stay in bed and periodically gave him medicine in his wine.[50]

One evening two fishermen came on board to do some trading. The weather got bad, so they decided to stay for the night and party. Everyone save for Smith and the captain fell into an alcohol-induced sleep. Smith dropped an opiate into the captain's wine to ensure he did not wake, then in the early hours of the morning stole away on one of the fisherman's painters, letting it drift out of hearing before raising the sail. Out of the sight of land, he used the navigation instruments he had brought with him to make his way to Havana.[51] Known at this time as the "Paris of the Antilles," Havana had a population of about 13,000, including hundreds of slaves, and a garrison of Spanish

This 1768 illustration, drawn by Elias Walker Durnford and engraved by Pierre Charles Canot and Thomas Morris, shows Havana around 1768 (Library of Congress Prints and Photographs Division, John Bowles, 1768).

troops that ranged between 20,000 and 40,000, stationed here because Spain had lost the rest of its American empire and had nowhere else to put them. Hot, dry, and smelly, the city's narrow, unpaved streets and lack of sidewalks made travel by foot a precarious thing.[52]

Despite this, Smith managed to find a ship along the wharf commanded by a friend, Captain Williams, who promised he could get him a first mate's berth on another vessel. He told Smith to rest while he effected this. Upon waking, Smith found Williams had gone to shore but had left directions as to where he could find him. As Smith made his way to meet his friend, one of his former pirate comrades saw him, then ran away. He returned with several Spanish soldiers, one of whom had sailed upon a ship taken by the pirates for whom Smith served. The solider accused him of having stolen from him during this encounter, so Smith was arrested for piracy.[53]

After weeks of incarceration in a vile prison, Smith had his day in court and, despite a bad interpreter, managed to tell his story to the judge well enough to convince him of his innocence. The magistrate informed Smith that the British Admiralty wanted him, and he had to consider whether nor not to release him to the RN. Three days later he did. Smith felt relieved until the RN placed him into double irons, threw him on the HMS *Sybille,* and sent him to London, where he found himself incarcerated in the notorious prison of Newgate.[54] Originally built during the reign of Henry II on that monarch's orders, this prison, sometimes referred to as the English Bastille, held England's worst offenders. Its jailers ran it as a major moneymaking operation to enrich themselves. At one point in its history, prisoners had to pay to get in, get out, and avoid being shackled in irons. Those with money could purchase a better cell, itself empty until its occupant rented a bed, mattress, and blankets. Prisoners also had to buy their own food as well as coal or firewood. Though it had been banned by the time Smith arrived, the jailers had even run a tap.[55]

Smith's trial took place at the Old Bailey on December 19, 1823. Charged with a variety of crimes, including piracy, assault, and leading a boarding party onto the *Industry,* he also faced two counts of piracy for his part in the capture of the *Victoria*, from which he allegedly stole some gold and aided in the theft of 700 barrels of coffee. He pled not guilty. As part of his defense, a court surgeon examined his legs and acknowledged the burns on them could have come only from gunpowder, corroborating Smith's assertion he had cooperated with the pirates only after suffering from torture and the threat of further bodily harm or death.[56]

Smith gave a brief but effective speech to the jury before it adjourned to deliberate: "Now I ask you, Gentlemen of the Jury, what earthly motive could I have to join these unrelenting savages. Ask yourselves that simply question." He went on to explain how "England was every thing to me" and mentioned all the wonderful things his native land had to offer him.[57] After the jury acquitted him of the charges pertaining to the *Industry,* the judge dismissed those relating to the *Victoria*. A year later Smith published a book about his experience, *The Atrocities of Pirates; Being a Faithful Narrative of the Unparalleled Sufferings Endured by the Author During His Captivity Among the Pirates of the Island of Cuba; with an Account of the Excesses and Barbarities of Those Inhuman Freebooters.*

Five Bells

The British government believed those born as subjects of the Crown remained so for life, and that all its male subjects had a duty to serve in the military when called, including those who had become American citizens after the Revolution's conclusion. The RN used this legal philosophy as one of its justifications to press American citizens into its service after the Peace of Paris, the treaty that formally ended the War of Independence. Between 1796 and

1812, the RN pressed about 10,000 of the 106,757 American seamen registered in the United States. Of those, only 1,487, or 2 percent, had become American citizens after the Peace of Paris.[58]

The U.S. government tried to address the problem in 1796 by issuing American seamen an official identification paper called the sailor protection certificate, a document containing a man's name, birthplace, and a detailed physical description including significant scars and tattoos.[59] The RN often claimed those it pressed had deserted from its ships, an assertion with some justification because many of its men did flee to American vessels with the belief the U.S. flag would protect them from recapture. These deserters sometimes used false names or possessed forged certificates.[60]

Captain Salusbury Pryce Humphreys, commander of the HMS *Leopard,* used this reasoning when he attacked the USS *Chesapeake* on June 19, 1807. This incident had its origin in the port of Norfolk, Virginia. While ashore Humphreys saw three deserters from the HMS *Melampus* and followed them to the *Chesapeake.* The captain of the latter, James Barron, refused to allow British seamen on board to search for them. Barron swore he had no British subjects under his command and insisted that if he had, they would enjoy the protection of the U.S. flag.[61] Humphrey sailed off and waited for the *Chesapeake* to leave port, which she did three days later. The *Leopard* intercepted her prey "ten miles off the Virginia coast." Once in hailing distance, Humphrey demanded the *Chesapeake's* commander allow his men to board and search for the deserters. Barron refused. The *Leopard* opened fire on the *Chesapeake* and "made a perfect wreck of her," shattering her fore- and aft-masts, killing three men, and wounding twenty-three others, Barron among them.[62]

The British took the three deserters from the *Melampus,* plus a fourth they had unexpectedly found. The *Chesapeake* limped back to port. Barron faced a court-martial that found him guilty of negligence of duty for his lack of preparedness to fight another vessel of war. He received a five-year suspension from duty.[63]

Of the four men pressed by Captain Humphrey, only one had U.S. citizenship. Americans illegally pressed in this manner might serve for years on end, often released only at the conclusion of an ongoing war. Given the chance, illegally pressed Americans wrote to the U.S. consulate when they reached Britain because it could sometimes secure their release. If that did not work, a pressed man had only one other alternative to get out with his life and health still in tact: desertion. An American named Joshua Penny used both methods during his time as a deep sea mariner. Born on September 12, 1773, he came from a poor Long Island family of nine children. At the age of fourteen his father indentured him to a physician, a career path he hated with a passion.

He begged his father to cancel the apprenticeship and let him go to sea, which he did. Penny loved his first voyage; he felt ill-treated on his second, but did not allow this latter experience to deter him from continuing his new profession.[64]

In 1793 Penny sailed on the brig *Minerva* to Cork, Ireland. There he found himself pressed into service on a seventy-four-gun British warship, but upon seeing his protection certificate, the captain released him. After a six-month stay in Ireland, he went to Liverpool, where a recruiting officer of the RN got him drunk and tricked him into enlisting. Fortunately the American consul freed him from the obligation. Fearful of press-gangs, Penny took a berth on the *Budd,* which sailed to Africa to pick up slaves and then went on to Kingston to sell them.[65] At this latter destination a British press-gang captured the *Budd*'s crew and brought it to the HMS *Alligator,* a ship under the command of a Captain Africk. Penny and the three other Americans showed their certificates. Africk did not care. He needed men, so they would stay. During Penny's first night, a contagious fever raging on board took the lives of

This lithograph shows the *Chesapeake* attacking a British vessel near Quebec during the War of 1812 (Library of Congress Prints and Photographs Division, Detroit Publishing Co., ca. 1890–1901).

This wood engraving by Howard Pyle, which originally appeared in the April 1884 issue of *Harper's Monthly,* shows the impressment of Americans (Library of Congress Prints and Photographs Division).

eleven men. Within days, Penny himself came down with it and almost died of it.[66]

By the time the *Alligator* reached London, the outbreak had run its course. Captain Africk brought his newly pressed men onto the quarterdeck and offered them a choice. They could sign up as regular enlisted men, or he would send them to Spithead in Britain, from which they would sail to parts unknown to prevent them from writing to the American consulate. Penny refused, so Africk had him transferred to the sixty-four-gun *Stately,* a vessel belonging to a squadron bound for the Cape of Good Hope.[67]

This jut of land near the tip of Africa first came to Europe's attention when the Portuguese mariner Bartolomeu Dias rounded it. He named it the "Cape of Storms," an apt appellation because strong southeasterly gales create chronically bad weather there.[68] Because several of the Cape's bays offered good shelters, the Dutch company Vereenigde Oost-indische Compagnie (VOC) established it as a waypoint in the seventeenth century for its merchant vessels traveling to and from Batavia (now Jakarta).[69]

VOC ships usually anchored at Table Bay, a deep natural harbor well protected against storms in the summer, the time of year Dutch vessels made the journey to and from the East Indies. A more permanent settlement did

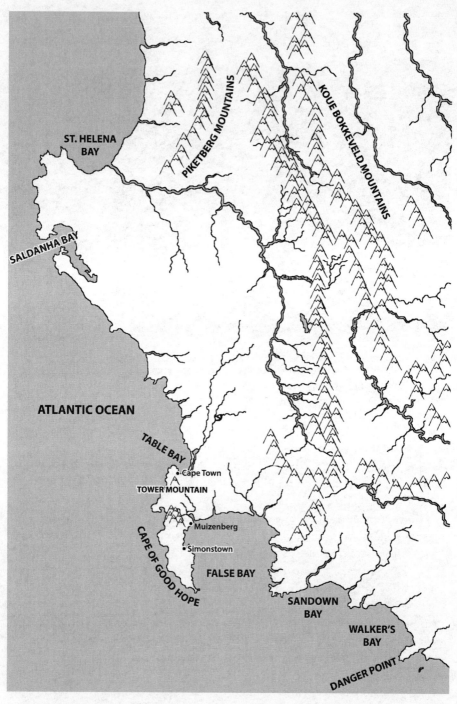

Cape of Good Hope area, based on an 1842 map by John Arrowsmith (redrawn by the author).

not appear along its shores until the shipwrecked crew of the Dutch vessel *Haarlem* became stranded there one winter. The camp they established evolved into Cape Town, a settlement with the added advantage of having Table Mountain about four miles away, from which foraging parties could procure ample firewood—at least until they stripped it bare. The mountain had a flat top that provided an excellent vantage point from which an observer could see the ocean for a good 100 miles out as well as watch the Cape's farthest point to the southwest.[70]

The British sent Penny's squadron to the Cape in 1795 as a move against the French Crown, with which it had an ongoing struggle. As part of its European strategy, France had recently ousted the existing Dutch government and replaced it with a friendly one. The British feared the French might follow this up with an invasion of the Cape, which would then disrupt the East India Company's spice trade. To prevent this the British government ordered a preemptive military occupation. Penny's squadron arrived in June, winter in the southern hemisphere. Because Table Bay offered poor shelter against storms in that season, the squadron sailed farther south into False Bay. The next morning six additional ships under the command of Admiral George Keith Elphinstone arrived carrying a regiment of the British Army led by General James Henry Craig.[71]

Along the bay's shores stood Simonstown, founded to serve as a winter base for the Dutch. Here General Craig landed and presented the man in charge of the colony, Commissary Sluysken, with a letter from William V, the Prince of Orange and Nassau and head of the Dutch government in exile. The epistle directed Sluysken to give the British permission to land and offer his full cooperation. He refused to recognize the prince's authority. Elphinstone and Craig ordered the entire Seventy-eighth Regiment plus about 300 marines to land and take the town by force, which they did.Captain Hardy of the HMS *Echo* and Captain Spranger of the HMS *Rattlesnake* then landed with their own forces to bolster General Craig's to about 1,600. The *Stately,* too, contributed men, Penny among them.[72]

The combined force marched toward Cape Town to the north. Eight miles into this thirty-mile trek, a ragtag militia of Dutch colonists and their native allies gathered at the coastal settlement of Muizenberg to make a fight of it. Disorganized and containing few professional soldiers, the defenders could not keep the well-disciplined British at bay or defend themselves against the offshore barrage from the *Stately.* After this routing the British force continued towards Cape Town, leaving a detachment behind that included Penny.[73]

One day Penny joined a party of eight pressed men under a sergeant and marched to the top of a nearby mountain in a downpour of rain. Along the way the detachment saw the Dutch militia and immediately surrendered, its men explaining how they had gotten there and that they just wanted to go home. The Dutch took them to their camp, and from there to Cape Town. Here the governor offered them a choice: they could either join the local garrison or just go free. Penny chose the latter. He and others who had decided the same stayed in town until an arriving British force caused them to flee.[74]

After a brief stint on a whale ship ruled by a despotic captain, Penny returned to the Cape and stayed with a friendly Dutchman for the next few months using the alias Jonas Ingelbergh. A plantation owner enticed him to work as his overseer, a position Penny held for six months until the British issued a warning that they would send anyone caught harboring a deserter to Botany Bay, the convict colony in Australia. Penny fled far inland. He found and joined a contingent of Dutch rebels and their local native allies in a valley in the Koue Bokkeveld Mountains.[75]

Penny called these natives the Hottentots, a derogatory term for the Nama, a people comprising mainly shepherds. Noted for their language filled with clicking sounds, they have virtually disappeared from the Cape's rural regions because of disease and intermarriage. Although the Nama had allied themselves with the Dutch, the hunter-gathering people native to the Cape known as the San had not. Insultingly referred to as Bosjesmannen, or bushmen, these nomads continuously encroached upon Dutch settlements. The colonials and their Nama allies pushed back with war parties that Penny sometimes joined to attack San camps.[76]

After a year of this life, Penny decided to make a break for home. To do this he needed to catch an outbound ship at Cape Town. As he made his way there, two other American deserters joined him. They went into town in disguise to avoid the search parties looking for deserters, but this failed to work, as he was apprehended and thrown into jail. Officers of the RN regularly visited to see if they recognized anyone, and one day a lieutenant from the *Stately* thought he knew Penny. But when Penny gave his name as Jonas Ingelbergh and said he had come from America, the officer dropped the matter.[77]

An admiral ordered those held in jail but not recognized as deserters to take berths upon the first available merchant ship in port. Soon enough they boarded an Indiaman, but before she departed, the admiral announced he knew of deserters on board and would press the whole crew if the captain did not hand them over. Someone in the boarding party recognized Penny and took him to the HMS *Sceptre,* a vessel stationed "in Table Bay [for] four or five months." The RN transferred him to the HMS *Rattlesnake* to serve in a squadron blockading the port of St. Louis, located on the French-held island of Mauritius in the Indian Ocean; then he was transferred to the HMS *Sphinx,* bound for the island of St. Helena.[78]

Never did a more desolate place exist. St. Helena was located in the middle of the Atlantic far from anywhere, and the British had annexed it in 1659 and made it into a watering station for the East India Company's fleet of ships. By 1700, the British had stripped the island of its forests, leaving it a barren wasteland.[79] It was little wonder Napoleon did not like staying here. Penny and four other crewmen used the stopover as an opportunity to desert. One night they swam for a nearby whale ship. When Penny realized he lacked the strength to reach her, he returned to the *Sphinx.* He refused to give up his three comrades and for this he suffered a flogging.[80]

The RN transferred him to the HMS *Jupiter,* on which he got into a brawl with an enlisted man. During the altercation he put his finger through his adversary's teeth, causing so much damage to this digit the surgeon listed him as unfit for duty. Penny played this for all he could, eventually convincing the surgeon to declare him incurable. Although the *Jupiter*'s captain had doubts about the severity of Penny's wound and its effect on his overall health, he nonetheless allowed the surgeon to send Penny ashore to a hospital just beyond the far side of Cape Town. Penny's deception involved making it seem he could not walk for long, so several men had to carry him in a sling made from a blanket and an oar.[81] As they made their way through town to the hospital, Penny saw a wine-house and "begged the sailors to set ... [him] down," claiming he desperately needed a drink. His fellow travelers readily agreed as they knew they would partake with him. Penny purchased "a bottle of Constantia wine and three tumblers." As his companions drank, he excused himself and went out the back door, presumably to urinate. He made a break for it, successfully winding his way through the maze of streets to avoid capture.[82]

He headed to Table Mountain, where he used the skills taught to him by the Nama to live off the land. Settling into a cave on the mountain's summit, he made himself a set of clothes out of antelope hide using a bone as a needle. An infestation of lice forced him to abandon his clothes and the cave, both of which he replaced. As he descended the mountain one day, he looked upon Cape Town and there in its harbor saw a brig with no topgallant masts, a sure sign she did not belong to a navy. Still dressed in his animal skins, he made his way there, his wild man look gaining him quite a few stares. Reaching the wharf, he happened to meet the captain of the brig upon which he desired to sail. Penny asked him if he needed an extra hand, to which the captain replied, "What in the name of God are you! Man or beast?"[83]

Satisfied Penny had no supernatural origins and not caring that he had deserted from the RN, the captain took him on board and gave him two suits of clothes and a chance to shave for the first time in fourteen months. The brig made her way to St. Helena, where she dropped anchor to wait several months for the arrival of a convoy of Indiamen with which she would sail to England. When the American ship *Indian Chief* came into port, Penny went out to her and asked if anyone had died, because he wanted someone's protection certificate to replace his own, now long gone. Luckily for Penny, a fellow named John Porter had recently passed away. Taking the poor fellow's papers back with him, Penny asked his captain to list him under this man's name.[84]

Upon their arrival in London, a British captain boarded the ships of the convoy to look for deserters. Penny gave his name as John Porter, presented his certificate, and went on his way. He found a berth on the American brig *Dauphin* and sailed to Charleston, South Carolina, where he obtained better papers to protect himself from future impressment. He never again served in the RN, which stopped the practice of impressment altogether in 1815. He returned to his home *"eleven years and six months"* after leaving. He settled down, married, started a family, and bought a coasting vessel.[85]

During the War of 1812 Penny determined to exact revenge on the RN by entering the fight against them. To that end he volunteered in a civilian capacity to assist Stephen Decatur's squadron, at the time blocked in at New London, Connecticut. Unfortunately a fellow American with a grudge against him told the British that Penny had once deserted from the RN and hated it with a passion. The RN responded by sending a force to Penny's house, which it surrounded. Penny, asleep at the time, had no chance to fight back. He confronted the ranking officer, Lieutenant Lawrence, and asked him what he wanted. Taking this response as an act of defiance, Lawrence pointed his pistol at Penny's face and pulled the trigger. It fortunately misfired. Lawrence decided to make Penny a prisoner instead. A waiting ship took him to Halifax, Nova Scotia, where he stayed for *"nine months and nine days"* until the British finally released him on the grounds that he did not qualify as a prisoner of war because he had only assisted the U.S. Navy as a civilian.[86]

8

The Oysterman Problem

In 1905 stories of men being shanghaied en masse to fill the crews of oyster dredgers operating in Chesapeake Bay prompted a reporter from *The Washington Times* to investigate. This journalist, who used the byline F.C.P., visited a shipping office in Baltimore at Canton Harbor in which someone drugged him. While he was still half-conscious, his abductors placed him into a cart. It stopped about three-quarters of an hour later at the wharf where his kidnappers met a "buy boat," a vessel that purchased oysters from dredgers working in the bay to sell them to the highest bidder on land; some of these had a side business of selling shanghaied men as well. One buy boat captain asked the reporter's kidnappers what they had. "Got a geeser [*sic*] what don' look for much, but might do at a pinch." The buy boat's captain paid $1.50 for him, fed him a piece of liver, then headed to Tangier Sound.[1]

The vessel stopped alongside a dredger and offered to sell the reporter to its captain, who thought little of the man before him and told the kidnappers to throw him overboard. They did. Fortunately the captain changed his mind and had the reporter fished out. After the buy boat took the reporter on, one of the mates ordered, "Bale out the lee scuppers, you d—n fool ... don't you see we're listing to port?" The reporter, having no idea what this meant and failing to comply, suffered a whack in the head from the mate.[2]

Two weeks of working the hand-powered wench caused the reporter's hands to bleed, and the meager rations of bad pork and hardtack kept him nearly starved. To remedy that, he ate a couple of oysters, but for doing so he received a kicking as punishment. He averaged about four hours of sleep a night and had for his bedfellow a man whose body odor wreaked. After two weeks of this ordeal the reporter escaped by jumping overboard into a passing buy boat on its way to shore.[3]

One Bell

The humble oyster once reigned in the United States as a daily staple. Throughout the nineteenth century Americans consumed more of these bivalves than any other type of seafood, and by the 1880s the U.S. became the world's biggest exporter of them, beating its nearest competitor, France, by millions of pounds. Only two species of oysters had any commercial viability in America, one found on the East Coast (*Crassostrea virginica*) and the other on the West (*Ostreola conchaphila*).[4] Neither produced jewel-quality pearls. The animal that creates those, a member of the *Pteridae* family, lives mainly in tropical waters and in biological terms has more in common with the muscle than the true oyster. The *Crassostrea virginica* and *Ostreola conchaphil* species usually eject foreign particles, and in the rare cases they cannot, produce a malformed grayish-colored "pearl" to envelope the irritant.[5]

A love of oysters produced some peculiar advocates for it. In his book *Oysters, and All About Them,* writer John R. Philpots dedicated an entire chapter to their benefits. Despite the fact a medical publishing house produced his work, he made a lot of dubious assertions. He claimed oysters cured acute depression, could alleviate the pains of gout, kept a person youthful, healed wounds, increased blood flow, relieved headaches, and helped ease the symptoms of influenza. He recommended pregnant women eat them twice a day with bread as a remedy for morning sickness. "If not a cure," he went on to say, "at all events an oyster diet, under medical supervision, brings unquestionable relief to those who are suffering from pulmonary complaints, indigestion, or nervous affections."[6]

In the eighteenth and first half of the nineteenth centuries, Americans harvested oysters between November and February because they fatten only when the warmer waters of the summer begin to cool in the fall. People ate fresh oysters between September and April. In 1870 Chesapeake-harvested oysters commanded on average forty-five cents a bushel, and overall sales made up the majority of revenues in America's $50 million-a-year seafood industry. With the exception of the coastal areas where they grew, only the wealthy could afford them until their prices started to fall in the 1880s. This occurred in large part because of the invention of a reliable steam canning process that allowed companies to ship them at low prices far into America's interior as well as abroad.[7]

Americans who settled in California during the gold rush found they disliked the western variety of oyster because it had a coppery taste. Entrepreneurs imported both canned and fresh ones from the East, the first batch of live ones arriving in 1869 via rail. The next year San Francisco businessmen brought barrels filled with live spat, or baby oysters. These they transplanted to the tidewaters around the bay, dousing them twice daily with nutrients to make them grow. Soon all of the West Coast's oysters came from just six fisheries located in San Mateo County. Because eastern oysters do not reproduce well in the colder waters of this area, harvesters had to import new crops annually, which had the effect of doubling the price.[8]

After 1886 the Morgan Company obtained a monopoly on all oysters harvested along the Pacific Coast, introducing its famous Eagle brand label in 1892. Its canned and fresh oysters dominated markets as far north as Victoria, south to San Diego, east to Salt Lake City, and west to Hawaii. Between 1895 and 1904 California's oyster crop amounted to one-sixth of all those harvested in America, and it generated millions of dollars in revenues annually. California's oyster beds became by the last years of the nineteenth century the biggest fishery in the state. Harvesters made an average of $500,000 a year between 1888 and 1904.[9]

San Francisco's oyster harvesters had to contend with a variety of local predators that did not exist along the East Coast. Of these, oystermen considered the bat ray the most destructive to their crop. This stingray, confined mainly to the Pacific along the coasts of California and Oregon, has a body shaped like a diamond with an uncanny resemblance to a bat and a long tail containing a poisonous barb capable of biting deep into anything it hits. Its powerful jaws can crush any shellfish. Harvesters surrounded their beds with stakes to keep them out, but spring tides often caused the water to rise higher than normal, allowing the rays to swim over these barriers, their flat bodies needing just a few inches of water to do so. They also squeezed between loosened stakes.[10]

Oystermen dealt with bat rays at low tide when the water level fell to just a few inches. Wrapping themselves up in several inches of cloth and thick boots to protect themselves against the rays' stingers, they climbed into the oyster beds and clubbed any they found, throwing them into piles with long forks so they could cook them later. A local reporter who witnessed one of these hunts counted over ninety dead in just one day's work. Ironically, the rays did not eat the oysters but rather feasted on the crabs that *did* consume them. Thus had the harvesters left the bat rays alone, their losses to predators would have dramatically decreased.[11]

Two Bells

Chesapeake Bay produced a wealth of oysters each year in large part because they can survive only in shallow saltwater, something the bay offers

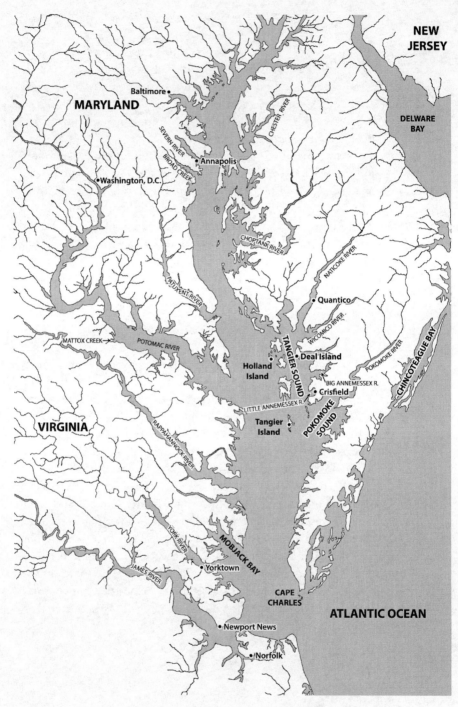

Chesapeake Bay, based on the map "Transportation Lines of Chesapeake Bay Serving the Port of Baltimore MD" by H.Y.B. (redrawn by the author).

in an ample supply. Of its 2,300 square miles, 65 percent of it has a depth of less than thirty-five feet, and only 8 percent is over forty feet. Oysters also like its low salinity, a phenomenon caused by the 419 freshwater rivers flowing into it. Before commercial harvesting began, oysters in the bay reproduced so well their high piles formed dangerous reefs.[12]

The industry's rapid growth after the Civil War created boom towns such as Crisfield. Founded by John Crisfield at Somers Cove, it stood at the entrance to Tangier Sound on a peninsula formed by the Little Annemessex River to the north and Pocomoke Sound to the south. Tangier Sound contained not only the most prosperous oyster beds in America, but also the world. By 1876 Crisfield became Maryland's busiest oyster port, its processing factories serving about six hundred vessels. In the 1870s millions of pounds of oysters went from here to places in America, Australia, and Europe, via either boat or rail-car.[13]

Behind the town grew pine trees broken by swaths of flat land on which oystermen and fishermen lived in cottages. The Eastern Shore Railroad, owned by John Crisfield, cut through this, terminating at the harbor, where large oyster processing factories stood. Even during a poor season, these facilities still produced a lot. In the low-yielding 1877–1888 season, for example, they filled "25,000 barrels of shell oysters and 300,000 gallons of shucked oysters."[14] Blacks made up the bulk of those who worked in the factories, some of whom could shuck an oyster in under five seconds. Owners showed their appreciation of them by throwing oyster fries complete with free beer and other types of food.[15]

Those who fished for the oysters themselves, the watermen, had a character unique to this former slave-owning area. White oystermen despised the elite and worked side by side with blacks despite the fact it broke the local taboo. Watermen of all races lived hard lives. Their bodies suffered from premature aging due in part to the damp, cold working environment, which also caused chronic rheumatism, fatigue, and cramps. Gray hair, deep lines, and facial crevices accentuated by persistent coughs accompanied by a disproportionate number of tuberculosis cases set them apart from their landsmen neighbors. Starting in childhood, they spent more time on water than land, which gave them an almost uncanny relationship with their boats.[16]

Life on an oyster boat offered nothing but abject misery. A surgeon named Walter Wyman who worked in the Marine Hospital Service reported seeing a number of men from the boats in his facility with frozen hands and feet as well as an uncommon number of oystermen who had suffered injuries after being knocked overboard by an irate officer. Because most oystermen worked on deck without proper protective clothing, they suffered from chronic wetness unrelieved by the unheated cabins in which they slept, and this resulted in a higher rate of pneumonia than normal.[17]

Oysters also caused lacerations on hands that often became infected, inflaming arms, and was cured only by the amputation of fingers. On dredgers the windlass, normally powered by four men working together, killed dozens and injured more every season, usually when the dredge struck something unexpectedly and caused the crank to suddenly reverse with such great force that anyone caught in the path of its spindles suffered either serious injury or death.[18]

Starting sometime during the mid–1700s, watermen used tongs to procure their oysters, an instrument resembling two garden rakes attached by a pivot that permitted its user to clamp into an oyster bed. In the earliest days of the industry, tongers used dugout canoes that could hold up to forty bushels, but as the demand for their catch increased, they started to use larger vessels, including the iconic skipjack. This sail-powered boat had a V-shaped bottom that allowed it to move easily through the shoal water in which it worked, yet gave it a good carrying capacity.[19]

This February 1911 photograph by Lewis Wickes Hine shows oyster shuckers working at the Barataria Canning Company in Biloxi, Mississippi (Library of Congress Prints and Photographs Division).

Oyster dredges sitting in a row in Baltimore (Library of Congress Prints and Photographs Division, Keystone View Co., 1905).

Watermen dreaded a frozen sea as much as farmers on land feared a drought, because it threatened their livelihood. Although the Chesapeake did not freeze with any regularity, when it did, these men filled their idle time with drinking and hell-raising until their meager savings ran out. At that point the whole area fell into economic hardship because of the loss of its biggest customer base.[20] When the Chesapeake froze in the winter of 1911–1912, it locked in the oystermen living on Holland Island in Tangier Sound, a sandbar about a mile long and "not more than 100 yards" in width on which about 300 inhabitants lived. For thirty days no one heard from them. Over several nights the residents of Deal Island, eight miles to the east, heard gunfire. Deal Island inhabitants reported them as distress signals coming from their neighbor. Maryland's governor ordered the steamer *Governor Howard* to investigate. Her commander informed him via telegraph he could do no such thing because the ice currently trapped his vessel in the Choptank River.[21]

On the morning of February 6 another Maryland revenue cutter, the *Apache,* began the arduous ice breaking voyage out to Holland Island, reaching her destination at eight the next morning. About the same time, two more steamers stocked with supplies, the *Governor Thomas* and *Governor McLane,* headed to the island as well.[22] In this case the Maryland government had gone to much trouble and expense for nothing. The *Apache*'s crew found the island's inhabitants perfectly fine; the gunshots had presumably come from elsewhere.[23]

After the Civil War, Chesapeake Bay's tongers found themselves in competition with oyster dredgers, vessels that dropped an iron-jawed contraption into the oyster beds upon which they dragged along until full. With this accomplished, four men started the backbreaking process of raising it up using a hand-powered windlass. The dredge dropped its contents onto the deck and the crew sorted its catch, throwing anything undesirable overboard. Although Virginia banned dredgers in 1811 and Maryland followed in 1820, a change in the latter's law in 1865 allowed them to return so long as they paid for a license.[24]

Dredgers worked too well. In 1885 complaints of them exhausting the Chesapeake's oyster beds emerged. In that year, watermen could no longer find the large oysters that brought between seventy and seventy-five cents apiece, but instead collected smaller ones worth thirty to thirty-five cents.[25] This increasing scarcity prompted dredgers from Maryland to operate illegally in Virginia's waters, causing much tension and spawning what ultimately become a war on the Chesapeake between the two states as well as tongers and dredgers.[26]

Virginia also required licenses for those who wished to fish for oysters, but it lost much of its revenue to oyster pirates. One Virginia newspaper suggested the state introduce tougher laws against them, reporting that in the first two months of the 1888–1889 season, pirates had already stolen about $200,000 worth of oysters.[27] To deal with them as well as the tensions between tongers and dredgers, Virginia and Maryland each formed special water police complete with well-armed boats to counter the arsenal of personal firearms usually carried by watermen.[28]

Maryland forbade dredgers from operating in shallow water to preserve it for tongers, and it did not allow those from out of state in without permits. Dredger captains ignored both prohibitions. State officials blamed the reduction in oyster harvests on overfishing by dredgers, but an argument existed that the elimination of every dredger on the bay would not put a stop to this because tongers would just come in and do the same thing. In any case, pirate dredgers reduced the revenues Maryland would otherwise have derived, so its police force cracked down on them. The pirates responded by working under the cover of darkness or in the fog.[29]

On Christmas Day 1888, the police steamer *McLane* found forty to fifty pirate dredgers working in the Chester River and got into a firefight with them, although neither side caused much damage.[30] In an incident along the Choptank River, the Maryland police sloop *Eliza Hayward* sailed into the midst of fourteen pirate dredgers with the idea of causing them to scatter. One dredger fired at the police vessel and the remaining thirteen tried to surround her, but the *Hayward*'s captain wisely maneuvered out of danger and retreated, although some of the pirates followed for a time.[31]

Some Maryland oyster pirates boldly worked within sight of major cities in which the state water police had bases. The police boat *Davy Archer* out of Annapolis, for example, found the *Virginia T. Lawson* working not far from the city's harbor. The *Archer*'s mate ordered the *Lawson*'s master, Captain Lutts, to surrender, but he sailed off. The *Archer* pursued her for two hours, during which time the vessels exchanged fire. The *Archer* finally ran alongside the *Lawson* and raked her with a broadside that shredded her sails, stopping her flight, then took Captain Lutts back to Annapolis for a trial.[32]

San Francisco Bay had its own unique brand of pirates. Although this offense qualified as a felony and had a corresponding punishment, its practitioners kept at it because the financial rewards made the risk acceptable. John Griffith Chaney got into the business at the age of fifteen during a period of his life when he had become utterly destitute. He borrowed $300 from a friend and purchased the sloop *Razzle Dazzle*. At night he made his way into the best oyster beds despite the possibility armed guards might catch him. Making $25 on a good night, he soon repaid his generous patron. A rival pirate burned his boat, so he worked with another for a few months, then retired from this dangerous business for good and turned to writing using the pen name Jack London.[33]

Oyster pirates did not limit themselves to Chesapeake Bay or San Francisco. New York City had its own productive beds, a prime target for New Jersey dredgers because they could quickly return to their own state and thus get out of New York's jurisdiction. When the owners of the beds in Prince's Bay off of Staten Island complained to Governor Theodore Roosevelt about this menace, he ordered a response. On March 23, 1900, the police boat *Patrol,* commanded by Captain Elbert O. Smith, headed into Prince's Bay and there saw a fleet of pirate dredgers. Before Smith could uncover his guns, the dredger lookouts shouted warnings, prompting the whole fleet to make its way safely into New Jersey waters.[34]

Smith decided to go into hiding and see if the dredgers would return. They did. Ordering his guns filled with powder but not shot, he sailed into their midst fast, targeting the fleet's largest sloop, *Frances Emma*. Once in hailing distance he ordered her captain to heave to. He refused, so Smith fired a warning shot. This so terrified the *Frances Emma*'s captain he immediately surrendered. The *Patrol* scattered the rest of the fleet and ended the problem—at least for a month or two.[35]

Three Bells

The number of men who willingly signed onto oyster dredgers on the Chesapeake did not come close to meeting the demand, so crimps operating along the East Coast, some as far north as Boston, got into the lucrative business of selling their victims to them. A spike of missing persons reports coincided with the oyster harvest season, peaking between September and April. Police figured many of those reported absent during that time had a fifty-fifty chance of returning.[36]

Philadelphia's crimps who shanghaied men for the oyster dredgers operated mainly along the waterfront's streets. They got men drunk in its bars, then offered them jobs on dredgers for $22 a month, very good money in the late nineteenth and early twentieth centuries. The crimps then took their victims—usually from ten to twelve in number—down to the Walnut Street railroad station and placed them on a Baltimore and Ohio train, making sure to give them plenty of liquor for the trip down. Upon the victims' arrival, confederates whisked them off the train and placed them into a Black Maria, the type of vehicle used by the police to transport felons, and took them to the docks to waiting buy boats.[37]

Baltimore crimps operated a bit more subtly, relying primarily on subterfuge because no sane citizen of that city would willingly board a dredger.[38] One favorite confidence trick worked like this. A runner approached a man standing along the waterfront and asked him if he wanted to make a couple of dollars. If he said yes, the runner explained he needed help to find someone to work on a dredger for a $2 finder's fee, which he would split fifty-fifty. The runner and his victim soon found just the person—actually a confederate of the runner—and took him to a shipping office. There the crimp who ran it told the victim that to receive his money he had to sign a document once there and again on the boat upon which the fellow he had found would work. When the victim stepped on board, the runner and his confederate rowed off, their victim forced to stay because he had just unknowingly signed the ship's articles.[39]

Baltimore crimps also recruited men by promising good wages for just a short time on a dredger. Those foolish enough to believe this quickly learned they would not get to leave as promised.[40] Baltimore crimps expanded this swindle by placing ads in other cities with the same promise. Nineteen-year-old John Drummond of Mt. Vernon, New York, answered such an ad, but once in Baltimore he found himself on a dredger from which he did not escape for nine weeks.[41]

New York crimps who sold men to dredgers liked to target recently arrived European immigrants. Jewish teenagers Jacob Friedberg and Joseph Rosenchanz found this out firsthand when they visited the Empire Labor Exchange at Battery Place on September 11, 1888, looking for work. Its sign, written in German, promised "light and easy work." Located in a run-down basement, a German named von Slomski ran it and promised the boys $12 a month for work in Baltimore. There they found themselves taken to a dredger operated by the brothers Ben and Sam Colburn. Friedman refused to sign the articles, but threat of bodily harm from the captain changed his mind. Forced to work a daily schedule that usually went from three in the morning to ten at night, they labored for the next four months in a state of near starvation, beaten if they did not meet the captain's expectations. For-

This 1884 wood engraving, *The Oyster War on the Chesapeake*, shows oyster pirates working their dredges under the cover of darkness (Library of Congress Prints and Photographs Division, publisher/creator unknown, March 1, 1884).

This 1909 photograph by Lewis Wickes Hines shows an oyster boat working along
the waterfront of Apalachicola, Florida (Library of Congress Prints and Photographs
Division).

tunately they suffered nothing worse than blister-covered hands and frostbitten
ears.[42]

The Jewish Immigrant Society in New York started a search but could
not find them. The New York newspaper *The World,* never one to miss an
opportunity to do good as a means a self-promotion, sent reporter Isaac D.
White to the Chesapeake to find them as well as any other shanghaied men
forced to work on dredgers. Using the *The World's* funds, White (the same
man who would later free shanghaied men in Mexico) hired the steam tug
Commodore S.F. DuPont to carry out his mission. He brought with him six
gunners, another reporter from his paper, an artist, Captain W. Parkers of the
Baltimore Society for the Protection of Minors, and U.S. deputy marshal J.C.
Lengrade Cole, the last of whom carried with him arrest warrants. The expedition successfully rescued the missing boys plus another twenty-two victims
of shanghaiing. Of the six captains Cole apprehended for offences against
their crews, two won acquittals for lack of evidence.[43]

Locating shanghaied men on oyster dredgers rarely brought results
because most of those taken never stepped foot on land during the oyster harvesting season. Instead, captains marooned them on a large oyster boat
anchored far out in the bay and there left them stranded until needed. Those
who died while working on the Chesapeake often wound up buried in shallow

graves on marshy Deal Island.[44]One body found in a ditch there on October 14, 1905, belonged to a shanghaied man named James McCabe, who had supposedly drowned. Upon hearing of this, his wife went there to have him exhumed. What she saw convinced her of murder: "The ditch where his body was found did not contain enough water to drown a three-year-old child.... [The body] was a mass of bruises, the head had been beaten almost to a pulp in the back, the skull was crushed, and his teeth had been knocked down his throat.... As long as I have strength to continue my mission I will hunt down his murderers, and if there is such a thing as justice, they will be punished."[45] To that end she went to Baltimore and there secured affidavits from three of McCabe's fellow hands who swore to having watched McCabe suffer from three beatings. Her persistence paid off. Authorities took the U.S. revenue cutter *Windom* out to investigate. This led to a grand jury indictment of shipping agent James Hodges for his assault on McCabe.[46]

Four Bells

State governments did not ignore Chesapeake Bay's shanghaiing problem. In 1888 a Maryland grand jury assembled to investigate the alleged abuses said to occur on oyster dredgers. It found solid evidence captains mistreated their crews, abusing them using a variety of tools that included pistols, axes, shovels, iron levers, and fists. Shipping agents often tricked men into signing onto dredgers, and many captains forced men to work past the end of their contracts, then refused to pay their due wages.[47]

Immigrant societies also got involved because crimps disproportionately targeted recent émigrés. The German Society placed signs along the waterfronts of Baltimore, Philadelphia, and New York in both English and German warning men not to sign onto dredge boats. In March 1893 it paid for an expedition to rescue shanghaied Germans. In that same month seven Baltimore humane societies pooled their resources to form a bureau of lawyers to investigate reports of shanghaiing and give their findings to the appropriate authorities in an effort to stop physical abuse and theft of wages, the latter of which affected about 1,000 immigrants in the 1892–1893 oyster harvesting season alone.[48] The Maryland legislature passed a law that went into effect on January 1, 1890, stipulating harbormasters and allied authorities had to register all dredge boats and keep copies of their ship's articles in their offices. Captains had to return with all the men who had shipped with him or they could face up to six months in jail.[49]

In 1905 U.S. District Attorney John C. Rose of Baltimore, tired of the shanghaiing problem in the Chesapeake, wrote a letter to the Treasury Department requesting assistance from the Secret Service. The U.S. district attorney of Philadelphia made a similar request. The Treasury Department responded by committing agents as investigators into the matter, promising revenue cutters if the need arose. This in turn prompted U.S. marshal John F. Langhammer of Baltimore to take out the revenue cutter *Windom* and start his own investigation.[50] He boarded around 100 vessels, made several arrests, and rescued a man named George Kissick, who was from the Philadelphia suburb of Kensington.[51]

In February of the next year U.S. Marshal Morgan Treat, his deputy Samuel Bendit, and a U.S. shipping commissioner named Stephenson from Norfolk, Virginia, took the *Windom* out on a similar mission. In Virginia's Mattox Creek they found a large number of dredgers blown there by a storm and trapped by ice. The *Windom* cut through to them and sent out a launch to visit each dredger, questioning the men on board about their treatment as well as how they got there.[52]

No one would tell them a thing until they boarded the *Daniel*. Here they interviewed a man named Thomas Cunningham, who reported suffering from rheumatism and having had to sleep in a flooded cabin. Other crewmen also testified to experiencing poor conditions on board, and many stated that a shipping agent in Baltimore named Charles Doherty had gotten them to sign onto dredgers by promising them $18 a month for those working in Maryland or $13 a month for those in Virginia, money they never saw. The marshals arrested the *Daniel*'s captain, William E. Justice, and a grand jury indicted him.[53] This crackdown of enforcing new anti-shanghaiing laws had the desired effect. Deputy U.S. Marshal Miller, while summoning witnesses on Tangier Island, learned most of the dredger captains had paid off their crews for fear of prosecution.[54]

The U.S. Navy also got involved in the effort, although it did so only because of the poor judgment of a dredger captain named Marion R. Coleman. In 1908 Coleman drugged an enlisted man, Charles F. Hammond, and locked him in his boat's hold. For three months Hammond toiled under terrible conditions until he escaped and made his way to Baltimore. Although charged with absence without leave, when the details of his ordeal came out during his court-martial, the navy went into action to right this wrong. It sent a revenue cutter into the Chesapeake that found and arrested Coleman for his crime.[55]

In 1911 the drowning of a shanghaied man named John McNamara from Williamsport, Pennsylvania, escalated the U.S. government's crackdown when the incident caught the attention of the Bureau of Navigation, a division of the Department of Commerce. It prompted commissioner Eugene Tyler

Chamberlain to launch an investigation into the matter with the help of a collector of customs from Crisfield, A. Lincoln Dryden. The two learned someone had drugged McNamara during his trip to Baltimore from Williamsport and took him to the oyster sloop *Irene and Ruth*, which was under the command of Captain Aldie Dorsey. While working along Broad Creek in Maryland, McNamara drowned on January 6, 1911, after jumping overboard to escape. Twenty-two days later three crewmen murdered Dorsey, but not before he had inflicted mortal wounds on two of them. After learning all of this, authorities arrested, tried and convicted the man who had shanghaied McNamara.[56]

The secretary of Commerce and Labor, Charles Nagel, ordered the yacht *Old Glory,* a vessel powered by two gasoline engines and armed with a powerful searchlight, to go on a cruise aimed at sailing all through the Chesapeake to look into the accusations of shanghaiing, brutality, and the poor food distributed on board the dredgers. During the cruise's first three days, the authorities sailing on her arrested twenty-one men for violations of laws, including an oyster boat captain who had attacked a crewman with a hatchet. To escape, his victim had jumped overboard into the icy water and nearly died of hypothermia before someone fished him out.[57]

Shanghaiing ended on the Chesapeake not because of laws and their enforcement but rather overfishing. In 1841 watermen discovered the beds in Tangier Sound that produced more oysters than any other place in the world, but by 1881 overfishing resulted in their exhaustion. In 1885, one of the industry's peak years, several thousand boats harvested around 600,000 tons of oysters. Maryland's beds produced 1,257,000 bushels of packed oysters in 1895 and a mere 260,000 bushels in 1905. In the early twentieth century the take of the entire bay produced about 80,000 tons.[58]

In 1911 the captain of an oyster boat found a "patch" of oysters with an area of between eighteen and twenty acres containing large ones found only in old, untapped beds. Being an old hand in the business, he knew he had to keep this find a secret. He came out only at night to work and from it took "nearly a thousand bushels of ... [oysters] first and last, which he sold at an average of eighty-five cents." This did not last long. "One day about sundown [he saw] ... four or five dredgers" headed towards his boat. "Within a few days there was practically not an oyster left on that bed."[59]

The loss of beds also caused trouble between independent watermen and corporate oyster fishery operations. In 1903, for example, a number of Maryland watermen raided the beds of the Tangier Packing Company along the Annemessex River in retaliation for its alleged violation of Maryland's law limiting a claim to five acres. Independent oystermen accused the company of having claimed more than 200 acres using false names. Although the independents had initially managed to get an injunction to stop Tangier Packing from operating in them, a judge reversed this decision. In response to the raid, the state sent boats out to round up those responsible.[60]

Two technologies made the decimation of Chesapeake oysters possible: mechanized tongs and the gas-powered wench. Mechanized tongs first appeared in 1887 and could dive to a depth of about eighty-two feet, much farther than the standard type. This allowed tongers to harvest in places they had never before reached. The gas-powered wench reduced the number of men needed on dredgers. Now instead of four turning a windlass by hand to pull one up, just a single person could do it. The combination of fewer oysters and the need for fewer men ended shanghaiing on the Chesapeake because the demand for laborers no longer exceeded the supply.[61]

9

The Hunt for Whales and Men

Sixty-one-year-old Bernard Morrison, a bricklayer and mason from Ann Arbor, Michigan, fell on hard times in 1888 and could no longer take care of his wife. To remedy this, he headed to San Francisco to try to make a living. There he met a man on the Broad Street wharf who offered to show him the city's sites. As the day went on the two stopped to have a drink or two. In a saloon along the waterfront, Morrison lost consciousness. He awoke in a tangle of ropes lifting him onto the deck of the whaling bark *Bounding Billow.*[1]

Her master, Captain Eugene O. Thaxter, demanded he sign the ship's articles for a hunting expedition to the South Seas and the Arctic. Morrison refused. Thaxter marooned him on Ascension Island in the South Atlantic with the expectation this would motivate his unwilling victim to sign on. A barren spit of land dotted with the volcanoes that had formed it, the island contained sparse vegetation that supported a few goats, sheep and cows. Even Darwin, who visited it during his famous voyage around the world, found little of interest here. The locals robbed the clothes off Morrison's back, leaving him with just his boots.[2]

About a month later Morrison caught passage on the steam whaler *Thrasher,* which found the *Bounding Billow* anchored in Guam. The *Thrasher*'s master, Captain Charles E. Weeks, went over to her to convince Thaxter to take Morrison back, which he did. At Yokohama, Morrison went to the American consulate and complained. For this the outraged consul threatened to arrest Thaxter. To make amends, Thaxter paid for Morrison's passage back to San Francisco out of his own pocket.[3]

One Bell

Ordeals like Morrison's happened all too often. The filthy process of hunting and processing whales had little appeal, the primary reason professional mariners called these vessels "hell ships."[4] Even those who did not mind the bloody mess of cutting a whale into pieces small enough to process could not get away from its awful smell, so terrible that in the seventeenth century the town of Southampton on Long Island forbade processing a whale any closer than 25 poles (137.5 yards) from the town's edge. Those who did received a £5 fine. Whaling never contributed a significant amount to America's overall economy. In 1850, one of the industry's peak years, it added a mere 1 percent, and by 1860, when the industry's decline had begun, this dropped to 0.5 percent. Many Americans nonetheless made their fortune from the business largely because their ships had the whaling grounds all to themselves until the late 1840s.[5]

Whaling by white settlers probably started in America around 1640 in Southampton. In the seventeenth century the infant industry expanded north into New England and as far south as North Carolina.[6] America's first whalers, Native Americans, practiced drift whaling, the finding and processing of whales that had washed ashore. In Southampton so many fights broke out over who had the rights to a find the town passed an ordinance dividing it into four wards, the residents of each drawing lots to decide which person received the rights to cut it up.[7]

Drift whaling gave way to killing passing whales by going out to them in boats. Known as coastal or shore whaling, it probably began around 1650. Records from 1672 indicate that the towns of Southampton, Easthampton, and Southwold on Long Island's east side had done so for at least twenty years. In Southampton all citizens had to take their turn watching for passing whales in a tower erected for this purpose.[8]

The island of Nantucket off of Massachusetts, a place lacking good soil for agriculture or any other land-based natural resources, started out as a fishing community. Nantucket was settled by Quakers looking for a place to escape from Puritan persecution; several of them bought the island on July 2, 1659. In 1712 a wind blew a Nantucket boat owned by Christopher Hussy far off-shore and straight to a sperm whale, which he and his crew quickly killed and brought back. His success prompted the island's whalers to abandon coastal whaling and take to the deep sea.[9] From this year until about 1775 Nantucket's whale ships dominated the industry, the number of them rising from six in 1715 to sixty in 1749 to 150 in 1775. Nantucket initially targeted northern right whales because they inhabited the local waters and swam slower than others of their species, but their near extinction and the better returns from sperm whales caused whalers to target the latter instead.[10]

Epitomized by Moby Dick, the sperm whale has a high, blunt head that makes up 25 to 35 percent of its entire body and contains a matter called spermaceti, a waxy substance that resembles semen (thus its name). Once extracted, its refinement could take up to two years depending on the final product desired. Those who processed the raw material did so by applying heat, pressure, cooling, and bleaching. No one knows the exact function of spermaceti, but several plausible theories exist. One says it helps sperm whales regulate their buoyancy during their incredibly long and deep dives, while another speculates it cushions head impacts during mating season. Still a third idea suggests these whales use it as an aid for echolocation.[11]

Around 1750, candle makers started to use whale oil for their products, but these smoked badly, smelled foul, and did not emit very good light. Spermaceti, on the other hand, burned nearly smokeless and produced far more illumination. Despite the higher cost, demand for it soared. It became especially desirable for use in lighthouses and locomotive headlamps. Oil derived from spermaceti could survive high temperatures, making it valuable for the machinery that fueled the Industrial Revolution.[12]

Sperm whales also produced a valuable substance known as ambergris. A hard substance with a waxy texture, throughout most of human history it appeared only as detritus that had washed onto beaches along the shores of the world's seas and oceans. When exposed to the air, it turns from gray to amber or, more rarely, black or brown. Its pungent smell changes into a fragrance so pleasant it became highly desirable as fixative for perfume. Although no longer the case, Europeans coveted it for its flavor. Those with money to spare added it to their coffee, tea, chocolate, and wines, and even used it as an ingredient for icing. King Charles II of England preferred eating it with his eggs more than any other dish. In medieval Europe it became a key ingredient in love potions.[13]

Also known as "Neptune's Treasure" because of its immense value, which even today can amount to a small fortune, ambergris found ashore usually weighs from a few to twenty pounds. For the longest time no one knew where it came from. In the late eighteenth century someone figured out a whale produced it, but not which one. Whalers answered that question when they cut into sperm whales and found the substance in their intestinal tracts. Unlike ambergris that washed up on a beach, the kind found inside a sperm whale could weigh up to nearly half a ton. A whale ship belonging to the Dutch company Vereenigde Oost-indische Compagnie once found a piece weighing 975 pounds. In 1912 a small whaling company avoided bankruptcy upon finding a 1,003-pound piece it sold for $60,000.[14]

Ambergris forms in a sperm whale because of its diet of squids. The squid is swallowed whole, and the whale's digestive track dissolves everything but the squid's beak. This sometimes gets trapped in the lining of the whale's stomach or intestines and becomes an irritant. To ease the discomfort, the whale produces a waxy substance called *amberein* to envelope the beak, and the substance can expand to cover even more of them. Ambergris comes out when the whale vomits or defecates.[15]

Those who owned Nantucket's whaling fleets, at least during its heyday, made enough profit that ambergris provided nothing more than a nice bonus. Part of their overall wealth derived from the fact they paid their crews—mainly Native Americans and some blacks in its earliest days—unconscionably low wages to keep them in perpetual debt, forcing them to repeatedly go out on voyages. By the 1750s the scarcity of willing laborers, the decline of the Native American population, and the increase in the cost of whale oil made sailing on a Nantucket whaler quite profitable even for the hands. This attracted white Yankees, many of whom by this time lacked other economic opportunities because settlers had already taken all the available land to the immediate west.[16]

The British decimated Nantucket's whale fleet during the American Revolution. By that time, too, much of its primary source of men, Native Americans, had died out from disease or suffered from chronic alcoholism, and the whites who replaced them demanded higher wages.[17] The Massachusetts town of New Bedford replaced Nantucket as the most important whaling port in the world, a status it kept into the 1850s. Originally a part of Dartmouth, it became its own municipality in 1787 and a city in 1847. It, too, had started out with drift whaling but soon expanded to coastal then deep sea hunting. Like the shipowners on Nantucket, those in New Bedford maximized their profits by paying crews obscenely low wages. Unlike Nantucket and other American whaling ports, New Bedford's hunters targeted a wide variety of whale species rather than just one, cushioning the city from the effects of over-fishing.[18]

In 1848 artists Benjamin Russell and Caleb Purrington celebrated New Bedford's success by painting the travelling 1,295 foot *Grand Panorama of a Whaling Voyage 'Round the World* depicting a view of New Bedford from the perspective of a ship coming into its harbor, a snapshot that captured the city during its peak; it would decline for the next sixteen years. Two catastrophes ended its dominance. In 1864 Confederate raiders captured twenty-eight of its whale ships, and the next year Arctic ice crushed another twenty-two.[19]

The American whaling industry on the whole began its decline around the time of the Civil War. By then whale ships had overfished so many of the world's whaling grounds they had to go much farther afield to find new ones, raising the overall costs of voyages. More efficient mineral-based sources for illumination and lubrication such as petroleum appeared, rendering comparable whale products obsolete. With this aspect of the industry dead, whalers began selling flexible whalebone, used in the nineteenth century for items such as canes, whips, umbrellas, and corsets.[20]

Two Bells

Whale ships hunted until they held as much as they could carry. Voyages usually took between one and three years, the bulk of that time spent looking for prey, especially in the industry's waning years when many types of whales had become virtually extinct. Ships spent the majority of their time searching for prey, and to that end placed a lookout to scour the horizon for them by seeking sprouts of water coming from their blowholes. A lookout who saw this cried, "A blooooow!" This he repeated several times to gain the attention of those on deck, pointing in the appropriate direction.[21]

The main whale ship rarely did the hunting directly. Instead her crew used whaleboats commanded by a mate and directed by the boat-steerer, who doubled as a harpooner. Crews maneuvered their boats through the water using sail power if possible and rowing when necessary. In heavy seas a man called the "waif" climbed to the top of the main ship's mast and signaled the boats with a flag to point them in the right direction because the boat crew, being so low in the water, could not see very far in such conditions. The harpooner used his weapons to catch but not kill the whale. He called his harpoons "irons" and always kept them in top shape. Harpoons consisted of an iron tip with one or two barbs (called flues) affixed to a hardwood shaft three to four feet long and attached to a long whale line.[22]

For about two thousand years most whalers used a one- or two-barbed harpoon that did not always stay secure. This problem virtually disappeared in 1848 when an African-American blacksmith named Lewis Temple invented, or rather rediscovered, an improved iron called the toggle harpoon. Its head flew parallel to the shaft, but upon hitting a target, a weak wooden stick holding it in place broke, allowing it to swivel perpendicularly to ensure a much better hold into the blubber.[23]

Whalers developed specialized words describing the different ways a whale reacted to a strike from a harpoon. One that dove into the deeps of the ocean "sounded," and if it resurfaced like a cannonball, it performed a "breach." Some swam away along the surface at top speed until worn out, taking the boat from which the harpoon had come on a "Nantucket Sleigh Ride." This might last for hours and could take a whaleboat many miles from the main ship. Upon stopping, the tired whale usually made fairly easy prey, but not

Sperm Whaling with Its Varieties (**Library of Congress Prints and Photographs Division, publisher/creator unknown, publication date unknown**).

always. Some turned on the boat and with its jaws and broke it into pieces, "chawing" it.[24]

A hand-thrown harpoon had a maximum range of about fifteen yards. Around 1730 the British invented the harpoon gun, a device capable of launching an iron up to eighty-four yards. Too heavy to hold like a regular firearm, it sat upon a swivel mounted to a boat's bow, giving it a wide sweep. Because whales in arctic waters might dive under the ice and never reappear within sight, it became vital to incapacitate if not kill the target on the first hit. To that end someone came up with the bomb lance, a weapon that dug into the whale's blubber then exploded from within to cause maximum damage. The Americans improved upon this with the shoulder-mounted bomb gun used for long-range attacks. The dart gun, another American innovation invented around 1880, fired both a harpoon and bomb lance simultaneously.[25]

To kill a whale, hunters came alongside and stabbed its vitals repeatedly with lances five to seven feet long and had an attached rope so a wielder could readily draw it back and strike again. Such struggles presented much danger to the hunters because a whale lashing out could do them much physical harm.[26]

Upon subduing of the beast, the main ship came alongside and its crewmen immediately began the process of "cutting in," the chopping of the whale into manageable pieces of blubber. These came on board and went into a brick-encased cauldron heated by a fire called the "try-works" as part of the "trying out" operation in which the men boiled the blubber to separate out its oil. One man stirred while others threw the scraps onto a wooden strainer to catch every last drop of oil, which quickly went rancid in temperate climates. Others removed, cleaned, and stored the whalebone.[27]

The whale ship *Grayhound* (Library of Congress Prints and Photographs Division, publisher/creator unknown, September 18, 1917).

Working on a whale ship had many dangers. On occasion a wounded whale went to war against those who dared to attack it. One verifiable incident of this occurred on August 20, 1851, and involved the New Bedford whaler *Ann Alexandra* during a hunting voyage in the South Pacific. On this day her lookout saw a pod of sperm whales. The captain, John S. Deblois, ordered two of the ship's whaleboats lowered to pursue. He took command of the starboard boat and his first mate took the larboard. The latter reached a whale first, its harpooner successfully striking a whale, which took the boat on a Nantucket Sleigh Ride. But, once tired, the whale did not passively await its fate. Instead it chawed the boat to bits, although fortunately no one suffered an injury.[28]

Although the incident occurred about six miles away from the *Ann Alexandra,* someone nonetheless saw it and dispatched the waist-boat to effect a rescue, but Captain Deblois reached them first and took all nine men on board. When the waist-boat arrived, he ordered half the men into it, placing his first mate in charge. The mate's boat reached the wounded whale ahead of the other, but its attack only enraged the beast further. It destroyed this boat as well, so Delbois once again rescued his men, all still unharmed.[29]

He then prudently decided to return to the *Ann Alexandra,* but as the remaining boat started its long trip back, the whale pursued, its jaws wide open. Fortunately it passed them by. Back on the main ship, Delbois ordered his vessel to continue the attack. The whale retaliated by swimming at high speed with the intent of ramming the *Ann Alexander,* but a bit of handy seamanship got her out of harm's way. Now the whale dove into the deep, appar-

Whale Fishery: Attacking a Right Whale (Library of Congress Prints and Photographs Division, Currier & Ives, ca. 1856–1907).

ently giving up. Except it had not. Past sundown it came at the ship again at a great speed and rammed her, knocking a big hole in her keel. Delbois tried to save his ship by dumping cables and ballast, but to no avail. She rolled onto her side.[30]Delbois rushed into his cabin to grab his chronometer, sextant and charts while his men scrambled to procure what supplies they could, which amounted to nothing more than twelve quarts of fresh water and no food. They climbed into two leaky boats they had to bail all night. Delbois had the men cut into the *Ann Alexander*'s hull to get at and salvage what supplies they could, but they found little of value. The survivors headed north to get into the rainier latitudes to at least procure some fresh water from the sky. Within two days of the incident they came across the whale ship *Nantucket,* which took them to Paita, Peru. From there they made their way home on a ship aptly named *Providence.*[31]

Another whale ship, the *Eliza,* faced a danger whalers working in Arctic waters feared: the weather. On October 18, 1890, a nasty gale blew in a snowstorm. It hit the *Eliza* as she passed the Diomede Islands in the Bering Strait. The blow lasted for weeks, pushing the *Eliza* north of St. Lawrence Island off the Alaskan coast and causing her to lose boats and several masts.[32]On November 12 Captain Kelly beached her off St. Lawrence Island. The crew escaped to shore in a boat, which they converted into a shelter. Natives living on the island gave them fish to eat, then took Kelly and his carpenter to the island's northwest side to some huts by which they lit a signal fire. This caught the attention of the steamer *Belvedere,* which picked up the marooned crew. In San Francisco four of the *Eliza*'s men went to the hospital for treatment of frostbite, and one reported having lost fifty-one pounds, thanks to the ordeal.[33]

Weather related disasters occurred in the Arctic all too frequently. One of the worst happened in 1871. In September of that year sea ice blown up from the south trapped a fleet of thirty-two whale ships, sinking three and causing two to take on dangerous amounts of water. Their captains gathered on board the *Florida* on September 12 to decide what to do. Predicting it would take a good nine months for the ice to break up and knowing they only had about three months worth of food to feed the 1,200 they collectively had on their vessels—including women and children—they decided upon a course of action.[34]

Although no ship could escape the ice, enough room remained between its pieces to allow a boat through. The *Florida*'s captain, David R. Fraser, took one south with the hope of finding some ships still free. Those left behind began the work of making their boats more seaworthy in anticipation of using them to evacuate. Fraser found two ships free of the ice and five more working their way loose. After apprising them of the situation, he made the seventy-mile trip back north to inform the trapped crews to man their boats. Boarding 150 of these, they made their way to the waiting ships, then sailed to Hawaii. The next year a salvage ship, the *Florence,* explored the area in which the trapped fleet had resided only to find just one vessel, the *Minerva,* still seaworthy.[35] With conditions like these, it ought to come as no surprise that men on whale ships deserted when possible. To make this more unlikely, their captains often chose to make port in out-of-the-way places that offered few diversions. A captain who stopped in a well-populated port usually made arrangements with local officials to bring back deserters for a fee, one deducted from the captured men's lay (a percentage of a ship's profit).[36]

Steve Cole arrived in San Francisco from Madera, a small town to the southeast, with $127 in his pocket and a desire to have some fun. He had no idea a man on the street who offered to show him the sites worked as a runner. For two days this fellow helped him spend all of his money. When that ran out, he got Cole drunk, whisked him into a shipping office to sign articles with a promise of a $50 advance (which Cole never received), then brought him on board the whaling brig *Alexander*, where Cole fell into a deep sleep.[37]

One crewman described the *Alexander* as "a stanch, seaworthy little vessel. She had no fine lines; there was nothing about her to please a yachtsman's eye." Built in New Bedford specifically for Arctic whale hunting and rigged as a brigantine, she had a sturdy oak hull that allowed her to break through ice and carried three boats for the pursuit and killing of whales. The forecastle, like that on most ships of this type, had little appeal. "It was a dark, malodorous, triangular hole below the deck in the bows" filled with double-tiered bunks.[38]

When Cole awoke and realized his predicament, he decided to swim to shore despite its being several miles away. The men to whom he confided this plan warned him not to try it, predicting he would drown. He thought that sounded better than sailing on a whale ship, so at two in the morning he stripped to his underwear and climbed down into the water via one of the mooring lines. He made it to shore in the frigid March water on or near Jackson Street, where a friendly watchman gave him a pair of overalls. He then went into a saloon to get warm. At dawn he found an acquaintance to help him contact his friends and family in Madera.[39]

Three Bells

Those who signed onto whale ships worked in a rigid hierarchal system of rank. The captain commanded his vessel with absolute authority and controlled the men with the help of his mates. Ranked just below his officers but above the hands came the boat-steerers, who, along with the steward and cooper, lived aft in cabins, another way of reinforcing their superiority over the hands, who lived forward in the cramped forecastle that, during foul weather, lacked any natural light or ventilation because of the closing of the hatch above to keep water out.[40]

Masters of American whale ships exacerbated their crew's misery by unnecessarily hoarding water. Rather than return to port every four months to resupply as stipulated by U.S. law, they stayed at sea much longer, forcing a conservation of fresh water used only for cooking or drinking. Men who wanted to wash themselves or their clothes had to collect rainwater for this purpose. A pump piped fresh water up from a lower deck to the main for drinking, but on many ships the captain placed a single drinking cup slightly aloft, forcing anyone who wanted it to make a climb. Its possessor could not pass it to another but had to return it, forcing the next man to climb for it as well. The captain did this to discourage his hands from drinking as much as they would have liked.[41]

Because whale ships roamed all over the earth, a captain could not readily make contact with the owners if something unexpected happened. Instead, he received a roaming commission giving him the authority to sell the ship or cargo as if he owned them. And most did not own them. Only half of New Bedford's captains, for example, held a share in the ships they commanded, and of these, on average, most possessed just one-sixteenth. Nor did this share necessarily protect him from dismissal; shareholders could remove him with just cause and majority vote, although this rarely happened.[42] Whale ship owners had little inclination to divide their take with anyone who made a living at sea. Owners of multiple vessels played their captains against one another to encourage competition among them. If that failed to get results, they might threaten to withhold bonuses or to keep them home the next season, reminding them that they had more skippers available than they needed.[43]

During the height of the American whaling industry, ships usually made large profits, prompting many New Bedford owners to demand their captains return with enough whale products to result in a 45 percent profit, of which they usually took 65 to 70 percent. The *Benjamin Tucker,* for example, arrived at the end of an 1851 voyage with a cargo of whalebone and oil that sold for $47,682.73. After deducting operating costs, this left $45,320 for distribution to all those with a share.[44]

Despite the privileges they enjoyed, the masters of whale ships got lonely, especially for the company of women. In 1906 this caused a minor scandal in Alaska. That summer the U.S. government sent a special commissioner to investigate reports of captains debauching the native Inuk women. The commissioner fined nine men, four of them skippers, and arrested Captain Edwin W. Newth of the whale ship *Jeanette* on a charge of statutory rape for having had sex with a twelve-year-old girl.[45] As it turned out, authorities already wanted him for questioning for an incident that had allegedly occurred the year before in which he and several other captains had gotten the natives of the Alaskan island Little Diomede drunk, then kidnapped a woman and her daughters for their pleasure, although they did eventually release them. This charge apparently went nowhere, although Newth did plead guilty to the charge of statutory rape. For this he received a mere one day's prison sentence plus a $2,500 fine and court costs.[46]

A year later Newth faced accusations of cruelty against a crewman. During the winter of 1904–1905 in the Arctic, ice had trapped the *Jeanette*. Newth, nearly always drunk, withheld food from the crew. One day he accused a hand named Stephen P. Talbot of stealing a pair of trousers. A mate forced Talbot to take them off and work in the Arctic cold without this protection. Talbot demanded the captain either prove his accusation of theft or return the confiscated apparel. Newth refused. He commanded Talbot to carry on with his duties. Talbot would not. Newth knocked him down and kicked him a few times, then had a mate tie him to the ratlines high enough to make his feet dangle over the deck (this last part Newth denied).[47]

Newth asked if Talbot would work now. At first Talbot refused, but after twenty-five minutes or so of this, he changed his mind. Talbot, who suffered from tuberculosis, left the *Jeanette* not long thereafter. He eventually went to the office of U.S. shipping commissioner Heacock and pressed charges for the incident. In 1907 Heacock brought Newth into his office for a trial. Gazing upon his former captain for the first time in about two years, Talbot saw not the monster he remembered but rather an old man sick and broken. Pity overcame him. He asked Heacock to dismiss the charge, which he did.[48]

Captains continued to use cruelty as a means of discipline because terrifying crews into submission usually worked. In 1902 an Australian man named Arthur Edwin Dihm came to San Francisco with the idea of getting a berth on a steamer. The owner of the boardinghouse in which he stayed convinced him to sign on to a whaler with promises he could easily jump ship in Alaska and go hunting for gold. Once on board Dihm and four others plotted their escape, but the captain caught wind of their plans and warned he would not allow this.[49]

While in the Arctic, the captain spent most of his efforts on trading with the Inuit rather than hunting for whales. One day a crewman disguised himself as an Inuk and accompanied some of them back to shore in their boat. The captain forced the boat's return. As it came alongside, he grabbed the escaped man by the hair and brought him on deck, had him tied up by the hands and feet so he lay prone, then kicked him relentlessly. Thereafter he had him raised aloft by his thumbs, a technique called tricing. The sound of the poor fellow's thumb joints popping and his accompanying screams caused Dihm to have nightmares for days afterward.[50]

Unlike merchant vessels, those who signed onto a whale ship earned a percentage of the profit—called the lay—rather than a set amount per month. Crimps often told potential recruits they could earn 300 or 600 without mentioning this represented 1/300 or 1/600 of the total earnings rather than a fixed dollar amount, the irony being the higher the number promised, the less was earned. Not surprisingly, experienced seamen rarely signed onto whale ships of their own free will. This suited captains just fine because they could pay inexperienced men less and control them easier.[51]

Crewmen did receive free room and board, but they had to buy most of what they needed—needles, thread, knives, tobacco, clothing, and so forth—from the captain on credit at an inflated cost, and the captain had the goal of deducting as much as he could from each share of the crew's lay so as to increase his own. He also subtracted the cost of each man's access to the medicine chest (whether or not he used anything from it) and for any equipment damaged while in his care.[52]

A man who sailed on a whale ship for three or four years could earn up to $100, but because of all these deductions, by the time he reached shore, he might well *owe* money. To pay off his debt, he signed on for another voyage. The crimps took their cut as well, their fees coming from the crew's lay, not the captain's pocket. By the 1890s, when whale oil became worthless thanks to petroleum, this vicious circle only worsened.[53]

Arthur Dihm, the mariner who had seen a man hanged from the rigging by his thumbs, worked hard for seven months with the expectation of receiving a share of the profits from the whales his ship caught. But during this period her boats went out only once and found nothing, leaving him with no earnings whatsoever at the voyage's end despite months of hard work. The captain hardly cared. He had made a profit selling the Inuit items such as bad flour and obsolete rifles in exchange for skins, whalebone, and boots he sold for $10 a pair in San Francisco.[54]

Frank Trusdale from Oakland did not do much better than Dihm. Lacking work to support his wife and five children, Trusdale headed across the bay to San Francisco in March 1897 to look for a job. A man told him he could earn $2 a day unloading lumber from a ship, and, as a bonus, receive free room and board on her. Someone drugged his first supper with a strong sedative.

He and four or five other shanghaied men awoke to find themselves 300 miles out to sea on the *Alexander*. Trusdale pleaded with the captain to let him go, but he would not relent, unmoved even by tears. The *Alexander* headed to the Arctic and returned to San Francisco with the oil and bone of nine whales several months later. Trusdale received a paltry $16.26 as his lay despite all the hard work he had done. He believed he had more due to him.[55] Onshore a fellow named Colonel Dimpel of the Society for the Prevention of Cruelty to Children had him charged with not providing for his family, refusing to believe his story of being shanghaied. Thrown in the county jail, Trusdale contacted the *Alexander*'s owners, the Pacific Trading Company, to see if he could get more of the pay owed to him. The company replied that it had withheld $170 of his lay for the cost of his clothes but did admit to still owing him $10.26.[56]

Another story with a similar outcome sounds as if it could have inspired Rudyard Kipling's *Captains Courageous* had it not occurred after that book's publication. Nineteen-year-old David Hammond, Jr. enjoyed a life of leisure and indulgence. His millionaire father, who ran the Chicago facilities of G.H. Hammond—the third-largest pork packing company in the country and one owned by the syndicate of J.P. Lyman—insisted his son stop his "follies" and either go off to a university or start working for him in the stockyards. To avoid either fate, Hammond ran away to San Francisco in March 1905.[57] There he went to the waterfront to look at the ships. A man driving a buggy noticed him and stopped. The stranger asked if he would he like a ride. Hammond acquiesced. His new friend said he could get him a job on a ship that would pay between $500 and $10,000. Having never sailed on the ocean before, Hammond agreed. The man then took him to a sailor's boardinghouse. Here Hammond bunked with rough men of all nationalities and slept for the first time in his life on an uncomfortable cot.[58]

The man in the buggy took him to a shipping office and there got him to sign articles for the whaling vessel *Monterey* under the command of Captain Charles H. Foley. For this Hammond received a $40 advance, some of which went to pay for his room and food at the boardinghouse, and the rest to outfitting himself for the sea with items such as gum boots, an oil skin, a blue flannel shirt, overalls, a jumper, tobacco, and a tin plate and cup.[59]

Hammond took to his situation quite well. The work buffed him up and made his soft hands hard, reducing his fingernails to the quick. He washed his own clothes and ate from a tin plate he set on his legs. About the food, though, he commented, "I wouldn't feed a dog on the kind of grub I ate." He found he liked going whale hunting in an open boat and the entire experience made him grow up fast, although he got terribly homesick. As they sailed, Hammond had to replace his clothes from the slop chest and undoubtedly buy other things needed for work on board, and this cost him much. The voyage ended seven months later. Even though he earned only one dollar after deductions from his 1/170 of the lay, he felt proud to have received it. Upon returning home he planned to work for his father if he would allow him to.[60]

Hammond had the unfortunate luck of sailing on a whale ship during the waning days of that industry at a time when conditions had fallen to an all-time low. By now seamen avoided these vessels at all costs, forcing captains to rely on shanghaiing more than ever before. One former whaler, Henry A. Clock, estimated in 1895 that half the men working on any whaling vessel had gotten there because someone had shanghaied them. The crimps who had done this procuring usually tricked their victims to sign their articles without the presence of a shipping commissioner—which the law stipulated—because this person would have warned them of the perils of whaling.[61]

As whale ship masters became more desperate to fill out their crews, they took on anyone the crimps offered, even if nothing save for divine intervention would give such persons the ability to do the job, such as happened to Charles Orton. Originally from Minneapolis, Orton came to San Francisco with the hope the change of climate would improve his tuberculosis, but unfortunately a crimp shanghaied him and he wound up on the *Alexander,* which took him to the Arctic. Her captain tried to get some work out of the poor fellow by beating him, but it soon became apparent that would accomplish nothing. He dumped his useless man onto the U.S. revenue cutter *Thetis.* Orton died with the photograph of a young girl in his hand before reaching San Francisco.[62]

American revenue cutters such as the *Thetis* first came to the Arctic in 1880 to enforce U.S. customs laws, rescue wrecked crews, and provide a refuge for sick seamen.[63] Cutter officers also took complaints against the captain and his mates from the crew, but few hands made them for fear of retaliation either in the form of a beating, extra work, or a bad discharge. Cutter captains also tended to believe the word of a whale ship's officers over that of the hands, often dismissing their complaints using the flawed logic that the men would not have signed on if such terrible conditions really existed.[64]

Harsh realities did not entirely discourage volunteers. Romance about the whaling industry flooded American popular culture and lured men in. George Fred Tilton of Martha's Vineyard answered its call. Born on January 12, 1861, he came from a prosperous family, but by the age of fourteen could no longer resist the temptation of whaling. He and a friend acquired fake sailing permits and signed on board the *Spartan.* Before she could depart, Tilton's father noticed his son missing, so he and the boy's grandfather chased down and stopped him from going (but not his friend). Tilton tried to run away to sea a couple more times, but his extended family kept a close eye on him.[65]

When he learned the whale ship *Union* would soon depart from New Bedford the next year, he determined to get onto her. To that end he asked the captain of a packet heading to New Bedford for a day trip if he could accompany him. The captain, being a friend, agreed. There Tilton jumped ship and stowed away on the *Union*. Once well at sea, he appeared on the main deck. Someone asked him where he had come from. He explained. The man told him to see the captain on the poop deck. The captain could not turn the ship around, so Tilton joined on. Fourteen months later Tilton returned home much stronger and bigger. He spent the rest of his life on whale ships, working his way up to captain.[66]

Four Bells

Although whale ships worked in all the world's waters in which their prey roamed, the Arctic Ocean and its environs presented one of the hardest places to operate. One man who spent his career living and hunting there, George Grover Washington Cleveland of Beetlebung, Martha's Vineyard, originally went to sea at the age of fourteen with the idea of sailing to China to fulfill "his ambition ... to verify at firsthand some anatomical peculiarity of Chinese women."[67] A man of simple pleasures, he enjoyed above all else liquor and the company of women. About the latter, one Inuk woman recalled, "I certainly know of Suquortaronik, the harpooner. He went off the ships to hunt muskox and left many children in the camps."[68] When whalers first came to the North and began trading with the Inuit, some asked for Inuk women in exchange for items. Cleveland acquired at least one of his girlfriends that way and with her fathered a child. One of this union's descendants told her daughter-in-law, "He had children all over the place ... in South Baffin, Pangirtung, and the Hudson Bay and Keewatin areas."[69]

Whiskey appeared only rarely in the Canadian Arctic, with a limit of six bottles per person per year "for medicinal purposes." Cleveland, upon getting his hands on it or any other liquor, drank the lot at once, only grudgingly sharing it with one of his many Inuk girlfriends. One visiting friend, a Danish anthropologist and explorer named Peter Freuchen, always brought Cleveland items he could not otherwise acquire. Cleveland did not care what he received, but insisted his friend bring him "three of anything.... Always three. If one of these terrible girls who hang around me sees that another gets a kettle, she will make life a hell for me until I give her one also."[70]

Cleveland's stubbornness could get the better of him. Once, after harpooning a whale, two men in another boat, both experienced Inuk whale

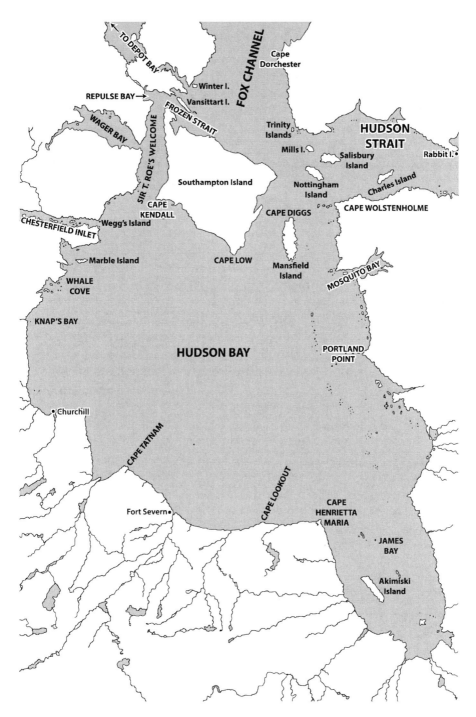

Hudson Bay, based on the 1857 map "Alaskan Boundary Tribunal" by John Arrow-smith (redrawn by the author).

hunters, warned him not to chase it because the beast had breached; when it came back up it might hit his boat with a flipper or its tail. Cleveland ignored their advice and sure enough the whale capsized his boat. Fortunately the hunters who had cautioned him about this possibility picked him and his men out of the water before they froze.[71]

Cleveland's early attempts to get to China brought him to Boston, where one night in 1895 someone knocked him over the head, tied him up, and threw him onto the whale ship *A.R. Tucker* bound for Hudson Bay. Two years later he suffered the same fate in this city, this time winding up on the Arctic-bound schooner *Francis Allyn*. While on this latter voyage he learned the trade of harpooner. Upon his return to America he signed onto still another whale ship bound for the Arctic, but this one wrecked. He became separated from the crew, but fortunately the *Francis Allyn*—at the time on a trading voyage— happened upon him and took him on board. His stay on her gave him valuable experience doing business with the Inuit.[72]

In 1899 the *Francis Allyn*'s owner, Thomas Luce & Company, hired Cleveland to work for them as a whale hunter and trader. He would stay on the *Francis Allyn* for another year, then set up a post and run it for the next five. Cleveland's last voyage on the ship proved especially difficult because the crew consisted mainly of shanghaied men who had no interest in their new vocation. He forced them at gunpoint to roll casks filled with whale oil up hills every day to keep them in shape.[73]

During the summer thaw he divided them up into three whale hunting boat crews manned mainly by local Inuit. Cleveland became acquainted with an Inuk named Keedluk (whose name referred to the soapstone lamps his people favored), and the two became close friends. At the end of the whaling season in September 1898, he left the *Francis Allyn* with some supplies and built a shack on Wager Bay, an inlet of Hudson Bay, to serve as his base. This he shared with Charles Clemmons from Connecticut. The *Francis Allyn*'s captain promised to return the next year.[74]

That summer Cleveland hunted bowhead whales, an animal living exclusively in the Arctic. Its mighty triangular-shaped head could break through up to six feet of ice. Hunters preferred it because of the high amount of whalebone it contained, which made up about 70 percent of its total value. As Hudson Bay's supply of bowheads dwindled, hunters started to target smaller ones as well as females, causing them to become virtually extinct by 1915.[75]

Cleveland returned to his shack at the conclusion of his hunt and there found two notes tacked to his door. One had come from his family, the other from the *Francis Allyn*'s captain, Manuel F. Santos, who informed Cleveland his ship would winter in Depot Bay, a distance of 600 miles overland via dogsled. Cleveland lacked supplies, so he sent Santos a note using two Inuk couriers asking for some. Santos replied he barely had enough provisions for his own crew and therefore could spare none, nor would he likely send any the next year.[76] The following summer Santos informed Cleveland of the unexpected discovery of provisions, but before he could send them, the *Francis Allyn* went up in smoke on July 15, 1902. Fortunately her crew all survived, rescued by the steamer *Active,* a vessel owned by the Scottish company Robert Kinnes and Sons.[77]

In that same year Thomas Luce fired Cleveland for stealing equipment (probably liquor), leaving him stranded.[78] He moved in with his friend Keedluk. To stay long term with Keedluk's tribe, which belonged to the Iglulik people, Cleveland either had to marry into it or go through an initiation ceremony. He chose the latter. The ritual involved having "a circle of hair from the top of ... [his] head [cut off] with a snow knife," then ten days of meditation alone in an igloo. Upon his finishing this and other rituals, his adoptive tribe made him a shaman because he had once used some medicine to cure some of its people's minor ills.[79]The Iglulik called their shamans *anakkuq.* To become one, another shaman served as a mentor and taught his pupil "illumination." Shamans took on the responsibility of divining the future, healing, affecting the weather, finding game, looking for stolen souls, fighting evil spirits, and speaking with friendly ones.[80]

Cleveland stayed with the Iglulik for three years, living with Keedluk's family the whole time. In the summer he went hunting with his new brethren. Two years after Thomas Luce fired him, several Inuit brought him some tobacco—a rare commodity in the Arctic—along with a note from Captain John Murray of the whaling ketch *Ernest William* inviting him to meet on board. He would find the ship anchored in Repulse Bay, a ship belonging to Robert Kinnes and Sons, the same that owned the *Active.* The company had established its first whaling station in the Arctic in 1899 "near Cape Low, the southern extremity of Southampton Island" close to the mouth of Repulse Bay. The base consisted of three whites and about 150 Inuit, all hired to hunt whales in the summer and trap furs the rest of the year.[81]

For such a desolate place, the Arctic had a surprisingly wide variety of fauna, including polar bears, foxes, wolverines, minks, seals, and musk-ox. Before the age of synthetic materials, the naturally thick coats of such animals made them highly desirable because of the warmth they offered. Trappers preferred the wild varieties over those farmed because the latter produced a lower quality of fur.[82]

Cleveland and several of his fellow tribesmen got into a boat and started for Repulse Bay, but during their trip the season's first snowstorm hit. They waited for nine days and still it did not let up. With their food running low, Cleveland decided to try for the *Ernest William* anyway. Their boat hit a piece of ice, damaging it so severely it started to take on dangerous amounts of water. The men scrambled onto a piece of the floe and dragged the boat with them to effect repairs. This accomplished, they started out once more, finally reaching their goal. Captain Murray asked Cleveland if he would like a job. Although he found it difficult to speak English after not using his native language for two years, he managed to accept, hoping this work would allow him to earn enough money to return home.[83]

When Captain George Comer, master of the whale steamer *Era* and an employee of Thomas Luce, learned of Cleveland's new job on August 8, 1904, he decided to go to the Wager Bay station and pick up the skins Cleveland had gathered for the company. Comer did not like what he found: "Every one of the skins is spoiled by being wet. Many of them the maggots are thick on them, not good skins in the first place. Evidently all the best skins have been taken out, including all the fox skins." Comer also confiscated "1 vice, 1 grindstone, 6 lantern globes, 1 shoulder gun and 2 dozen bars [of] soap."[84]

Cleveland's account of Comer's visit varies considerably. In his version, he returned to his shack one day and there found Comer burning it down while at the same time confiscating his furs, whale products, and two whaleboats. Cleveland challenged Comer to a fistfight over this matter and won. Although Cleveland placed this event before his abandonment by Thomas Luce, Comer's more accurate chronology puts it after the company had fired him. In his private journal Comer made no mention of meeting Cleveland in person at the Wager Bay shack nor of a fistfight.[85]

While working for Kinnes and Sons and under Captain Murray's tutelage, Cleveland achieved the rank of captain. In 1905 he took passage on the *Active* and headed back to New Bedford for the first time in seven years. Upon arriving home, he found he could no longer walk in American-crafted boots since he had not done so during most of his stay in the Arctic.[86]

In 1908 Robert Kinnes decided to set the *Ernest William* up as a trading post in Repulse Bay and placed Cleveland in charge of her. Aside from a white harpooner, cook, and carpenter, he had an all Inuk crew. The ship traded or hunted mainly walrus furs, but in the summer she went in pursuit of whales. *Ernest William* had no set port but rather stayed anchored in the summer and allowed the ice to hold her in the winter. Upon returning from his first whaling expedition, Cleveland found her missing. It turned out the spring melt had created such a powerful ice flow that it had dragged her away, the might of this natural force snapping her two anchor cables. Inuit who had seen where she went guided him to her. Fortunately for him he found her still intact.[87]

In 1909, upon his return to Repulse Bay after a summer of hunting, he learned of an outbreak of a deadly disease among his adopted people living on Rabbit Island. As a medicine man he had an obligation to give them aid. Here he found many had died from an apparent outbreak of dysentery, the majority of those affected being children. He blamed this on the pools of stagnant water from which the Inuit drank, which he conjectured had become contaminated by their dead, whom they covered with stones rather than using interment. Although he had no formal medical training, he knew enough about hygiene to have made this educated and probably correct guess. Bacillary dysentery spreads through contaminated water and hits children harder than any other group.[88]

He gave orders to his companions to acquire water from a different island, mixing it with flour to create a thin gruel fed to those afflicted to help them swallow it without throwing up. "I ordered that the children should have nothing else for food or drink until I gave permission, but I had to disguise this simple measure elaborately with [an] angikok [*sic*] ceremonial to give the Eskimos confidence in it. I wore my angikok belt and went through the ritual for exercising [*sic*] evil spirits. What I had done was a fumble in the dark, but the prescription worked. My patients began to mend, and there were no more deaths. My fame as an angikok grew accordingly."[89]

In time Robert Kinnes fired Cleveland as well.[90] Despite Cleveland's womanizing, thieving, and love for liquor, his experience in the Arctic made him a valuable commodity, so he found another job with the trading concern Lambson & Hubbard. When it sold out to the Hudson Bay Company, he considered going home, but the company enticed him to stay on by offering a pension, something he hoped to use to finance a trip to China.[91] Sometime in the mid–1920s he became ill and departed from the Arctic for good. An Inuk took him on a dogsled to Churchill, a Canadian town along Hudson Bay's west coast in Manitoba Province, for medical attention.[92] Cleveland settled in New Bedford and there told the story of his northern adventures to journalist Minna Littmann. These she turned into a series of articles that appeared in the New Bedford newspaper *The Sunday Standard* under her own and Cleveland's byline.

10

The Struggle to
End Shanghaiing

An unnamed mariner went to a shipping office with the intent of taking a berth on a vessel going to Shanghai. When he saw the vessel onto which he had signed, he stopped on the gangplank and said, "Not for me. That's a whaler. You don't shanghai this chicken. I'm wise, I am." Apparently he had little wisdom when choosing his friends, because one of them whacked him "behind the ear" to force him onto the deck. He tried to get off but too many men surrounded and shuffled him to the forecastle and out to sea.[1] Escape would have done him little good. By signing the articles, he had a legal obligation to sail, thanks to existing laws. Even if he had gotten away, authorities could have tracked him down and compelled him to sail against his will.

One Bell

From its inception, U.S. law treated sailors differently than they did other free citizens. Both the merchant marine and U.S. Navy had special laws that applied only to those services.[2] In the United States, federal judges doubled as admiralty jurists, their rulings on cases pertaining to the sailing world becoming the law of the sea on American ships.[3] Legal historians have traced British and U.S. maritime regulations back to medieval Europe, particularly to the highly influential Laws of Oléron. Named after an island off the French coast and probably written by Eleanor, Duchess of Guienne, King Richard I brought them back to England upon his return from the Crusades.[4]

These and similar laws of that era outlined harsh discipline against common sailors. A seaman who deserted, for example, suffered either death by hanging or had a hot iron branded onto his face with the letter of the town from which he came. A seaman who fought with another or struck a superior officer might lose a hand. While a captain had absolute authority, the codes encouraged him not to act in a tyrannical manner. He could strike a subordinate only once. After that, this fellow had the right to defend himself. Seamen received their pay in three parts, one-third as an advance, one-third when they reached their destination, and the last third when they returned to their home port, plus extra for doing the work of longshoremen. If a vessel wrecked, those who helped to salvage the cargo received a bonus.[5]

American shipowners embraced the more oppressive aspects of these ancient laws because doing so made it easier for them to exploit and control their crews. In the earliest days of the American Republic shipowners lobbied for and got Congress to pass harsh laws to control sailors, such as giving authorities the power to arrest those who deserted and to make refusing the order of an officer an act of mutiny. These earliest laws also established the shipping contract, or ship's articles, a document stipulating that each man who signed on received an advance of one-third of his total earnings, something later exploited by crimps.[6]

Congress also recognized the economic importance of America's merchant marine. To ensure it remained fully manned, Congress passed a law to protect the health of those who served in it. Using a British system established during the reign of Queen Elizabeth I as a model, in 1798 Congress enacted a law establishing a series of marine hospitals in American ports to keep merchant mariners in good health, financing the system by deducting a tax from sailors' wages, something collected by customs agents. A seaman who needed medical care went to the customs house for an examination. If an agent determined he needed attention, he sent the man to a marine hospital or, if one did not exist in that particular port, arranged for him to see a local doctor.[7]

The U.S. government's paternalism toward American seamen became more intrusive in 1823 because of an incident involving an officer named William Harding. He signed the articles for the merchant ship *Enterprize* for a voyage from Portland to Guadalupe and back with a guarantee he would still receive his pay if he became ill. Sickness overcame him in Guadalupe, so he went to shore for medical attention. When his captain, Joshua Gordon, deducted this cost from his wages, Harding sued. Gordon and his codefendants, the *Enterprize*'s owners, argued the terms of the articles entitled Harding only to free drugs from the medicine chest, not treatment on shore in a foreign port.[8]

The case made its way to a federal court with Judge Joseph Story, a Supreme Court justice at the time executing his duties as a circuit court jurist, presiding. Harding won the case, but Justice Story's opinion set a terrible precedent that pushed sailors' rights back for decades to come. Story designated seamen as "wards of the admiralty" and established the legal principle that they lacked the ability to take care of themselves and therefore the American government had this responsibility, an idea he borrowed from his understanding of Britain's treatment of its sailors.[9]

Unfortunately this paternalism did not extend to a seaman's retirement. Retired sailors had to live on their life's savings (presuming they had any), move in with family, or beg on the streets. Fortunately local governments and private individuals established retirement communities for them known as sailors' homes. One of the earliest of these appeared in the New York City area in the nineteenth century, although its origins stretched back into the eighteenth. Thomas Randall made his fortune as a privateer during the Seven Years' (French and Indian) and King George's wars. A man of conscience, in 1768 "he headed the committee that drew up the articles leading to a royal charter for The Marine Society of the City of New York, which would care for distressed shipmasters, their widows and orphans."[10]

His son, Robert Richard, bought some Manhattan farmland on November 25, 1783, for this purpose. The father died in 1797, and the son followed in 1801. The latter's will stipulated the family fortune would go to the establishment and construction of a seamen's retirement home on the land he had bought for this purpose. Called Sailor's Snug Harbor, Randall's will called for the creation of a board of trustees to govern the facility, naming the men he wished to take its seats. For its president and vice president he chose members of the Marine Society. Before the board could carry out its official duties, the New York legislature had to incorporate it, but that body at first refused with hope an heir would come forward and stop this nonsense of wasting money on mere sailors. Five years later DeWitt Clinton, nephew of Governor George Clinton, pushed the incorporation through, but the board faced still more obstacles.[11]

By now, New York, then limited to Manhattan Island, had crept upon the farmland set aside for Snug Harbor, making its value too high for the board to pass up selling. In 1828 it did so, figuring it would purchase land elsewhere. It also had to contend with potential heirs claiming the Randall fortune, including an Episcopal bishop, John Inglis of Canada, who demonstrated his Christian piety by putting his own personal gain ahead of the men who would benefit if the Harbor ever got built. The case made its way to the Supreme Court where Inglis lost, allowing the board to finally proceed with its plans.[12]

The board purchased land on Staten Island in 1831. Sailor's Snug Harbor opened in 1833 with thirty-seven residents, most of them foreigners. At first allowing men only from tall ships to take rooms, it eventually accepted those who had served on steamers as well, despite the fact the former held the latter in contempt. To qualify for a room, a mariner had to have sailed for a minimum of ten years, five of them on U.S.-registered ships. The Harbor facility offered each resident his own quarters connected via "enclosed bridges" to common rooms used for things such as recreation and reading. The board later had an adjoining hospital constructed to serve the residents' medical needs.[13]

Chronic neglect by the board and a reduction of income generated by the rental properties it owned in Manhattan caused the Harbor to fall into disrepair by the 1960s. This state of affairs turned around on July 1, 1969, when Captain Leo Kraszeski became its governor and began a successful program of renewal. Despite his efforts, the high cost of operating in New York City made it too expensive to run the facility there. The board sold off all the Harbor's New York assets and purchased land at Sea Level, North Carolina, on which it had a new facility built. It transferred all its residents there in 1976. New York City bought the Staten Island facility and transformed it into the Snug Harbor Cultural Center and Botanical Garden.[14]

Two Bells

The effective enslavement of sailors by American and British Admiralty laws did not end when they came to shore. Some American colonies, for example, regulated them on land in much the same way they controlled their indentured servants and slaves. White men had the power to chase down "runaway" seamen in South Carolina. New York allowed the whipping of those who misbehaved. The colony of Virginia required them to carry travel passes and prohibited them from going to shore after sunset. As with slaves, the system sought to break the will of those it affected by making them feel inferior to and dependent on their so-called betters.[15]

One of colonial Virginia's lieutenant governors, Alexander Spotswood, used his power over sailors to locate the pirate Edward Teach, better known then and now as Blackbeard, the infamous rogue who operated in the Caribbean and along America's eastern seaboard between 1716 and 1718. His downfall began when the governor of North Carolina, Charles Eden, gave him and his crew a royal pardon at the beginning of 1718. This allowed his quartermaster, William Howard, to return home to Virginia without fear of being charged with piracy. Or so Howard thought. Spotswood had him seized on the grounds he had no lawful business in the colony, confiscated his two slaves, then forced him to become an enlisted man on the British warship *Pearl*.[16]

Spotswood did this with the idea it would intimidate Howard into telling him where his former captain resided, but he did not panic so easily. For three ounces of gold he hired a lawyer named John Holloway and sued the *Pearl*'s captain and first officer for unlawfully detaining him. Howard won his case, so Spotswood charged him with piracy and tried him in an Admiralty Court. As Spotswood had planned, this forced Howard to reveal Blackbeard's current location. The court convicted Howard and sentenced him to hang, but a last-minute royal pardon saved his neck. Blackbeard did not get so lucky. He lost his head.[17]

Despite their harshness, American laws did offer seamen some legal protections. A 1790 law, for example, stipulated that any ship 150 tons or heavier had to carry a medicine chest. It also gave crews on merchant ships the power to demand the captain return to port if they believed they sailed upon an unseaworthy vessel. After an inspection, a judge would rule whether the ship needed repairs or could sail without further delay. If the latter, the captain received compensation out of the crew's wages for this loss of time.[18] An 1835 amendment to an existing law reduced a crew's resistance to the authority of an officer from an act of mutiny to a lesser type of insubordination. It changed the penalty for mutiny from death to a maximum of five years in prison or a $1,000 fine, and it forbade officers from exacting cruel and unusual punishments against the crew, including beatings, unjustified imprisonment, and the withholding of food or water.[19]

Shipowners naturally resisted such laws. When they could not outright stop them, they lobbied to have them watered down. Take the 1872 law that established the office of the shipping commissioner. Appointees would serve as a witness when a man or boy signed his ship's articles to ensure he did so willingly with a full understanding of the contract's stipulations. Shipowners convinced Congress to include a provision that punished desertion with up to three months imprisonment and empowered authorities to apprehend deserters without a warrant, then force them to sail against their will. Congress also failed to appropriate enough money to make the new office of shipping commissioner effective, so crimps ignored it.[20]

Beyond the force of law, owners used wages as a means of control. In the late 1750s and early 1760s, for example, New York City's shipowners formed an association with the sole purpose of lowering the wages of able-bodied seamen, ships carpenters, and other better-paid laborers involved in the shipping industry. To weed out troublemakers, the association insisted those who signed onto a vessel present a written certificate of approval from their last employer or they would find themselves blacklisted.[21]

By the turn of the twentieth century, seamen received their pay based not on their personal experience but rather on the type of vessel on which they sailed and the port from which they departed. Men who worked on a barge made less than those who sailed on the deep sea. Those shipping out on an American vessel from London made less than if they sailed on that same ship out of New York City, while crews departing from West Coast ports made more than those almost anywhere else in the world.[22]

Many captains took on boys as midshipmen for a fee in exchange for training them to become officers. In the late nineteenth century some captains assigned them duties no able-bodied seaman would do, then taught them nothing of value. Unscrupulous masters did this to bolster their personal incomes, which had severely declined along with their power over crews at the same time their legal responsibility for what happened to them increased. Such circumstances drove many captains to drink heavily, commit suicide, or go mad, a problem exasperated by the fact that most shipping companies no longer allowed them to bring their loved ones with them on voyages.[23]

Ships' mates also found their lot had worsened. Previously they received their pay based on how long they sailed on a given ship, but to save money owners started to hire them per voyage. Experienced mates had to compete with young and foreign officers willing to work for less. The authority and living conditions of the second and third mates deteriorated to the point where they had it no better than the hands, whose own lot had become so bad they started to form unions in an effort to reverse this situation.[24]One of the earliest of these appeared in New York City and served the interests of black seamen working out of this port. Called the American Seamen's Protective Union Association (ASPUA) and founded by William P. Powell, the son of a former slave, it "incorporated on April 15, 1863," and accepted all black mariners except for officers. The ASPUA aimed to stop the exploitation of black sailors both in New York and onboard ships. Powell also ran the "Colored Sailor's Home on Cherry Street ... [a place] supported financially by the American Seamen's Friend Society." He used it as the union's headquarters as well as a place to help destitute members.[25]

A July 1863 event beyond Powell's control caused the home and ASPUA to shut down for three months.[26] At this time the Civil War raged on and the North desperately needed men, so in March 1863 it implemented a draft, avoidable by paying $300, something only the well-off could afford. The city's recently arrived Irish population resented this, in part because they lacked the funds to pay for exemptions and in part because they did not want to fight a war on behalf of blacks. When New York City's provost marshal started to draw draftee names using a lottery system on July 13, it sparked a riot.[27]

This began in the Twelfth Ward when an angry mob attacked the district's headquarters to get at the Board of Enrollment and its provost master within. The mob found and beat the deputy provost marshal, then burned the building down. They then turned on blacks, destroying their homes and businesses. They grabbed one black man, hanged him on a tree, then set it, and therefore him, on fire. They also burned down the Colored Orphan Asylum, but fortunately everyone within escaped.[28]

At some point in the day rioters invaded the Colored Seamen's Home, looting its rooms and doing some significant damage. Powell, his family, and the home's residents climbed to the roof and fled to safety. Powell later returned to effect repairs. From 1862 to 1867 he ran the Seamen's Saving Bank out of it. The last record of ASPUA's existence dates to 1870. After this it presumably ended, although why remains undiscovered.[29]

Similar and more successful attempts to unionize by seamen followed. Mariners living in San Francisco who sailed on coastal vessels along the Pacific penned the "Sailor's Declaration of Independence." Read aloud on March 6, 1885, on Fulsom Street from atop of a pile of lumber—a symbolic choice because most coastal seamen sailed on ships that transported this commodity—it called for them to organize. Although wages mattered to this new movement, especially since a depression gripped the United States at the time, it had formed primarily in response to the city's crimps who kept shanghaiing coastal seamen and forcing them to sail on deep sea vessels.[30]

The declaration inspired the formation of the Coastal Seamen's Union (CSU), which has, because of mergers with other unions, evolved into the present day Sailors' Union of the Pacific, AFL-CIO. Founded primarily by those of Nordic descent, in 1886 its members made the racist choice of railing against Chinese immigrants taking good "white" jobs. To that end, they refused to sail on any ships owned by Speckles Brothers, a company that used a lot of Chinese labor for its shipping of sugar from Hawaii to San Francisco. Speckles Brothers refused to negotiate until the CSU coordinated its efforts with an Australian union.[31] This action and others like it rankled San Francisco's shipowners so much that in 1885 they formed the Pacific Shipowners' Association. Its members only hire would seamen who signed through its offices and carried a grade book containing their skills and history of employment. The CSU went on strike over this, well knowing crimps could use these books to control victims.[32] A spokesman for the Shipowners' Association outright denied the existence of both crimps and shanghaiing and insisted his organization had nothing but San Francisco's mariners' best interests in mind.[33]

Although the CSU failed to keep lumber ships from sailing south from San Francisco, it did prevent them from returning. Members accomplished this by mimicking the tactics of runners. Whenever a coastal vessel came into port, they rowed out to her and enticed men to join their union with promises of higher wages. Ships so affected could leave if they took on union crews.[34] The strike crumbled when the Shipowners' Association hired enough scabs to break it, a successful tactic frequently repeated throughout the nineteenth century.[35]

In 1875 the CSU received bad publicity when a conflict with a crimp named "One-Eyed" John Curtin became explosive. Curtin, originally a ship's carpenter, ended that career when he lost an eye. In 1875 he came ashore and established the Fulton House for seamen in San Francisco, from which he shipped nonunion men on coastal vessels against the CSU's wishes. On September 24, 1893, someone dropped a black valise in front of his boardinghouse.[36] His son, John Junior, saw it in the street and investigated. Within he found dynamite. He shouted a warning but few nearby paid him any heed, and some even laughed at the notion. Although he ran for it and escaped harm, those who had not died or suffered terrible wounds.[37]

The explosion blew off the front of Fulton House and killed five people inside. One newspaper reported, "Men were thrown from their beds across the street.... Four groaning victims lay in the street near by. Beside them lay two corpses, stripped of nearly every bit of clothing."[38] California's governor issued a $1,000 reward for the arrest and conviction of those responsible. The head of San Francisco's police department blamed the CSU, as did Curtin. Police arrested John Tyrell, James Wood, and Terrace Tracy for the bombing, but of these, Tracy had never belonged to the CSU and the other two no longer did because they had stopped paying their dues. A jury failed to convict them.[39]

This bad publicity did not deter the CSU. In late 1887 it started its own newspaper, *Coast Seamen's Journal,* and on February 14, 1894, ran the first of its "Red Record" features, so called because they appeared in red ink. These had the purpose of highlighting atrocities committed on ships by captains and officers in the last seven years. Although it did not run for long, the next year an editor collected the articles into a pamphlet containing sixty-four incidents of cruelty, including fourteen murders. For all these crimes, prosecutors secured convictions for a mere three.[40]

In 1892 the CSU formed a committee to outline the sort of legislation needed to stop the bad treatment of merchant mariners, a tactic made viable thanks to the lobbying abilities of one of its members, Andrew Furuseth, a man who had a talent for influencing politicians. Within nine years of his going to Washington, D.C., for this purpose, Congress passed the legislation he wanted, an effort earning him the appellation "the Abraham Lincoln of the Sea." He was born on March 12, 1854, in the Norwegian village from which he took his last name. His father had trouble caring for him and his nine siblings. To alleviate this burden, he sent Andrew away to work on a farm in Romedal owned by Jonas S. Schjotz, who quickly recognized his eight-year-old ward's keen intelligence and, not wanting it to go to waste, sent him to school. Furuseth left the farm in 1870 and three years later went to sea. He worked as a deep sea mariner until 1880 when he tired of the brutal conditions on board ships and came to America, there becoming a fisherman on the Columbia River.[41]

Although he did not help to found the CSU, Furuseth joined it shortly after its formation and became its secretary in 1887. In this position he expanded it, but after two years he resigned his post. When his successor suffered a major scandal in 1891, members asked Furuseth to replace him, and he did. Dissatisfied, he resigned several months later and returned to fishing, but a guarantee of higher pay enticed him to return. He would stay in this office until 1935.[42]

In 1891 he effected a merger of the CSU with the Steamship Sailors' Protective Union, and this became the Sailors' Union of the Pacific. Two years later he gained the ear of San Francisco's congressman James Maguire, con-

This illustration, *Our Merchant Marine: The Rip Van Winkle of the Sea,* appeared in the November 15, 1911, issue of *Puck;* it parodies the troubles the American merchant marine faced at the time (Library of Congress Prints and Photographs Division).

vincing him to represent the interests of the professional mariner.[43] Maguire introduced a bill bearing his name that, when passed in 1895, did two important things for seamen in the coastal trade. It voided punishment for desertion—stripping the power of captains to compel men to serve against their will—and disallowed the legal concept of "original creditor" in which a person could sell debts owed to him or her to another. This last kept crimps from selling their victims' debts to a shipping office or a captain.[44]

Three Bells

The U.S. Merchant Marine, one of the world's mightiest in the mid-nineteenth century, had rapidly declined by its end. In the late 1890s U.S. businesses wanted to expand into East Asian markets but found it impossible to use American vessels to do so, a deficiency that became startlingly clear during the Spanish-American War when the U.S. military found itself forced to lease mostly foreign ships as transports for its supplies to Cuba and the Philippines.[45]

In his December 1903 message to Congress, President Theodore Roosevelt called for the formation of a commission to investigate the decline of the merchant marine and come up with ways to fix it. Congress responded by establishing the Merchant Marine Commission on April 28, 1904. Filled with five members of the House and five from the Senate, it began hearings in New York City the next month, then moved to other cities across the nation with the same purpose. To its frustration, the committee discovered few willing to testify who had a personal interest in the problem.[46]

The committee learned U.S. manufacturers exported no goods to South America on U.S. ships, and the foreign-owned ones they used often proved unreliable, sometimes even damaging their cargo. U.S. mail going to England did so on British ships. By 1903 only 10 percent of all goods went abroad on American vessels, costing U.S. manufacturers an estimated additional $1 million a year. Foreign ships rarely used American seamen and even refused to purchase provisions while in American ports.[47]

Those who ran what remained of the U.S. shipping industry blamed the state of things on American seamen and on shore laborers, claiming their demands for wages higher than those in other countries made it impossible to remain competitive. P.A.S. Franklin, a vice president at the International Mercantile Company, said it cost 40 percent more to build a steamship in America than in Britain. Thomas Clyde, who ran a steamship company operating along the coasts of the Carolinas and Florida, blamed the industry's problems on sailors' unions because they insisted foreigners make the same as Americans, keeping him and other shipping companies from undercutting their wages. Companies that refused to comply found themselves targets of union actions.[48]

The commission concluded the industry's decline and its inability to compete with foreign shipping companies had come about because, unlike the rest of the world's nations with important merchant fleets, the United States did not heavily subsidize its own to keep it competitive with commercial rivals. The American line Pacific Mail, for example, received a $63,902 subsidy for shipping mail to Alaska, while the Japanese paid $600,000 to a smaller mail-carrying line, and Germany and Britain gave even larger supplements to some of theirs. America had stopped subsidizing its merchant marine after the Civil War, instead allocating this money for internal improvements such as railroads.[49] American cargo tramps faced intense competition with Danish and Norwegian syndicates. Norwegian captains who did not make at least a 25 percent profit often reduced their crew's size or their allotment of food to made up the difference. The small size of American syndicates owning these vessels had little surplus with which to operate, explaining why so many of their ships, even new ones, looked run down.[50]

The commission also looked into why Americans no longer became professional mariners in the numbers they once had. It found some answers when it interviewed Otto Parsons, the New York agent for the Atlantic Coast Seamen's Union. He explained professional American mariners refused to sail on many ships because they lacked sufficient crews with too few able-bodied seamen, making sailing on them more dangerous than necessary. Moreover, most Americans had no interest in becoming mariners, because, unlike other careers, those who quit suffered arrest for desertion. Even with that deterrent removed, they still could not resign at will because if they didn't complete their entire voyage, they did not get paid. Parsons thought it would help if men received wages for however long they sailed rather than having to blindly commit themselves to an entire voyage.[51]

Nothing exemplified this better than the *Arago* case, its infamy marking a major turning point in the mariners' struggle for better conditions. In May 1895 four of this vessel's crewmen, Robert Robinson, P.H. Olsen, John Bradley, and Morris Hansen, jumped ship in Astoria. They had signed articles for this coastal vessel in San Francisco with the expectation of sailing to Valparaiso and any other ports in between that the captain decided upon. The four found conditions on board not to their liking, so they left believing the Maguire Act protected them from apprehension for desertion. Authorities nonetheless detained them for sixteen days, then forced them to sail on the *Arago* when she left port. Her captain had a U.S. marshal arrest them in California for refusing to work.[52]

For this the four sued the federal government as well as the marshal who had arrested them in California. They argued their apprehension for desertion violated the outlawing of indentured servitude found in the Thirteen Amendment. As American citizens, no one had a right to make them work against their will. The case made its way to the U.S. Supreme Court. The court decided authorities could indeed arrest seamen who refused to honor their contracts. More infamously, it ruled that the Thirteenth Amendment did not apply to military personnel, merchant mariners, or minors

Robert M. La Follette (Library of Congress Prints and Photographs Division, Harris & Ewing, 1911).

and those under guardianship, this last being a double strike against a seaman's liberty, considering Judge Story had made all American sailors wards of the state with his 1823 ruling.[53]

Justice Henry Billings Brown, who had throughout his career specialized in admiralty law, wrote the *Arago* case's opinion. It reinforced Story's ruling by stating seamen could no more take care of themselves than children could. Their inability to make mature decisions meant they had to fulfill any contract to which they agreed. The decision voided the Maguire Act's prohibition against arresting coastal seamen for desertion.[54] About this ruling the editors of *The Broad Ax,* a newspaper out of Salt Lake City, opined, "We confess that we cannot see the justice or reason of this decision. Can it be possible that the Thirteenth Amendment looked only to the inception of the contract? If a person contracts to do certain service upon terra firma, and having entered upon its performance, refuses to complete it, can he be compelled to go on or be subjected to fine and imprisonment? We think not. He has a perfect right to dispose of his time and skill as he sees fit."[55]

Cases like this motivated Andrew Furuseth to continue his search for political supporters in Washington who would change existing laws that allowed such outrages. He brought the plight of the U.S. merchant mariner to a progressive Republican senator from Wisconsin named Robert Marion La Follette. Known to his constituents as "Fighting Bob" La Follette, once he took up a cause, he saw it through.[56]

Born in Primrose, Wisconsin, on June 14, 1855, he began his public life in 1880 as the attorney general of Dane County and four years later became a U.S. congressman, an office he held until 1890. He became a progressive in 1891 when one of Wisconsin's U.S. senators, Philetus Sawyer, offered him a bribe. Sawyer, a wealthy lumberman, wanted him to influence a lawsuit over which La Follette's brother-in-law presided as judge. La Follette angrily refused. The incident awakened him to the corrupting influence of big money and caused him to become a populist who would fight for the rights of the common people. After a stint as state governor, during which time he went after the power of the railroads and advocated for the direct election of senators, he began his career as one of Wisconsin's U.S. senators in January 1905. He introduced a bill, known as the Seamen's Act, in 1910 that, among other things, removed penalties for desertion, but it went nowhere.[57]

Like so many important laws passed by Congress, it took a major tragedy to get this one through that body, and even then this had less to do with the plight of the seaman than it did the death of women and children. On the night of Sunday, April 14, 1912, the White Star Line's newest ship, *Titanic*, struck an iceberg and quickly sank. About 1,500 passengers (many quite rich) died for lack of sufficient lifeboats to carry them, a situation made worse by an inexperienced and untrained crew. The White Star Line had violated no laws in this matter. The *Titanic* carried *more* lifeboats than required.[58]

A subcommittee of the Senate Committee on Commerce recommended all ships leaving or entering U.S. ports had to have a sufficient number of lifeboats for passengers, and each boat have no less than four trained crewmen assigned to it with drills for their use occurring a minimum of twice monthly. Ships should also carry two searchlights and a dedicated wireless operator, and have ready communication among all parts of the vessel.[59] The recommendation about lifeboats made its way into a new version of Senator La Follette's Seamen's Act bill. Although it passed both houses of Congress on October 13, 1913, President Howard Taft vetoed it.[60] His decision to do so came about in part because of intense lobbying by the shipping industry. Its representatives convinced him that the bill's passage would allow seamen's unions to create a giant trust that could then take complete control of their vessels, rendering the captain and his officers powerless and therefore endangering the passengers.[61] The matter really had less to do with passenger safety than it did a loss of the power owners had over crews. Captain Allen Luckhurst, the marine superintendent of the American and Red Star Lines, predicted the act would give the seamen's unions the ability to demand that crews receive the same rations as the captain, including ham, rolled oats, baked potatoes, and coffee. Indeed, these men (his attitude suggested he would have preferred the word "peons" or "peasants") would insist on eating three full meals a day![62]

Luckhurst found the idea of giving up a shipowner's or captain's ability to have deserters arrested particularly offensive, couching this in terms meant to convince those listening of the inherent dangers: "If this bill became law the big liners carrying passengers and mails would be liable to be held up for hours while a new crew was being obtained, and then have to go to sea with incompetent men. Deserters are not to be punished or arrested and taken back to their ship, so a vessel could be abandoned at a port where another crew could not be signed."[63] Then he started to contradict his own argument: "Today ... the sailor is better off than the unskilled laborer ashore, as he has comfortable quarters.... That the men are contented with their lot is proved by the fact that a big percentage of our crews remain voyage after voyage.... Men on their arrival in New York, Boston, or any other port in this country can demand money in order that they may go ashore and spend it on liquor, and possibly leave their ship and go to a sailors' boarding house."[64]

The International Seamen's Union of America countered the shipping industry's lobby by submitting a petition to Congress entered into the congressional record on June 4, 1914. It capitalized on the *Titanic* disaster by arguing Congress needed to limit the number of hours a mariner could work in order to ensure passenger safety. At present men sometimes worked for up to thirty to forty hours uninterrupted, leading to their utter exhaustion. Tired men could not effectively see to the safety of the ship and especially her passengers, who in any case often numbered more than the ship could safely take on. To that end, shipping companies needed to place far more able-bodied seamen on board because without a sufficient pool of experienced hands the chances of survival during a crisis seriously diminished. Shipping companies kept experienced men to a minimum to save money.[65]

Andrew Furuseth met with President Woodward Wilson and convinced him to sign the Seamen's Act into law, which Wilson did on March 4, 1915.[66] Fearing it would destroy the American shipping industry, the National Foreign Trade Council petitioned him to suspend it because of the ongoing world war.[67] Congress convened a committee to give the shipping industry a place to present its reasons for this. A manager at the Pacific Mail Steamship Com-

pany predicted the law would mean the end of his company's business; its
stockholders planned on voting as to whether or not it would shut down.[68]

Yet this ire against government's intrusion into the shipping business
demonstrated Pacific Mail's hypocrisy; without government intrusion the company never would have started or prospered. In his 1846 address to Congress,
President James Polk requested the establishment of a mail service along the
Pacific Coast, an idea suggested to him from an Oregon resident named John
M. Shively. Congress appropriated the money for this venture, and Shively
became Oregon's first postmaster general. Congress stipulated the mail route
would span from the Isthmus of Panama to Astoria and serve many points in
between. The shipping company to which it awarded the contract would
receive no more than $100,000 annually for the service. It would carry letters
at forty cents apiece and had to make deliveries no less than once every two
months.[69]

Arnold Harris, a speculator from Arkansas, won the contract on November 16, 1847, by committing to run the service at $199,000 a year. Three days
later he turned it over to William H. Apsinwall, who, along with several others,
formed the Pacific Mail Company to fulfill the contract. The company incorporated in the State of New York on April 12, 1848, for a period of twenty
years, and its first fleet of ships consisted of wooden side-wheel steamers sup-
plemented by sail power because of the side-wheelers' inefficient one-stroke

**Pacific Mail steamer *Korea* (Library of Congress Prints and Photographs Division,
publication date unknown).**

steam engines. Despite the high expense of running them with imported coal, the company nonetheless turned a good profit, in large part because of its lucrative California Gold Rush passenger service, which ultimately transported thousands to and from the Isthmus of Panama.[70] For those who could pay, the average twenty-one day trip from Panama to San Francisco proved quite luxurious. First- and second-class passengers slept in carpeted staterooms with good ventilation. On some vessels they even had access to a barbershop and bath. Passengers who could only afford steerage accommodations slept on canvas bunks stacked three high. Although poor food plagued the line's ships in its earliest days, even this improved.[71]

The completion of the Union and Central Pacific railroads shortly after the Civil War prompted Congress to subsidize a shipping line that would establish a regular route from West Coast ports to Japan and Hong Kong. Pacific Mail won this in addition to its existing mail contract. It had four ships built for this purpose, all side-wheel wooden steamers with masts. Its first ship to travel from San Francisco to Hong Kong, the *Colorado,* departed on January 1, 1867, and stayed in service until 1876.[72]

Pacific Mail lost its first government contract for mail in 1875 when it got caught using some of this allotment of money to buy congressional votes for a second subsidy. Besides its regular vessels, between 1904 and 1915 it also ran four huge steamers, nicknamed the Big Four. To reduce labor costs, the company hired a significant number of Chinese, something other Pacific lines did as well. The Seamen's Act stipulated 75 percent of all seamen on board an American ship had to speak English, and since few Chinese mariners could do so, this effectively reduced their numbers on Pacific Mail ships to 25 percent.[73]

From 1876 to 1906 American lines paid Chinese seamen shipping out of Hong Kong between $7 and $15 a month and Americans on the same route between $25 and $55 a month. Despite any language barrier, Chinese seamen proved quite competent and just as good as Americans. The number of Chinese mariners wanting to sail on American ships far outstripped the demand. Many Chinese had lost work in their own country when its river and ocean-going shipping converted to steam and thus reduced the number of mariners needed to operate. Over a period of thirty years the use of Chinese seamen saved Pacific Mail and one of its rivals, Occidental and Oriental, about $1,444,000 in wages.[74]

A Pacific Mail representative argued before the congressional hearings on implementing the Seamen's Act that his company could not operate profitably without Chinese mariners, nor could it replace them with willing Americans. He warned that the new law's requirement that ships carry only able-bodied seamen who had received official certification would ruin his company because few Chinese mariners qualified despite attempts to train them. A rival line, the Chinese Mail Steamship Company, dispelled this falsehood when it reported that on the day of the law's official implementation, November 5, 1915, seven of its Chinese crews had passed their certification tests on its ship *China*.[75] The law also required that crewmen receive lifeboat certification. One master, Captain Van Borkerck of the *Androscoggin,* reported that 35 percent of those on his ship who tried to get it had failed, warning this would cause a severe shortage in the number of available seamen on American ships.[76]

Unable to stop the law's implementation, Pacific Mail sold five of its vessels to the Atlantic Transport Company, including its Big Four, then sold itself to two rival shipping concerns. The new board of directors met at the beginning of 1916 and immediately decided to purchase three large steamers, a move that made economic sense because of the ongoing European war in which the United States had not yet gotten involved. At this time neutral vessels such as theirs commanded premium shipping rates. Even after America entered what became known as World War I, Pacific Mail did so well that at the conflict's conclusion it purchased surplus ships no longer needed for the war effort, a total of forty by 1922.[77]

The Seaman's Act put a complete stop to shanghaiing by eliminating the power crimps and captains had over mariners. A seaman who deserted no longer suffered any punishment, and this fact took away the ability of crimps to trick men into signing a ship's articles, then force them to sail. Nor could crimps use debt as a means of blackmailing men who owed them money into sailing against their will. Unscrupulous captains could no longer steal crewmen's wages by running them off before their term of service ended because seamen now had the right to demand half their wages when leaving early. And the law's requirement that at least 75 percent of the crew speak English with a minimum of three years' experience to ensure good communication prevented shipping companies from undercutting wages by employing cheap foreign labor.[78]

Chapter Notes

Databases (Abbreviations in Parenthesis)

California Digital Newspaper Collection database (CDNC)
Cornell University Library: Making of America database (CUL: MOA)
EBSCO: America: History & Life database (A: H&L)
EBSCO: Historical Abstracts database (HA)
EBSCO: MasterFILE Premier database (MFP)
ESBCO: Academic Search Premier database (ASP)
ESBCO: Legal Collection databases (LC)
Infotrac: 19th Century Newspapers database (NCN)
JSTOR
Library of Congress: Chronicling America: Historic American Newspapers database (LOC: CA: HAN)
NewsBank: Cleveland Plain Dealer Historical Newspaper database (CPDHN)
NewspaperARCHIVE database (NA)
Oxford English Dictionary database (*OED*)
Project Muse database (PM)
ProQuest: Historical Newspapers: New York Times (1851–2007) database (HN: TNYT)
ProQuest: Humanities Module database (HM)

Chapter 1

1. "A Shanghaied Crew: Tailors, Barbers, Shoemakers, Carpenters and Grocers Doing Duty Before the Mast," *Daily Alta California,* October 10, 1873, p. 1; "A Shanghaied Crew: The United States Commence Proceeding to Recover Damages for Violation of the Passenger Act," *Daily Alta California,* October 11, 1873, p. 1 (both in CDNC database [accessed August 31, 2011]).

2. "Shanghai," in *OED* database (accessed October 19, 2011).

3. See, for example, Eric Partridge, *Origins: A Short Etymological Dictionary of Mod-*

ern English (New York: Greenwich House, 1983), 613, and Ernest Weekly, *An Etymological Dictionary of Modern English: L–Z,* vol. 2 (New York: Dover, 1967), 1327.

4. Stewart H. Holbrook, "Article No. 1— Shanghai Days in the City of Roses: Larry Sullivan, the Astoria Boy Who Moved to Portland; and Who, as Master of a Sailor Boarding House, Became a Big Shot of the '90s," *Sunday Oregonian,* Magazine Section, October 1, 1933, p. 7.

5. "Shilling," in *OED* database.

6. Gina Bardi, J. Porter Shaw Library, e-mail to author, March 21, 2011.

7. Denise M. Alborn, "Crimping and

Shanghaiing on the Columbia River," *Oregon Historical Quarterly* 93:3 (Fall 1992): 263, in JSTOR database (accessed December 26, 2010).

8. Holbrook, "Article No. 1," *Sunday Oregonian,* 7; Rev. William Taylor, *Seven Years' Street Preaching in San Francisco, California; Embracing Incidents, Triumphant Death Scenes, Etc.* (New York: Carlton & Porter, 1857), 225.

9. Steve Wilson, "Of Crimps and Shanghaied Sailors," *American History,* June 2006, 59, in ESBCO: ASP database (accessed October 7, 2010).

10. Alborn, "Crimping and Shanghaiing on the Columbia River," 264; Taylor, *Seven Years' Street Preaching in San Francisco, California,* 22, 227–228.

11. Holbrook, "Article No. 1," *Sunday Oregonian,* 7.

12. "The New York Land Sharks," *North-China Herald,* March 9, 1888, in NA database (accessed April 3, 2010), 21.

13. Ibid; Robert D. Foulke, "Life in the Dying World of Sail, 1870–1910," *Journal of British Studies* 3:1 (November 1963): 130, in JSTOR database (accessed October 5, 2010).

14. United States, U.S. Congress, Merchant Marine Commission, *Report of the Merchant Marine Commission, Together with the Testimony Taken at the Hearings; Report and Recommendations of the Commission (Including the Views of the Minority) and Hearings on the North Atlantic Coast,* vol. 1 (Washington, D.C.: Government Printing Office, 1905), 54.

15. "A Shanghaied Crew: The United States Commence Proceeding to Recover Damages for Violation of the Passenger Act," *Daily Alta California,* 1; "The New York Land Sharks," *North-China Herald,* 21; United States, "An Act for the Government and Regulation of Seamen in the Merchants Service," in *Statutes at Large,* vol. 1 (1789–1799) (Washington, D.C.: Microcard Editions, 1972), 131.

16. "H.B.M.'s Police Court," *North-China Herald,* April 9, 1903, p. 33, in NA database (accessed April 3, 2011).

17. Holbrook, "Article No. 1," *Sunday Oregonian,* 7.

18. William Morris Barnes, *When Ships Were Ships and Not Tin Pots: The Seafaring Adventures of Captain William Morris Barnes* (New York: Albert & Charles Boni, 1930), 304.

19. "'Shanghai'-ing a Seaman," *North-*

China Herald, April 6, 1887, p. 20, in NA database (accessed April 3, 2011).

20. Frederick Stonehouse, *Great Lakes Crime: Murder, Mayhem, Booze and Broads* (Gwinn, MI: Avery Color Studios, 2004), 26–27.

21. Taylor, *Seven Years' Street Preaching in San Francisco, California,* 226–228, 281.

22. Luc Sante, *Lures and Snares, Low of Life: Old New York* (New York: Farrar, Straus, and Giroux, 1991), 108–109.

23. Steve Wolf, *The Science Behind Movie Stunts and Special Effects* (New York: Skyhorse, 2007), 183.

24. Alborn, "Crimping and Shanghaiing on the Columbia River," 275.

25. Barnes, *When Ships Were Ships and Not Tin Pots,* 301–302; Judith Fingard, "The Decline of the Sailor as a Ship Labourer in 19th Century Timber Ports," *Labour/Le Travail* 2 (1977): 37, in EBSCO: A: H&L database (accessed June 16, 2011).

26. "A Badly Treated Sailor," *New York Times,* June 9, 1886, p. 8, in ProQuest: HN: TNYT database (accessed February 25, 2011).

27. "A Will O' The Wisp: A Millionaire Is Pursued Almost Around the World," *Cleveland Plain Dealer,* August 1, 1894, p. 2, in NewsBank: CPDHN database (accessed December 23, 2010).

28. "Seeking His Inheritance," *New York Times,* August 2, 1893, p. 9, in ProQuest: HN: TNYT database (accessed February 28, 2011).

29. Ibid.

30. "Friday Evening, December 8, 1848," *Star and Banner,* December 8, 1848, p. 3, in NA database (accessed October 30, 2011).

31. Malcolm J. Rohrbough, "The California Gold Rush as a National Experience," *California History* 77:1 (Spring 1998): 17, in JSTOR database (October 31, 2011).

32. George D. Dornin, "Thirty Years Ago," in *Gold Rush: A Literary Exploration,* ed. Michael Kowalewski (Berkeley, CA: Heyday Books, 1997), 59–60; John Walton Caughey, *The California Gold Rush,* with Vignettes by W.R. Cameron (Berkeley: University of California Press, 1975), 57–58.

33. Walter A. Douglas, *Let the Sea Make a Noise: A History of the North Pacific from Magellan to MacArthur* (New York: Perennial, 1993), 246–247; Bayard Taylor, "El Dorado," in *Gold Rush: A Literary Exploration,* 66; H.W. Brand, *The California Gold Rush and the New American Dream* (New York: Doubleday, 2002), 74.

34. Ralph J. Roske, "The World Impact of the California Gold Rush, 1849–1857," *Arizona and the West* 5:3 (Autumn 1963): 206, in JSTOR database (accessed October 16, 2011).

35. Charles R. Schultz, *Forty-Niners 'Round the Horn* (Columbia: University of South Carolina Press, 1999), 176–177; Oscar Lewis, *Sea Routes to the Gold Fields: The Migration by Water to California in 1849–1852* (New York: Alfred A. Knopf, 1949), 80–81; Paul G. Merriam, "Riding the Wind: Cape Horn Passage to Oregon, 1840s–1850s," *Oregon Historical Quarterly* 77:1 (March 1976): 41, 43, in JSTOR database (accessed December 26, 2010).

36. Lewis, *Sea Routes to the Gold Fields,* 82; Merriam, "Riding the Wind," 43.

37. Julia Cooley Altrocchi, "Paradox Town: San Francisco in 1851," *California Historical Society Quarterly* 28:1 (March 1949): 31–33, in JSTOR database (accessed December 26, 2010).

38. James P. Delgado, *To California by Sea: A Maritime History of the California Gold Rush* (Columbia: University of South Carolina Press, 1990), 173.

39. Fred Rosen, *Gold! The Story of the 1848 Gold Rush and How It Shaped a Nation* (New York: Thunder's Mouth Press, 2005), 71–72.

40. Delgado, *To California by Sea,* 173–174; Roske, "The World Impact of the California Gold Rush, 1849–1857," 207.

41. H.M. Downing, "Shanghaiing Sailors," *Boston Daily Globe,* December 24, 1889, p. 3, in NA database (accessed April 10, 2011).

42. Rohrbough, "The California Gold Rush as a National Experience," 19; Roske, "The World Impact of the California Gold Rush, 1849–1857," 187, 207.

43. Richard Cavendish, "The Australian Gold Rush Begins," *History Today* (February 2001): 50–51, in EBSCO: ASP database (accessed June 14, 2011).

44. Philippa Mein Smith, *A Concise History of New Zealand* (New York: Cambridge University Press, 2005), 79.

45. "China and the Foreign Devils," *Bulletin of the Business Historical Society* 3:6 (November 1929): 11, in JSTOR database (accessed December 26, 2010).

46. Glenn Melancon, "Peaceful Intentions: The First British Trade Commission in China, 1833–5," *Historical Research* 73:180 (February 2000): 36, in ESBCO: ASP data-

base (accessed November 14, 2010); J.A.G. Roberts, *A Concise History of China* (Cambridge, MA: Harvard University Press, 1999), 156.

47. "China and the Foreign Devils," *Bulletin of the Business Historical Society,* 11–14; Roberts, *A Concise History of China,* 156, 164.

48. Sarah Rose, *For All the Tea in China: How England Stole the World's Favorite Drink and Changed History* (New York: Viking, 2010), 23–25, 54, 59–60; Huw V. Bowen, "400 Years of the East India Company," *History Today* 50:7 (July 2000): 47, in ESBCO: ASP database (accessed November 14, 2010); John Keay, *China: A History* (New York: Basic Books, 2009), 457.

49. Hunt Janin, *The India-Opium Trade in the Nineteenth Century* (Jefferson, NC: McFarland, 1999), 57.

50. Melancon, "Peaceful Intentions," 37.

51. Larry Sawers, "The Navigation Acts Revisited," *Economic History Review* 45:2 (May 1992): 262–263, in JSTOR database (accessed March 17, 2011).

52. James A. Williamson, *A Short History of British Expansion* (London: Macmillan, 1922), 482.

53. Carl C. Cutler, *Greyhounds of the Sea: The Story of the American Clipper Ship,* 3rd ed. (Annapolis, MD: Naval Institute Press, 1984), 145–146; Richard Woodman, *The History of the Ship: The Comprehensive Story of Seafaring from the Earliest Times to the Present Day* (New York: Lyons, 1997), 111, 148.

54. Ian Dear and Peter Kemp, eds., *An A–Z of Sailing Terms* (New York: Oxford University Press, 1992), 36, 178.

55. Woodman, *The History of the Ship,* 152.

56. "The American Commercial Navy," *Nautical Standard,* July 12, 1850, 8, in NA database (accessed February 20, 2011).

57. Gerald S. Graham, "The Ascendancy of the Sailing Ship 1850–85," *Economic History Review* 9:1, new series (1956): 76, 79, in JSTOR database (accessed May 29, 2011).

58. Foulke, "Life in the Dying World of Sail, 1870–1910," 108, 119–120.

59. Kenneth Giggal, *Classic Sailing Ships* (Stamford, CT: Longmeadow, 1998), 83.

60. Alexander Laing, *American Ships* (New York: American Heritage, 1971), 292; David W. Shaw, *Flying Cloud: The True Story of America's Most Famous Clipper Ship and the Woman Who Guided Her* (New York: William Morrow, 2000), 51, 81.

61. Shaw, Flying Cloud, 83, 159, 161–163, 165, 237; Giggal, Classic Sailing Ships, 83.

62. Shaw, Flying Cloud, 247–250.

63. Giggal, Classic Sailing Ships, 83–84.

64. Keay, China: A History, 457; W. Travis Hanes III and Frank Sanello, The Opium Wars: The Addiction of One Empire and the Corruption of Another (Naperville, IL: Sourcebooks, 2002), 20–21.

65. Yangwen Zheng, "The Social Life of Opium in China, 1483–1999," Modern Asian Studies 37:1 (February 2003): 10, 16; Jonathan D. Spence, The Search for Modern China (New York: W.W. Norton, 1990), 87; Martin Booth, Opium: A History (New York: St. Martin's, 1996), 105.

66. Spence, The Search for Modern China, 87; Keay, China: A History, 458–459; Yangwen, "The Social Life of Opium in China, 1483–1999," 21; Hanes III and Sanello, The Opium Wars, 21, 24; Booth, Opium: A History, 5.

67. Booth, Opium: A History, 3, 5–7.

68. Yangwen, "The Social Life of Opium in China, 1483–1999," 10, 16 19–21; Hanes III and Sanello, The Opium Wars, 11, 22, 105.

69. Janin, The India-Opium Trade in the Nineteenth Century, 57, 63; Hanes III and Sanello, The Opium Wars, 42; "China and the Foreign Devils," Bulletin of the Business Historical Society, 17.

70. Joyce Madancy, "Unearthing Popular Attitudes Toward the Opium Trade and Opium Suppression in Late Qing and Early Republican Fujian," Modern China 27:4 (October 2001): 447, in JSTOR database (accessed November 1, 2010).

71. Hanes III and Sanello, The Opium Wars, 33, 36–37.

72. Keay, China: A History, 460; Shijie Guan, "Chartism and the First Opium War," History Workshop 24 (Autumn 1987): 18, in JSTOR database (accessed December 25, 2010).

73. Spence, The Search for Modern China, 152.

74. Janin, The India-Opium Trade in the Nineteenth Century, 104; Hanes III and Sanello, The Opium Wars, 116.

75. J.K. Fairbank, "Chinese Diplomacy and the Treaty of Nanking, 1842," Journal of Modern History 12:1 (March 1940): 1, 5, in JSTOR database (accessed November 30, 2010).

76. Peter Tamony, "Shanghai," Western Folklore 25:1 (January 1966): 43, in JSTOR database (accessed March 12, 2011); Spence, The Search for Modern China, 159.

77. Earl Cranston, "Shanghai in the Taiping Period," Pacific Historical Review 5:2 (June 1936): 147, in JSTOR database (accessed February 15, 2011); Linda Cooke Johnson, Shanghai: From Market Town to Treaty Port, 1074–1858 (Stanford: Stanford University Press, 1995), 176, 185–187.

78. Adonis Johnson Aloysius Diomede, "Reminiscence, 1837–1864," Journal, 1864, typescript copy, G.W. Blunt White Library, Manuscripts Division, Mystic Seaport: Museum of America and the Sea, 44; Johnson, Shanghai: From Market Town to Treaty Port, 1074–1858, 40–41; "Shanghai Gets Supersized," Smithsonian, November 2011, p. 77.

79. Albert L. Freeman, Letter to Charles Cullis, May 30, 1885, Box 1, folder 3, Albert L. Freeman Papers, G.W. Blunt White Library, Manuscripts Division, Mystic Seaport: Museum of America and the Sea.

80. Kurt Bloch, "The Basic Conflict Over Foreign Concessions in China," Far Eastern Survey 8:10 (May 10, 1939): 113, in JSTOR database (accessed October 16, 2011).

81. Teemu Ruskola, "Canton Is Not Boston: The Invention of American Imperial Sovereignty," American Quarterly 57:3 (September 2005): 860; Pearl S. Buck, "China and the West," Annals of the American Academy of Political and Social Science 168 (July 1933): 126; Earl H. Prichard, "The Origins of the Most-Favored-Nation and the Open Door Policies in China," Far Eastern Quarterly 1:2 (February 1942): 161–172 (all in JSTOR database [accessed October 16, 2011]).

82. Stephen Schwartz, Brotherhood of the Sea: A History of the Sailors' Union of the Pacific, 1895–1985 (New Brunswick: Transaction, 1986), xii; Taylor, Seven Years' Street Preaching in San Francisco, California, 236.

83. William Rosen, The Most Powerful Idea in the World (New York: Random House, 2010), 277–278.

84. Woodman, The History of the Ship, 140.

85. The Book of the Ocean and Life on the Sea: Containing Thrilling Narratives and Adventures of Ocean Life in All Countries, from the Earliest Period to the Present Time (Auburn, NY: John E. Beardsley, ca. 1835), 44–48.

86. Max E. Fletcher, "The Suez Canal and World Shipping, 1869–1914," Journal of Economic History 18:4 (December 1958): 556–558, in JSTOR database (accessed October 31, 2010); Graham, "The Ascendancy of the

Sailing Ship, 1850–85," 86–87; Rosen, *The Most Powerful Idea in the World,* 210; William J. Bernstein, *A Splendid Exchange: How Trade Shaped the World* (New York: Atlantic Monthly Press, 2008), 328–329.

87. Zachary Karabell, *Parting the Desert: The Creation of the Suez Canal* (New York: Alfred A. Knopf, 2003), 260, 264–265.

88. Fletcher, "The Suez Canal and World Shipping, 1869–1914," 558–559, 562; Foulke, "Life in the Dying World of Sail, 1870–1910," 114–115.

89. Ibid., 122–123; W. Clark Russell, "The Life of the Merchant Sailor," *Scribner's Monthly,* July 1893, 14, in CUL: MOA database (accessed October 16, 2010).

Chapter 2

1. Barnes, *When Ships Were Ships and Not Tin Pots,* viii.
2. Simon P. Newman, "Reading the Bodies of Early American Seafarers," *William and Mary Quarterly* 55:1 (January 1998): 67–68, in JSTOR database (accessed February 16, 2011).
3. Edwin Radford and Alan Smith, *To Coin A Phrase: A Dictionary of Origins* (London: Hutchinson, 1973), 54; William Morris and Mary Morris, *Morris Dictionary of Word and Phrase Origins,* 2nd ed. (New York: HarperCollins, 1988), 317; Admiral W.H. Smyth, *Chapman: The Sailor's Lexicon: The Classic Source for More Than 15,000 Nautical Terms* (New York: Hearst, 1996), 675; Melvin Maddocks and the Editors of Time-Life Books, *The Atlantic Crossing* (Alexandria, VA: Time-Life, 1981), 92.
4. Newman, "Reading the Bodies of Early American Seafarers," 61–63.
5. Maarten Hesselt van Dinter, *The World of Tattoo: An Illustrated History,* Trans. S. Green (Amsterdam: KIT, 2005), 42–43.
6. van Dinter, *The World of Tattoo,* 43; Ira Dye, "Early American Merchant Seafarers," *Proceedings of the American Philosophical Society* 133:4 (December 1989): 553, in JSTOR database (accessed November 9, 2012).
7. Newman, "Reading the Bodies of Early American Seafarers," 69; Craig Burns, *Skin and Bones: Tattoos in the Life of the American Sailor* (Philadelphia: Independence Seaport Museum, 2011), 17, 55.
8. Burns, *Skin and Bones,* 40–42.
9. Malcolm Cooper, "Maritime Labour

and Crew List Analysis: Problems, Prospects, and Methodologies," *Labour/Le Travail* 23 (Spring 1989): 182–183, in EBSCO: *HA* database (accessed March 17, 2011).
10. Anton Otto Fischer, *Focs'le Days: The Story of My Youth* (New York: Charles Scribner's Sons, 1947), xiii, 2–3, 6, 7, 12, 15.
11. Jeffrey W. Bolster, *Black Jacks: African American Seamen in the Age of Sail* (Cambridge, MA: Harvard University Press, 1997), 2.
12. Frederick Douglass, *Autobiographies: Narrative of the Life of Frederick Douglass, an American Slave; My Bondage and My Freedom; Life and Times of Frederick Douglass* (New York: Library of America, 1994), 80–84.
13. Ibid., 641, 643–645.
14. Ibid., 641, 643–645; Smyth, *Chapman: The Sailor's Lexicon,* 656; Bolster, *Black Jacks,* 75–77, 93; Margaret S. Creighton, *Dogwatch and Liberty Days: Seafaring Life in the Nineteenth Century* (Worchester, MA: Peabody Museum of Salem, 1982), 35.
15. James Farr, "A Slow Boat to Nowhere: The Multi-Racial Crews of the American Whaling Industry," *Journal of Negro History* 68:2 (Spring 1983): 161–162, in JSTOR database (accessed December 27, 2010).
16. Ibid., 162, 164.
17. Sidney Kaplan, "Lewis Temple and the Hunting of the Whale," *New England Quarterly* 26:1 (March 1953): 78, in JSTOR database (accessed December 27, 2010).
18. Walter Noble Burns, *A Year with a Whaler* (New York: Outing, 1913), 22, 27–28.
19. Robert J. Schwendinger, "Chinese Sailors: America's Invisible Merchant Marine, 1876–1905," *California History* 57:1 (Spring 1978): 58, in JSTOR database (accessed December 25, 2010); "Exclusion in Washington," *Chinese American Forum* 26:4 (April 2011): 18, in EBSCO: MFP database (accessed August 12, 2012).
20. Schwendinger, "Chinese Sailors," 59–62.
21. "Exclusion in Washington," *Chinese American Forum,* 19–20.
22. Shaw, Flying Cloud, 52.
23. Hattie Atwood Freeman, *Around the World in 500 Days: The Circumnavigation of the Merchant Bark Charles Stewart, 1883–1884: Recounted with Zest and Detail by the Captain's Daughter, Hattie Atwood Freeman,* ed. Curtis Dahl (Mystic, CT: Mystic Seaport: Museum of America and the Sea, 1999), 23–24, 32–33.
24. David Cordingly, *Women Sailors and*

Sailors' Women: An Untold Maritime History
(New York: Random House, 2001), 63–64.
    25. Ibid., 64–66.
    26. Joan Druett, *She Captains: Heroines
and Hellions of the Sea* (New York: Simon &
Schuster, 2000), 168–170.
    27. Cordingly, *Women Sailors and Sailors'
Women*, 64.
    28. Brian J. Rouleau, "Dead Men Do Tell
Tales: Folklore, Fraternity, and the Forecas-
tle," *Early American Studies: An Interdiscipli-
nary Journal* 5:1 (Spring 2007): 37–38, 41, in
PM database (accessed March 12, 2011);
Burns, *Skin and Bones*, 19.
    29. Burns, *Skin and Bones*, 19.
    30. Ibid., 15, 18, 19.
    31. Angelo S. Rappoport, *Superstitions of
Sailors* (Mineola, NY: Dover, 2007), 79, 161–
162.
    32. Russell, "The Life of the Merchant
Sailor," 11–13; Creighton, *Dogwatch and Lib-
erty Days*, 12.
    33. Russell, "The Life of the Merchant
Sailor," 13; Creighton, *Dogwatch and Liberty
Days*, 12.
    34. Captain George Fred Tilton, *"Cap'n
George Fred" Himself* (Garden City, NY:
Doubleday, Doran, 1928), 51–52.
    35. Ibid., 53; Creighton, *Dogwatch and
Liberty Days*, 12; Richard Ellis, *Men and
Whales* (New York: Lyons, 1991), 504;
Richard Henry Dana, *Two Years Before the
Mast: Twenty-Four Years After* (London:
Everyman's Library, 1969), 16.
    36. Freeman, *Around the World in 500
Days*, 23.
    37. Ibid; Kenneth F. Kiple, ed., *The Cam-
bridge Historical Dictionary of Disease* (Cam-
bridge, England: Cambridge University Press,
2003), 295; William Smart, "Notes on Sea-
Scurvy," *British Medical Journal* 2:879 (No-
vember 3, 1877): 617.
    38. Kiple, ed., *The Cambridge Historical
Dictionary of Disease*, 296; Smart, "Notes on
Sea-Scurvy," 617–618.
    39. Kiple, ed., *The Cambridge Historical
Dictionary of Disease*, 296; Derek Wilson,
The Circumnavigators (New York: M. Evan,
1989), 123.
    40. "The Oakes Towed In," *New York
Times*, March 22, 1897, p. 1, in ProQuest:
HN: TNYT database (accessed December
23, 2010); "At Sea's Mercy: A Vessel Adrift on
the Ocean for Over Eight Months," *Cleveland
Plain Dealer*, March 22, 1897, p. 2, in News-
Bank: CPDHN database (accessed Decem-
ber 23, 2010).

    41. "The Oakes Towed In," *New York
Times*, 1; "At Sea's Mercy," *Cleveland Plain
Dealer*, pp. 1–2; "The Oakes's Sad Voyage,"
New York Times, March 23, 1897, p. 5, in Pro-
Quest: HN: TNYT database (accessed De-
cember 23, 2010).
    42. Merchant Marine Commission, *Re-
port of the Merchant Marine Commission*, 58.
    43. Creighton, *Dogwatch and Liberty
Days*, 9, 18, 178; Foulke, "Life in the Dying
World of Sail, 1870–1910," 110–111; Interview
with Otto Parsons, *Report of the Merchant
Marine Commission*, 58.
    44. Russell, "The Life of The Merchant
Sailor," 8; Dana, *Two Years Before the Mast*,
13.
    45. James Lees, *Dana's Seamen's Friend:
Containing a Treatise on Practical Seaman-
ship, with Plates; A Dictionary of Sea Terms;
and the Customs and Usages of the Merchant
Service; with the British Laws Relating to
Shipping, the Duties of Master and Mariners,
and the Mercantile Marine* (London: George
Philip and Son, 1856), 128–192; Dana, *Two
Years Before the Mast*, 12; Creighton, *Dog-
watch and Liberty Days*, 18; Smyth, *Chap-
man: The Sailor's Lexicon*, 256.
    46. Lees, *Dana's Seamen's Friend*, 128.
    47. Foulke, "Life in the Dying World of
Sail, 1870–1910," 111.
    48. Dorothy Denneen Volo and James M.
Volo, *Daily Life in the Age of Sail* (Westport,
CT: Greenwood, 2002), 136–137.
    49. Ibid., 140–141; Margaret S.
Creighton, *Rites and Passages: The Experience
of Whaling, 1830–1870* (New York: Cam-
bridge University Press, 1995), 177;
"Scrimshaw," *Voyages: Stories of America and
the Sea*, Exhibit, Stillman Building, Mystic
Seaport: Museum of America and the Sea.
    50. Terry Breverton, *Breverton's Nautical
Curiosities* (Guilford, CT: Lyons, 2010), 14.
    51. E-mail from Clarissa Dean, National
Museum of the U.S. Navy, to author, June 9,
2012.
    52. Volo and Volo, *Daily Life in the Age of
Sail*, 143.
    53. Donna Dennis, *Licentious Gotham:
Erotic Publishing and Its Prosecution in
Nineteenth-Century New York* (Cambridge,
MA: Harvard University Press, 2009), 136–
137, 202–203.
    54. Volo and Volo, *Daily Life in the Age of
Sail*, 143, 147.
    55. Ibid., 148.
    56. David M. Hovde, "Sea Colportage:
The Loan Library System of the American

Seamen's Friend Society, 1859–1967," *Libraries and Culture* 29:4 (Fall 1994): 389, 391–392, in JSTOR database (accessed March 12, 2011).

57. Ibid., 397, 399–40.

58. Maddocks, *The Atlantic Crossing,* 126, 128.

59. George C. Bugbee, Journal, and "Biography of George C. Bugbee," George C. Bugbee Collection 1866–1917, G.W. Blunt White Library, Manuscripts Division, Mystic Seaport: Museum of America and the Sea.

60. *The Book of the Ocean and Life on the Sea,* 18–19.

61. Lees, *Dana's Seamen's Friend,* 130.

62. Russell, "The Life of The Merchant Sailor," 116–117.

63. Ibid., 116.

64. *Chelsea* log entry, December 10, 1839, in MacDonald Steers, "Research Notes," G.W. Blunt White Library, Manuscripts Division, Mystic Seaport: Museum of America and the Sea, no page numbers.

65. Paul C. Nicholson, ed., *Abstracts from a Journal Kept Aboard the Ship* Sharon *of Fairhaven on a Whaling Voyage in the South Pacific* (Providence, RI: Private Printing, 1953).

66. Hiram P. Bailey, *Shanghaied Out of 'Frisco in the Nineties* (Boston: Charles E. Lauriat, 1925), 129–131.

67. Janin, *The India-Opium Trade in the Nineteenth Century,* 132.

68. Ibid., 132.

69. Ibid., 133.

70. Jacques M. Downs, "American Merchants and the China Opium Trade, 1800–1840," *Business History Review* 42:4 (Winter, 1968): 425–426, in JSTOR database (accessed October 16, 2011).

71. Robert Fortune, *Three Years' Wanderings in the Northern Provinces of China, Including a Visit to the Tea, Silk, and Cotton Countries, with an Account of the Horticulture of the Chinese, New Plants, Etc.* (New York: Garland, 1979), 1, 384–385.

72. Ibid., 385–388.

73. Ibid., 389.

74. Benerson Little, *Pirate Hunting: The Fight Against Pirates, Privateers, and Sea Raiders from Antiquity to the Present* (Washington, D.C.: Potomac, 2010), 246.

75. Janin, *The India-Opium Trade in the Nineteenth Century,* 133–134; Smyth, *Chapman: The Sailor's Lexicon,* 415.

76. Fortune, *Three Years' Wanderings in the Northern Provinces of China,* 381, 393–395, 397–399.

77. Ibid., 380–381; Janin, *The India-Opium Trade in the Nineteenth Century,* 132.

78. Charles Ellms, *The Pirates Own Book; or, Authentic Narratives of the Lives, Exploits, and Executions of the Most Celebrated Sea Robbers with Historical Sketches of the Joassamee, Spanish, Ladrone, West India, Malay, and Algerian Pirates* (Portland: Sandborn & Carter; Philadelphia: Thomas, Cowperthwait, 1844), 263–264; Janin, *The India-Opium Trade in the Nineteenth Century,* 132.

79. Ellms, *The Pirates Own Book,* 264–266.

80. Dian Murray, "Cheng I Sao in Fact and Fiction," in *Bandits at Sea: A Pirates Reader,* ed. C.R. Pennell (New York: New York University Press, 2001), 258–259, 258.

81. Shelley Klein, *The Most Evil Pirates in History* (London: Michael O' Mara, 2006), 159.

82. Oscar Chapuis, *A History of Vietnam: From Hong Bang to Tu Duc* (Westport, CT: Greenwood, 1995), 134–136.

83. Ibid., 137, 140, 143.

84. Druett, *She Captains,* 55.

85. Klein, *The Most Evil Pirates in History,* 160–162.

86. Ibid., 163–164; Murray, "Cheng I Sao in Fact and Fiction," 259; Druett, *She Captains,* 56.

87. Ellms, *The Pirates Own Book,* 268.

88. Ibid., 266–270.

89. Ibid., 272–275.

90. Murray, "Cheng I Sao in Fact and Fiction," 259.

91. Ellms, *The Pirates Own Book,* 275.

92. Ibid., 275–276.

93. Christopher E.S. Warburton, *Slaves, Serfs, and Workers: Labor Under the Law* (Pittsburgh: Dorrance, 1998), 56–57.

94. Howard Zinn, *A People's History of the United States: 1492–Present* (New York: Harper, 1998), 274.

95. Ibid., 275.

96. Hardy Green, *The Company Town: The Industrial Edens and Satanic Mills That Shaped the American Economy* (New York: Basic Books, 2010), 57–58.

97. Ibid., 58–59.

Chapter 3

1. Nicholson, ed., *Abstracts from a Journal Kept Aboard the Ship* Sharon *of Fairhaven on a Whaling Voyage in the South Pacific,* 7–9.

2. Ibid., 9–10.

3. Ibid., 11–12.

4. Ibid., 12–13.

5. Matthew Raffety, "Discipline But Not Punish: Legality and Labor Control at Sea, 1790–1861," in *Pirates, Jack Tar and Memory: New Directions in American Maritime History,* ed. Paul A. Gilje and William Pencak (Mystic, CT: Mystic Seaport: Museum of America and the Sea, 2007), 184, 191–192.

6. Dana, *Two Years Before the Mast,* 11; Breverton, *Breverton's Nautical Curiosities,* 95.

7. Angus Konstam, *Scourge of the Seas: Buccaneers, Pirates and Privateers* (Oxford: Osprey, 2007), 180; Dana, *Two Years Before the Mast,* 11.

8. Dana, *Two Years Before the Mast,* 11; Smyth, *Chapman: The Sailor's Lexicon,* 509, 617; Schwartz, *Brotherhood of the Sea,* xi.

9. Myra C. Glenn, "The Naval Reform Campaign Against Flogging: A Case Study in Changing Attitudes Toward Corporal Punishment, 1830–1850," *American Quarterly* 35:4 (Autumn 1983): 414–415, in JSTOR database (accessed April 1, 2011).

10. J. Ross Browne, *Etchings of a Whaling Cruise, with Notes of a Sojourn on the Island of Zanzibar, to Which Is Appended a Brief History of the Whale Fishery, Its Past and Present Condition* (New York: Harper & Brothers, 1846), 49.

11. Smyth, *Chapman: The Sailor's Lexicon,* 172.

12. Association for the Prevention of Torture (APT) and Center for Justice and International Law (CEJIL), *Torture in International Law: A Guide to Jurisprudence* (Geneva: SRO-Kunding, 2008), 114; Glenn, "The Naval Reform Campaign Against Flogging," 415.

13. Dana, *Two Years Before the Mast,* 84.

14. Breverton, *Breverton's Nautical Curiosities,* 10.

15. "Flogging British Seamen: How the Cat Was Formerly Used in the English Navy," *Bangor Daily Whig & Courier,* January 13, 1894, p. 1, in Infotrac: NCN database (accessed August 29, 2012).

16. Raffety, "Discipline But Not Punish, 182, 188; Glenn, "The Naval Reform Campaign Against Flogging," 419–422.

17. Raffety, "Discipline But Not Punish, 187.

18. Bailey, *Shanghaied Out of 'Frisco in the Nineties,* 38–39; "And there in ..." 39.

19. Godfrey T. Anderson, "The Captain Lays Down the Law," *New England Quarterly* 44:2 (June 1971): 305–306, in JSTOR database (accessed December 27, 2010).

20. Ibid., 307–308.

21. Ibid., 309–310: "itinerant preacher," 310.

22. United States, "An Act in Amendment of the Acts for Punishment and Offense Against the United States," in *Statutes at Large,* vol. 4, (1824–1835) (Washington, D.C.: Microcard Editions, 1972), 113–115.

23. Shaw, Flying Cloud, 147–148, 164, 167–168, 170.

24. Creighton, *Dogwatch and Liberty Days,* 546–547.

25. Earl Swisher, "The Adventure of Four Americans in Korea and Peking in 1855," *Pacific Historical Review* 21:3 (August 1952): 237–238, in JSTOR database (accessed December 27, 2010).

26. Ibid., 239.

27. F.A. McKenzie, *The Tragedy of Korea* (London: Hodder and Stoughton, 1908), 239, 241; Djun Kil Kim, *The History of Korea* (Westport, CT: Greenwood, 2005), 86; William W. Rockhill, "Korea in Its Relations with China," *Journal of the American Oriental Society* 13 (1889): 18, in JSTOR database (accessed February 9, 2011).

28. Kim, *The History of Korea,* 85; Rockhill, "Korea in Its Relations with China," 16; McKenzie, *The Tragedy of Korea,* 2–3.

29. McKenzie, *The Tragedy of Korea,* 2; Swisher, "The Adventure of Four Americans in Korea and Peking in 1855," 239–240; Keay, *China: A History,* 467.

30. Franz Michael, "Revolution and Renaissance in Nineteenth-Century China: The Age of Tseng Kuo-fan," *Pacific Historical Review* 16:2 (May 1947): 145–146, in JSTOR database (accessed January 10, 2011).

31. W.J. Clennell, *The Historical Development of Religion in China* (New York: E.P. Dutton, 1917), 235–237; Keay, *China: A History,* 467.

32. Swisher, "The Adventure of Four Americans in Korea and Peking in 1855," 239, 239–240.

33. Ibid., 239, 240–241.

34. Cranston, "Shanghai in the Taiping Period," 153–154.

35. Swisher, "The Adventure of Four Americans in Korea and Peking in 1855," 241.

36. Lisa Manning, "The Model of a Mutiny: An Examination of Insurrection Aboard American Whaleships from 1820–

1860" (Research Paper, G.W. Blunt White Library, Manuscripts Division, Mystic Seaport: Museum of America and the Sea), 5–6, 8.

37. William Bligh, *Narrative of the Mutiny of the* Bounty, *on a Voyage to the South Seas to Which Are Added Some Additional Particulars, and a Relation to the Subsequent Fate of the Mutineers, and of the Settlement in Pitcairn's Island* (London: William Smith, 1853), 39–40, 42, 45.

38. Ibid., 43–44, 57.

39. "The Story of the Jefferson Borden—Sailors Driven to Mutiny by Their Officers," *Grenville Advance,* January 27, 1876, p. 1, in NA database (accessed April 7, 2011).

40. Ibid.

41. A.B.C. Whipple, *The* Challenge (New York: William Morrow, 1987), 50–51, 195; Giggal, *Classic Sailing Ships,* 88; Laing, *American Ships,* 208.

42. Laing, *American Ships,* 199–200.

43. Whipple, *The* Challenge, 115; Giggal, *Classic Sailing Ships,* 88; Laing, *American Ships,* 209.

44. Giggal, *Classic Sailing Ships,* 88.

45. Whipple, *The* Challenge, 150–151; Giggal, *Classic Sailing Ships,* 88.

46. Whipple, *The* Challenge, 159; "Law Courts: U.S. District Court—Before H.B. Jones, Commissioner," *Daily Alta California,* November 7, 1851, p. 2 (accessed May 18, 2011) and "Law Courts: U.S. District Court—Trial of Capt. Waterman Continued—Jas. Douglass, Mate of the *Challenge,*" *Daily Alta California,* December 20, 1851, p. 2, (accessed August 29, 2012), both in CDNC database.

47. "Law Courts: U.S. District Court—*Trial of Capt. Waterman Continued*—Fourth Day," *Daily Alta California,* December 21, 1851, p. 2, in CDNC database (accessed May 18, 2011); "Law Courts—*Trial of Capt. Waterman Continued,*" *Daily Alta California,* 2.

48. "Sixteen Days Later from California," *New-York Daily Times,* December 1, 1851, p. 1, in NA database (accessed November 15, 2010).

49. Whipple, *The* Challenge, 199; "City Intelligence," *Daily Alta California,* November 4, 1851, p. 2, in *CNDC* database (accessed August 29, 2012).

50. "Sixteen Days Later from California," *New-York Daily Times,* 1; "California: Events Since the Sailing of the Last Steamer," *New-York Daily Times,* December 26, 1851, p. 1, in ProQuest: HN: TNYT database (accessed November 15, 2010).

51. Whipple, *The* Challenge, 205, 210, 211.

52. David Cordingly, "Introduction Notes," in *A General History of the Robberies and Murderers of the Most Notorious Pirates,* Captain Charles Johnson (Guilford, CT: Lyons, 2002), 365; Klein, *The Most Evil Pirates in History,* 170; Gabriel Kuhn, *Life Under the Jolly Roger: Reflections on Golden Age Piracy* (Oakland, CA: PM, 2010), 15, 17–18.

53. Marcus Rediker, "'Under the Banner of King Death': The Social World of Anglo-American Pirates, 1716 to 1726," *William and Mary Quarterly* 38:2, 3rd series (April 1981): 206–209, in JSTOR database (accessed March 14, 2011).

54. Rediker, "'Under the Banner of King Death,'" 209–211; Kuhn, *Life Under the Jolly Roger,* 87–88.

55. Ibid., 159–160.

56. Konstam, *Scourge of the Seas,* 223–224.

57. Ibid., 224–225.

58. Pirate expert David Cordingly assessed this phenomenon in full with his invaluable book *Under the Black Flag: The Romance and Reality of Life Among Pirates* (San Diego: Harcourt, Brace, 1995).

59. "Pirates Seize a Schooner," *Hawaiian Star,* April 6, 1908, pp. 1, 8, in LOC: CA: HAN database (accessed September 1, 2012); Lewis R. Freeman, *In the Tracks of the Trades: The Account of a Fourteen Thousand Mile Yachting Cruise to the Hawaiis, Marquesas, Societies, Samoas and Fijis* (New York: Dodd, Mead, 1920), 24.

60. "Lady Is Found," *Hawaiian Star,* April 7, 1908, pp. 1, 5 (accessed September 2, 2012), and "Pirate Pals Are in Prison," *Hawaiian Star,* April 8, 1908, p. 5 (accessed September 1, 2012), and "Bold Pirates Run to Earth and Captured," *Evening Bulletin,* April 8, 1908, p. 2 (accessed September 2, 2012), all in LOC: CA: HAN database.

61. United States, U.S. Department of the Interior, *Historical American Landscapes Survey: Fort Shafter Military Reservation, N.C.O. Housing Area (Fort Shafter Military Reservation, Rice Manor Housing Area)* (Oakland, CA: National Park Service, 2011), 5.

62. "Pirate Pals Are in Prison," *Hawaiian Star,* 1; "Bold Pirates Run to Earth and Captured," *Evening Bulletin,* 2; "Pirates at the Bar," *Hawaiian Star,* April 9, 1908, p. 5, and "Pirates of the Schooner Lady," *Hawaiian Gazette,* April 10, 1908, p. 6, both in LOC: CA: HAN database (accessed September 2, 2012).

63. "Pirate Pals Are in Prison," *Hawaiian*

Star, 1: "as pirate princes"; "Pirates of the Schooner Lady," *Hawaiian Gazette*, 6; "Bold Pirates Run to Earth and Captured," *Evening Bulletin*, 2.

64. "Pirates of the Schooner Lady," *Hawaiian Gazette*, 6; "Bold Pirates Run to Earth and Captured," *Evening Bulletin*, 2; "Pirate Pals Are in Prison," *Hawaiian Star*, 1.

65. "Pirate Pals Are in Prison," *Hawaiian Star*, 1, 5; "Bold Pirates Run to Earth and Captured," *Evening Bulletin*, 2.

66. John R. Musick, *Hawaii: Our New Possessions; An Account of Travels and Adventure, with Sketches of the Scenery, Customs and Manners, Mythology and History of Hawaii to the Present, and an Appendix Containing the Treaty of Annexation to the United States* (New York: Funk & Wagalls, 1898), 416, 420.

67. "The 'Pirates' Are a Joke," *Hawaiian Star*, April 25, 1908, p. 1, in LOC: CA: HAN database (accessed September 2, 2012).

68. "Pirates Held for Grand Jury," *Hawaiian Gazette*, April 10, 1908, p. 5, in LOC: CA: HAN database (accessed September 2, 2012).

69. "Pirates at the Bar," *Hawaiian Star*, 5; "Pirates Are Not Guilty of Piracy: Men Who Stole Schooner Lady to be Charged with Larceny," *Evening Bulletin*, April 9, 1908, p. 1, in CA: HAN database (accessed September 2, 2012).

70. "Pirates of the Schooner Lady," *Hawaiian Gazette*, 6.

71. "Pirates of the Lady Get a Light Sentence," *Hawaiian Gazette*, April 28, 1908, p. 2, in CA: HAN database (accessed September 2, 2012).

72. "Soldier Pirates Escape and Still at Large," *Hawaiian Gazette*, June 30, 1908, p. 3, and "Pirates Break from the Fort," *Hawaiian Star*, June 26, 1908, p. 1, both in LOC: CA: HAN database (accessed September 3, 2012).

73. "Pirates Break from the Fort," *Hawaiian Star*, 1.

74. "Pirates Eat at Scotty's," *Hawaiian Gazette*, June 27, 1908, p. 1, in LOC: CA: HAN database (accessed September 3, 2012); Thos. G. Thum, ed., *Hawaiian Almanac and Annual for 1906: The Reference Book of Information and Statistics Relating to the Territory of Hawaii, of Value to Merchants, Tourists and Others* (Honolulu: Thos. G. Thrum, 1905), 18–19.

75. "Pirate Smith Is Captured," *Hawaiian Star,* July 14, 1908, p. 1, in LOC: CA: HAN database (accessed September 3, 2012).

76. "Pirates to Prison," *Hawaiian Star*, September 22, 1908, p. 6, in LOC: CA: HAN database (accessed September 3, 2012); Henry Shindler, *History of the United States Military Prison* (Fort Leavenworth, KS: Army Service School Press, 1911), 74–75.

Chapter 4

1. "Three Bold 'Shanghaiers,'" *New York Times*, September 24, 1877, p. 5, in ProQuest: HN: TNYT database (accessed February 28, 2011).

2. Downing, "Shanghaiing Sailors," *Boston Daily Globe*, 3.

3. Bill Pickelhaupt, *Shanghaied in San Francisco* (San Francisco, California: Flyblister, 1996), 125.

4. "Whitehall Boats," *Our Grandfather's Boats*, Exhibit, North Boat Shed, Mystic Seaport: Museum of America and the Sea.

5. Downing, "Shanghaiing Sailors," *Boston Daily Globe*, p. 3.

6. Ibid., 3.

7. H.H., "Puget Sound," *Atlantic Monthly*, February 1883, p. 218, in CUL: MOA database (accessed May 19, 2011).

8. Fischer, *Focs'le Days*, 54–56.

9. Ibid., 58–59.

10. "A Soldier Shanghaied," *New York Times*, May 17, 1882, p. 8, in ProQuest: HN: TNYT database (accessed February 28, 2011); *Historical Guide to New York Compiled by Frank Bergen Kelley from the Original Contributions Made by Members and Friends of the City History Club of New York with Seventy Maps and Diagrams and Forty-six Illustrations* (New York: Frederic A. Stokes, 1909), 256, 258.

11. "A Soldier Shanghaied," *New York Times*, 8.

12. "A Sea Captain 'Shanghaied,'" *New York Times*, May 6, 1881, p. 2, ProQuest: HN: TNYT database (accessed February 28, 2011).

13. Ibid., 2.

14. Alborn, "Crimping and Shanghaiing on the Columbia River," 282; "The Sailor Boarding-House Abuse," *Morning Oregonian*, February 5, 1889, p. 4, in NA database (accessed May 18, 2011).

15. Stewart Holbrook, "Jim Turk Shanghaied His Own Son: He Ran a Sailor's Boarding House and Sent Men to the Sea in Ships, Says Spider Johnson," *Sunday Oregonian*, magazine section, October 22, 1933, p. 8; Al-

born, "Crimping and Shanghaiing on the Columbia River," 267.

16. Ibid.

17. "The Sailor Boarding-House Abuse," 4.

18. Alborn, "Crimping and Shanghaiing on the Columbia River," 279.

19. Ibid., 267.

20. Holbrook, "Jim Turk Shanghaied His Own Son," *Morning Oregonian,* 8; "Astoria Pirates," *Morning Oregonian,* March 23, 1890, p. 6, in NA database (accessed May 18, 2011).

21. "Astoria Pirates," *Morning Oregonian,* 6; "An Infamous Business," *Morning Oregonian,* February 28, 1890, p. 6, in NA database (accessed May 18, 2011).

22. Ibid., 6.

23. "Corning Charged with Kidnapping," *Morning Call,* May 6 1899, p. 4, in CDNC database (accessed May 18, 2011).

24. Ibid., 4; "Shipowners, 'Crimps,' and 'Blood Money,'" *Morning Call,* May 5 1899, p. 4, in CDNC database (accessed May 18, 2011).

25. "Corning Charged with Kidnapping," *Morning Call,* 4; "Howard D. Troop Sailors," *Record-Union,* May 9, 1899, p. 8, in CDNC database (accessed September 10, 2012).

26. Alborn, "Crimping and Shanghaiing on the Columbia River," 282.

27. Stewart Holbrook, "No. 2: Shanghai Days in the City of Roses: More About Larry Sullivan, Plus Introduction to Bunco Kelley; Also, a Few Notes on Nancy Boggs," *Sunday Oregonian,* magazine section, October 8, 1933, p. 5.

28. Joseph Kelley, *Thirteen Years in the Oregon Penitentiary* (Portland, OR, 1908), 141; Holbrook, "No. 2: Shanghai Days in the City of Roses," 5.

29. Kelley, *Thirteen Years in the Oregon Penitentiary,* 139.

30. Richard H. Bradford, *The Virginius Affair* (Boulder: Colorado Associated University Press, 1980), 31, 33, 35–37.

31. Ibid., 40–41, 43, 47, 51–53; "Interesting Particulars of the Capture of the *Virginius,*" *Cleveland Plain Dealer,* November 13, 1873, p. 3, in NewsBank: CPDHN database (accessed December 23, 2010).

32. Kelley, *Thirteen Years in the Oregon Penitentiary,* 135, 137, 139–140; Alborn, "Crimping and Shanghaiing on the Columbia River," 275; Holbrook, "No. 2: Shanghai Days in the City of Roses," 5.

33. Holbrook, "No. 2: Shanghai Days in the City of Roses," 5; "Crimping and Shanghaiing on the Columbia River," 275.

34. Ibid.

35. "Swam for Liberty and Shore: A Landsmen's Daring Escape from a British Vessel," *Daily Morning Astorian,* October 26, 1890, p. 1; "That Sailor Kidnaping [*sic*] Case: 'Bunco' Kelly Placed Under Arrest in Portland Yesterday," *Daily Morning Astorian,* October 27, 1890, p. 3, both in LOC: CA: HAN database (accessed December 29, 2012).

36. "That Sailor Kidnaping [*sic*] Case," *Daily Morning Astorian,* 3; "Bold 'Bunco' Kelly's Case: Another Continuance Granted to the Accused Shanghaier," *Daily Morning Astorian,* October 30, 1890, p. 3, and "'Bunco' in a Portland Court: The Shanghaier to Be Tried in the City Up River," *Daily Morning Astorian,* November 4, 1890, p. 1, both in LOC: CA: HAN database (accessed December 29, 2012).

37. Alborn, "Crimping and Shanghaiing on the Columbia River," 276.

38. Kelley, *Thirteen Years in the Oregon Penitentiary,* 6; Holbrook, "No. 2: Shanghai Days in the City of Roses," 5; "Says Jurors Cursed Him: X.N. Steeves Has Something More to Say Before Going Away," *Daily Capital Journal,* May 15, 1896, p. 1, in LOC: CA: HAN database (accessed December 29, 2012).

39. Kelley, *Thirteen Years in the Oregon Penitentiary,* 6–8.

40. Ibid., 8; Holbrook, "No. 2: Shanghai Days in the City of Roses," 5; Alborn, "Crimping and Shanghaiing on the Columbia River," 277.

41. "Portland Mystery: Singular Circumstances of a Recent Suicide in That City," *San Francisco Call,* November 25, 1895, p. 3, in CDNC database (accessed December 29, 2012).

42. *The Quebec Guide, Comprising an Historical and Descriptive Account of the City and Every Place of Note in the Vicinity with a Plan of the City* (Quebec: W. Cowan and Son, 1844), 58–50, 72.

43. Frederick William Wallace, *In the Wake of the Wind-Ships: Notes, Records and Biographies Pertaining to the Square-rigged Merchant Marine of British North America* (New York: George Sully, 1927), 117–118; Letter from John Maguire to T. Lee Terrill, October 24, 1856, in *Appendix to the Fifteenth Volume of the Journals of the Legislative Assembly of the Province of Canada, from the 26th February of the 10th June, 1857, both days inclusive, in the Twentieth Year of the Reign of Our Sovereign Lady Queen Victory, Being the*

3rd Session of the 5th Provincial Parliament of Canada, by Canada, Legislature, Legislative Assembly Session (Toronto: John Lovell, 1857), no page numbers.

44. Judith Fingard, *Jack in Port: Sailortowns of Eastern Canada* (Toronto: University of Toronto Press, 1982), 187; Wallace, *In the Wake of the Wind-Ships,* 118.

45. Fingard, *Jack in Port,* 205; Letter from Henry Fry to John Maguire, October 20, 1856, in *Appendix to the Fifteenth Volume of the Journals of the Legislative Assembly of the Province of Canada,* no page numbers.

46. Wallace, *In the Wake of the Wind-Ships,* 119–120.

47. Fingard, *Jack in Port,* 204.

48. E. Smith, "British Seamen East of the Cape," *Nautical Magazine and Naval Chronicle for 1837: A Journal of Papers on Subjects Connected with Maritime Affair* (London: Simpkin, Marshall, 1837), 433–441.

49. Fingard, "The Decline of the Sailor as a Ship Labourer in 19th Century Timber Ports," 43.

50. Letter from Henry Fry to London's *Times,* September 13, 1856, and letter from M.H. Warren to John Maguire, October 21, 1856, in *Appendix to the Fifteenth Volume of the Journals of the Legislative Assembly of the Province of Canada,* no page numbers.

51. Letter from E. Parent to John Macguire, October 10, 1856, in *Appendix to the Fifteenth Volume of the Journals of the Legislative Assembly of the Province of Canada,* no page numbers.

52. Letter from David Gilmour to John Macguire, November 3, 1856, in *Appendix to the Fifteenth Volume of the Journals of the Legislative Assembly of the Province of Canada,* no page numbers.

53. Ibid.

54. Fingard, *Jack in Port,* 200.

55. Letter from David Gilmour to John Macguire, November 3, 1856, in *Appendix to the Fifteenth Volume of the Journals of the Legislative Assembly of the Province of Canada,* no page numbers.

56. Ibid.

57. Letter from J.W. Dunscomb to E. Parent, October 21, 1856, in *Appendix to the Fifteenth Volume of the Journals of the Legislative Assembly of the Province of Canada,* no page numbers.

58. Ibid.

59. Ibid.

60. Fingard, *Jack in Port,* 200, 206–208; John Robinson, "Half a Century at Sea," *The*

Bellman, July 7, 1917, 11; William White, *History Gazetteer and Directory of the County of Devon Including the City of Exeter, and Comprising a General Survey of the County* (London: Simpkin, Marshall, 1878–79), 102–103.

61. Fingard, *Jack in Port,* 200, 209–210.

62. Lance S. Davidson, "Shanghaied! The Systematic Kidnapping of Sailors in Early San Francisco," *California History* 64:1 (Winter 1985): 13, 15, in JSTOR database (accessed December 26, 2010).

63. Herbert Asbury, *The Barbary Coast: An Informal History of the San Francisco Underworld* (New York: Garden City, 1933), 213.

64. Ibid., 217.

65. Pickelhaupt, *Shanghaied in San Francisco,* 12.

66. Asbury, *The Barbary Coast,* 215–217.

67. Ibid., 217–218.

68. Ibid., 218.

69. "The Chicken: John Devine Under the Shadow of the Gallows," *Daily Alta California,* May 8, 1873, p. 1, in CDNC database (accessed August 29, 2012); Davidson, "Shanghaied! The Systematic Kidnapping of Sailors in Early San Francisco," 15.

70. Ibid; Asbury, *The Barbary Coast,* 220–221.

71. "The Chicken," *Daily Alta California,* 1.

72. Ibid., 1.

73. Stonehouse, *Great Lakes Crime,* 138.

74. Ibid., 138–139; J. Sam'l Vandersloot, *The True Path; or, Gospel Temperance: Being the Life, Work and Speeches of Francis Murphy, Dr. Henry A. Reynolds, and Their Co-laborers, Embracing also a History of the Women's Christian Temperance Movement* (New York: Henry S. Goodspeed, 1878), 469–470.

75. Richard H. Dillon, *Shanghaiing Days* (New York: Coward-McCann, 1961), 35–37.

76. Ibid., 29, 37.

77. Taylor, *Seven Years' Street Preaching in San Francisco, California,* 220, 223.

78. "The Floating Church of the Redeemer," *New-York Organ,* "A Family Journal Devoted to Temperance, Morality, Education, and General Literature," November 1848, p. 171.

79. Dillon, *Shanghaiing Days,* 48–49.

80. Taylor, *Seven Years' Street Preaching in San Francisco, California,* 224–225, 238–240.

81. Hovde, "Sea Colportage," 395–396.

82. Alister E. McGrath, *Christianity's Dangerous Idea: The Protestant Revolution; a History from the Sixteenth Century to the Twenty-First* (New York: Harper One, 2007), 164.

83. Judith N. McArthur, "Demon Rum on the Boards: Temperance Melodrama and the Tradition of Antebellum Reform," *Journal of the Early Republic* 9:4 (Winter 1989): 520, 527–528, in JSTOR database (accessed February 6, 2011); Hovde, "Sea Colportage," 392; John W. Frick, *Theater, Culture and Temperance Reform in Nineteenth-Century America* (Cambridge, UK: Cambridge University Press, 2003), 27–29.

84. Frick, *Theater, Culture and Temperance Reform in Nineteenth-Century America,* 19.

85. Christine Sismondo, *America Walks into a Bar: A Spirited History of Taverns and Saloons, Speakeasies and Grog Shops* (New York: Oxford University Press, 2011), 125.

86. Frick, *Theater, Culture and Temperance Reform in Nineteenth-Century America,* 20–21.

87. McArthur, "Demon Rum on the Boards," 518–519; Dillon, *Shanghaiing Days,* 29, 38.

88. Myra C. Glenn, "Troubled Manhood in the Early Republic: The Life and Autobiography of Sailor Horace," *Journal of the Early Republic* 26:1 (Spring 2006): 81–82, in JSTOR database (accessed December 26, 2010).

89. Ibid., 86, 89–90.

90. Trip Hammer, "Short Sermon for the Poor No. 1: 'Time Is Money,'" *New-York Organ,* "A Family Journal Devoted to Temperance, Morality, Education, and General Literature," March 4, 1848, p. 283, G.W. Blunt White Library, Manuscripts Division, Mystic Seaport: Museum of America and the Sea.

91. McArthur, "Demon Rum on the Boards," 520, 522.

92. "A Boon to the Seamen," *New York Times,* August 11, 1888, p. 8, in ProQuest: HN: TNYT database (accessed December 23, 2010).

93. Ibid., 8.

94. Rowena L.D. Alcorn and Gordon D. Alcorn, "Tacoma Seamen's Rest: Waterfront Mission, 1897–1903," *Oregon Historical Quarterly* 66:2 (June 1965): 101–102, in JSTOR database (accessed December 26, 2010).

95. Ibid., 104–106, 107, 122–123.

96. H.A. Page, "In Safe Haven," in *Good Words for 1874,* ed. Rev. Donald MacLeod (London: Daldy, Isbister, 1874), 458–462.

97. "Men of the Sea," *Atlantic Monthly,* January 1859, 44–52, in CUL: MOA database (accessed May 19, 2011), 48.

98. Rouleau, "Dead Men Do Tell Tales, 30–31.

99. Ibid., 34.

100. Charles Whitehead, "The Wandering Sailor Brought Home to God," *The Friend,* "A Monthly Journal Devoted to Temperance, Seamen, Marine and General Intelligence," September 1, 1866, pp. 82–83, G.W. Blunt White Library, Rare Books, Mystic Seaport: Museum of America and the Sea.

101. Ibid., 83.

Chapter 5

1. Jacob Nagle, *A Diary of the Life of Jacob Nagle, Sailor, from the Year 1775 to 1841,* ed. John C. Dann (New York: Weidenfeld & Nicolson, 1988), 150.

2. Ibid., 147, 158 (editorial commentary), 161–163.

3. Frank H. Shaw and Ernest H. Robinson, eds., *The Sea and Its Story: From Viking Ship to Submarine* (London: Cassell, 1910), 194.

4. Breverton, *Breverton's Nautical Curiosities,* 14, 15, 19, 22.

5. Mara L. Keire, "Dope Fiends and Degenerates: The Gendering of Addiction in the Early Twentieth Century," *Journal of Social History* 31:4 (Summer 1998): 810 (accessed February 6, 2011); Ivan Light, "From Vice District to Tourist Attraction: The Moral Career of American Chinatowns, 1880–1940," *Pacific Historical Review* 43:3 (August 1974): 371–372 (accessed March 30, 2011), both in JSTOR database.

6. Creighton, *Dogwatch and Liberty Days,* 64–65.

7. Stewart Holbrook, *The Columbia* (New York: Holt, Rinehart and Winston, 1956), 226.

8. David G. Schwartz, *Roll the Bones: The History of Gambling* (New York: Gotham, 2006), 269.

9. Richard Sasuly, *Bookies and Bettors: Two Hundred Years of Gambling* (New York: Holt, Rinehart and Winston, 1982), 67–69, 75.

10. Richard L. Frey, *According to Hoyle: Official Rules of More Than 200 Popular Games of Skill and Chance with Expert Advice on Winning Play* (New York: Fawcett Columbine, 1970), 212; Sasuly, *Bookies and Bettors,* 67–69.

11. Shaw and Robinson, eds., *The Sea and Its Story,* 194; Creighton, *Dogwatch and*

Liberty Days, 60; Elizabeth B. van Heynin-gen, "The Social Evil in the Cape Colony 1868–1902: Prostitution and the Contagious Diseases Acts," *Journal of Southern African Studies* 10:2 (April 1984): 170–171, in JSTOR database (accessed May 29, 2011).

12. Donna Dennis, *Licentious Gotham: Erotic Publishing and Its Prosecution in Nineteenth-Century New York* (Cambridge, MA: Harvard University Press, 2009), 22–23.

13. Marilynn Wood Hill, *Their Sisters' Keepers: Prostitution in New York City, 1830–1870* (Berkeley: University of California Press, 1993), 187–188.

14. Dan Cruickshank, *London's Sinful Secret: The Bawdy History and Very Public Passions of London's Georgian Age* (New York: St. Martin's, 2009), 8, 42, 44, 173–174.

15. Bracebridge Hemyng, "Prostitution in London," in *London Labour and the London Poor: A Cyclopædia of the Condition and Earnings of Those That Will Work, Those That Cannot Work, and Those That Will Not Work,* vol. 4, ed. Henry Mayhew (New York: Augustus M. Kelley, 1967).

16. Hill, *Their Sisters' Keepers,* 255–256; Heyningen, "The Social Evil in the Cape Colony, 1868–1902," 170; Bonnie Ripp-Shucha, "'This Naughty, Naughty City': Prostitution in Eau Claire from the Frontier to the Progressive Era," *Wisconsin Magazine of History* 81:1 (Autumn 1997): 39, 41, in JSTOR database (accessed January 10, 2011).

17. Hill, *Their Sisters' Keepers,* 255–256; Heyningen, "The Social Evil in the Cape Colony, 1868–1902," 170; Ripp-Shucha, "'This Naughty, Naughty City,'" 37–38.

18. Hill, *Their Sisters' Keepers,* 255; Ripp-Shucha, "'This Naughty, Naughty City,'" 38–39.

19. Hill, *Their Sisters' Keepers,* 256; Ripp-Shucha, "'This Naughty, Naughty City,'" 41; Jeffery Scott McIllwain, *Organizing Crime in Chinatown: Race and Racketeering in New York City, 1890–1910* (Jefferson, NC: McFarland, 2004), 51.

20. McIllwain, *Organizing Crime in Chinatown,* 51, 55; Light, "From Vice District to Tourist Attraction," 373.

21. Hemyng, "Prostitution in London," 211–212.

22. Asbury, *The Barbary Coast,* 3, 106–108, 110–111.

23. B.E. Lloyd, *Lights and Shades in San Francisco* (San Francisco: A.L. Bancroft, 1876), 84–85.

24. Ibid., 85.

25. Ibid., 85–86.

26. Hemyng, "Prostitution in London," 211.

27. Ripp-Shucha, "'This Naughty, Naughty City,'" 39; Hill, *Their Sisters' Keepers,* 232.

28. Kiple, ed., *The Cambridge Historical Dictionary of Disease,* 150–152.

29. Ibid., 312, 314.

30. Hill, *Their Sisters' Keepers,* 232–234.

31. Heyningen, "The Social Evil in the Cape Colony, 1868–1902," 172–173.

32. Larry Whiteaker, *Seduction, Prostitution, and Moral Reform in New York, 1830–1860* (New York: Garland, 1997), 52, 55.

33. Ibid., 67, 69–70.

34. McIllwain, *Organizing Crime in Chinatown,* 44; Light, "From Vice District to Tourist Attraction," 368.

35. Light, "From Vice District to Tourist Attraction," 369; Helen Clark, "The Chinese of New York," *Century,* November 1896, p. 104, in CUL: MOA database (accessed May 22, 2011).

36. Light, "From Vice District to Tourist Attraction," 369; McIllwain, *Organizing Crime in Chinatown,* 107, 109–110.

37. "From Vice District to Tourist Attraction," 372–375, 377; McIllwain, *Organizing Crime in Chinatown,* 127; Light,

38. Light, "From Vice District to Tourist Attraction," 371, 374.

39. Herbert Asbury, *The Barbary Coast: An Informal History of the San Francisco Underworld* (New York: Garden City, 1933), 280.

40. Lloyd, *Lights and Shades in San Francisco,* 78–79; Asbury, *The Barbary Coast,* 49, 280; "Barbary Coast Fast Becoming a Relic of the Past," *Morning Call,* November 28, 1897, p. 32, in CDNC database (accessed May 23, 2011).

41. Albert S. Evans, *À la California: Sketches of Life in the Golden State* (San Francisco: A.L. Bancroft, 1873), 275.

42. Asbury, *The Barbary Coast,* 3, 104–106, 223.

43. Seymour Briscoe, "A Night with Topers and Dancers of the 'Barbary Coast': Strange Scenes the Barkeepers Witness and Queer Characters They Meet," *Morning Call,* March 25, 1900, p. 5, in CDNC database (accessed May 18, 2011).

44. Ibid.

45. Sismondo, *America Walks into a Bar,* 221–222.

46. Evans, *À la California,* 276–277.
47. Ibid., 277–279.
48. "Dive Doors Open," *Morning Call,* August 8, 1893, p. 10, in CDNC database (accessed May 23, 2011).
49. "Shot in the Thigh," *Daily Alta California,* September 29, 1890, p. 6, in CDNC database (accessed May 23, 2011).
50. Briscoe, "A Night with Topers and Dancers of the 'Barbary Coast,'" *Morning Call,* 5.
51. Ibid.
52. William P. Hood Jr., "Absinthe and Its Artifacts," *Antiques,* April 2005, pp. 134–136, in EBSCO: MFP database (accessed June 14, 2011).
53. "Slummers See Sailors in Tenderloin's Depths," *Morning Call,* May 10, 1908, p. 37, in CDNC database (accessed May 23, 2011).
54. Daniel E. Bender, *American Abyss: Savagery and Civilization in the Age of Industry* (Ithaca, NY: Cornell University Press, 2009).
55. "Barbary Coast Fast Becoming a Relic of the Past," *Morning Call,* 32.
56. Dan Kurzman, *Disaster! The Great San Francisco Earthquake and Fire of 1906* (New York: HarperCollins, 2001), 160–162, 164, 240.
57. Asbury, *The Barbary Coast,* 238–239, 299–314.
58. Hill, *Their Sisters' Keepers,* 187.
59. Julian Ralph, "The Bowery," *Century,* December 1891, pp. 227–238, in CUL: MOA database (accessed May 22, 2011), 227; Burns, *Skin and Bones,* 52.
60. Sante, *Lures and Snares,* 12–14.
61. Ralph, "The Bowery," 233.
62. Sante, *Lures and Snares,* 106.
63. Ralph, "The Bowery," 234: "Professor Blinkum's Charge"; Michelle G. Gibbons, "'Voices from the People,' Letters to the *American Phrenological Journal,* 1854–64," *Journalism History* 35:2 (Summer 2009): 72–73, 78, in EBSCO: A: H&L database (accessed June 14, 2011).
64. Daniel Czitrom, "Underworlds and Underdogs: 'Big Tim' Sullivan and Metropolitan Politics in New York, 1889–1913," *Journal of American History* 78:2 (September 1991): 536, 547, in JSTOR database (accessed December 26, 2010); "'Big Tim': The Career of Senator Sullivan of the Sixth, a Tammany Bluffer," *New-York Tribune,* September 29, 1901, p. 13, and "Croker in Danger: Leadership Threatened by Vice Protectors," *New-York Tribune,* September 19, 1901, p. 1 (ac-

cessed May 28, 2011), both in LOC: CA: HAN database.
65. Czitrom, "Underworlds and Underdogs," 536–537, 548, 551.
66. "'Big Tim,'" *New-York Tribune,* 13.
67. "All the Bowery There," *New-York Tribune,* December 27, 1904, p. 1, LOC: CA: HAN database (accessed May 28, 2011).
68. Czitrom, "Underworlds and Underdogs," 557–558; "'Big Tim' Sullivan Killed," *Middletown Times-Press,* September 13, 1913, p. 1, in NA database (accessed May 28, 2011).
69. Czitrom, "Underworlds and Underdogs," 551, 547.
70. Robert W. Snyder, *The Voice of the City: Vaudeville and Popular Culture in New York* (New York: Oxford University Press, 1989), 5–8; Sismondo, *America Walks into a Bar,* 106.
71. Horace Lane, *The Wandering Boy, Careless Sailor, and Result of Inconsideration: A True Narrative* (Skaneateles, NY: Luther A. Pratt, 1837), 75.

Chapter 6

1. Broughton Brandenburg, "The Deep Sea Sailor: Life Ashore," *Frank Leslie's Popular Monthly,* June 1903, pp. 110–111.
2. Ibid., 111–112.
3. Ibid., 112.
4. Ibid., 112–113.
5. Broughton Brandenburg, "The Deep Sea Sailor: Life on a Liner," *Frank Leslie's Popular Monthly,* May 1903, p. 17.
6. "Shanghaied in San Francisco and Stranded in South America," *Syracuse Herald,* November 17, 1907, p. 27, in NA database (accessed April 18, 2011).
7. Ibid; Melissa Graham and Andrew Benson, *The Rough Guide to Chile,* 4th ed. (London: Rough Guides, 2009), 204.
8. "Shanghaied in San Francisco and Stranded in South America," *Syracuse Herald,* 27.
9. Ibid.
10. Graham and Benson, *The Rough Guide to Chile,* 203.
11. "Agriculture and Livestock," *Mountain Research and Development* 4:2 (May 1984): 150, in JSTOR database (accessed October 12, 2011).
12. "Shanghaied in San Francisco and Stranded in South America," *Syracuse Herald,* 27.
13. Ibid; Theodore Child, "Across the

Andes," *Harper's New Monthly Magazine,* September 1890, pp. 498, 503, 505, in CUL: MOA database (accessed May 19, 2011).

14. Child, "Across the Andes," 494, 490; Michael Jacobs, *Andes* (Berkeley, CA: Counterpoint, 2011), 469; "Shanghaied in San Francisco and Stranded in South America," *Syracuse Herald,* 27.

15. Colin M. Lewis, *British Railways in Argentina, 1857–1914: A Case Study of Foreign Investment* (London: Athlone, 1983), 137–138.

16. "Shanghaied in San Francisco and Stranded in South America," *Syracuse Herald,* 27; Colin M. Lewis, *Argentina: A Short History* (Oxford: Oneworld, 2002), 3.

17. "Shanghaied in San Francisco and Stranded in South America," *Syracuse Herald,* 27.

18. Stewart Holbrook, "Article No. 1," and "I Was Shanghaied: The Narrative of A.E. Clark, of Camas, Wash., Who in 1891 Fell Victim to Blood Money—and Who Sailed from Astoria Chained to the Ship *T.F. Oakes*," *Sunday Oregonian,* magazine section, October 29, 1933, p. 1.

19. Holbrook, "I Was Shanghaied," 1, 5.

20. Ibid., 1.

21. Ibid.

22. Ibid., 1, 5.

23. Ibid., 5; Stewart Holbrook, "'I Was Shanghaied': The Trip to Le Havre; Johnson, the Mate, Heaves a Jap Sailor into the Sea—and Pays a Heavy Price for the Privilege," *Sunday Oregonian,* magazine section, November 5, 1933, p. 5.

24. Ibid.

25. Stewart Holbrook, "'I Was Shanghaied': A Mad Captain; Clark Skips from a Trial for Mutiny—and Subsequently Boards a Vessel Shunned by the Rats," *Sunday Oregonian,* magazine section, November 12, 1933, p. 5.

26. Ellen J. Prager with Sylvia A. Earle, *The Oceans* (New York: McGraw Hill, 2000), 89.

27. Marq de Villiers, *Windswept: The Story of Wind and Weather* (New York: Walker, 2006), 109.

28. Holbrook, "'I Was Shanghaied': A Mad Captain," *Sunday Oregonian,* 5.

29. Ibid.

30. Woodman, *The History of the Ship,* 175, 177.

31. Holbrook, "'I Was Shanghaied': A Mad Captain," *Sunday Oregonian,* 5.

32. Herbert H. Smith, "Rio de Janeiro,"

Scribner's Monthly, October 1879, pp. 890, 892–894, in CUL: MOA database (accessed May 22, 2011).

33. Holbrook, "'I Was Shanghaied': A Mad Captain," *Sunday Oregonian,* 5.

34. Stewart Holbrook, "'I Was Shanghaied': Treason Trial; A.E. Clark Enlists in the Rebellious Brazilian Navy and Finds Himself Slated for Firing Squad," *Sunday Oregonian,* magazine section, November 19, 1933, p. 5; Kiple, ed., *The Cambridge Historical Dictionary of Disease,* 74; "For Freedom: Admiral Mello Issues a Proclamation," *Boston Daily Globe,* September 26, 1893, p. 18, in NA database (accessed November 28, 2010).

35. Robert M. Levine, *The History of Brazil* (New York: Palgrave Macmillan, 1999), 62–63, 73.

36. Joseph Smith, "Britain and the Brazilian Naval Revolt of 1893–4," *Journal of Latin American Studies* 2:2 (November 1970): 179, in JSTOR database (accessed November 30, 2010).

37. "A Bill for a Ball: Was the Primal Cause for the Brazilian Revolt," *Cleveland Plain Dealer,* October 16, 1893, p. 4, in NewsBank: CPDHN database (accessed December 23, 2010).

38. Smith, "Britain and the Brazilian Naval Revolt of 1893–4," 179; "Raining Bombs: Mello Vigorously Resumes Shelling of Brazil's Capital," *World,* October 6, 1893, p. 5 (accessed November 28, 2010), and "Brazil Rebellion Ended," *Daily Gazette,* April 16, 1894, p. 1 (accessed September 7, 2011), both in NA database.

39. "Raining Bombs," *World,* 5.

40. Walter Lafeber, "United States Depression Diplomacy and the Brazilian Revolution, 1893–1894," *Hispanic American Historical Review* 40:1 (February 1960): 108, in JSTOR database (accessed November 30, 2011).

41. "For Freedom," *Boston Daily Globe,* 18; "Raining Bombs," *World,* 5.

42. "The Insurrection in Brazil," *New York Times,* September 24, 1893, p. 21, in ProQuest: HN: TNYT database (accessed October 14, 2011); Lafeber, "United States Depression Diplomacy and the Brazilian Revolution, 1893–1894," 108.

43. "Crisis Near: United States Ready to Act Promptly," *Boston Daily Globe,* December 21, 1893, p. 1, and "Deadly Cannonading: Deadly Aspects of the War in Brazil," *Evening Express,* December 30, 1893, p. 1, both in NA database (accessed November 28, 2010).

44. "Crisis Near," *Boston Daily Globe*, 1; Lafeber, "United States Depression Diplomacy and the Brazilian Revolution, 1893–1894," 113–115, 119; "Brazil Rebellion Ended," *Daily Gazette*, 1.

45. Holbrook, "'I Was Shanghaied': Treason Trial," *Sunday Oregonian*, 5.

46. Ibid; Kiple, ed., *The Cambridge Historical Dictionary of Disease*, 300.

47. Holbrook, "'I Was Shanghaied': Treason Trial," *Sunday Oregonian*, 5, 7.

48. Credit for this series appeared in an article by Hartley Davis, "Reporters To-day: Stories of Our Foremost Newspaper Men and 'Beats' They Have Scored," *Everybody's Magazine*, January to June 1906, vol. 14 (New York: Ridgeway-Thayer, 1906), 69; "'The World' Frees Slaves in Yucatan," *World*, July 13, 1889, p. 1, in NA database (accessed October 6, 2010); James McGrath Morris, *Pulitzer: A Life in Politics, Print, and Power* (New York: Harper, 2010), 302.

49. George Juergens, *Joseph Pulitzer and the New York World* (Princeton, NJ: Princeton University Press, 1966), 4–6.

50. Ibid., 6; Morris, *Pulitzer*, 206–207.

51. Juergens, *Joseph Pulitzer and the New York World*, 14, 25–27; Morris, *Pulitzer*, 208, 215, 212.

52. Morris, *Pulitzer: A Life in Politics, Print, and Power*, 330.

53. "Now, 'Liverpool Jack,'" *World*, September 25, 1889, p.3, in NA database (accessed October 21, 2010).

54. George J. Svejda, *Castle Garden as an Immigrant Depot, 1855–1890* (Washington, D.C.: National Park Service, Division of History, Office of Archaeology and Historic Preservation, 1968), 31, 34, 41.

55. Ibid., 35, 43–44; Robert Scally, "Liverpool Ships and Irish Emigrants in the Age of Sail," *Journal of Social History* 17:1 (Autumn 1983): 7–8, in JSTOR database (accessed March 12, 2011).

56. Ibid., 19; Antonio Almedia, *From the Old Country: An Oral History of European Migration to America*, ed. Bruce M. Stave and John F. Sutherland with Aldo Salerno (New York: Twayne, 1994), 34; Maddocks, *The Atlantic Crossing*, 144.

57. Scally, "Liverpool Ships and Irish Emigrants in the Age of Sail," 19; Maddocks, *The Atlantic Crossing*, 148, 150; Carlson, *From the Old Country*, 44.

58. Maddocks, *The Atlantic Crossing*, 150.

59. "Castle Garden Emigration Depot: Crime on Emigrant Ships," *New-York Daily Times*, July 24, 1855, p. 4, in ProQuest: HN: TNYT database (accessed March 12, 2011).

60. Svejda, *Castle Garden as an Immigrant Depot, 1855–1890*, 35–38, 90, 86, 77–78.

61. "Commissioners of Emigration: An Emigrant Ship Captured by Runners," *New-York Daily Times*, May 8, 1856, p. 2, in NA database (accessed November 28, 2010).

62. "The Attack on Castle Garden," *New-York Daily Times*, May 9, 1856, p. 2, in NA database (accessed November 28, 2010), 8.

63. Ibid.

64. "Now, 'Liverpool Jack,'" *World*, 3.

65. "'The World' Frees Slaves in Yucatan," *World*, 1.

66. "Threatened the Consul: Another of 'Liverpool Jack's' Slaves Bears Witness," *World*, June 25, 1889, p. 12, in NA database (accessed October 21, 2010).

67. Ibid.

68. "'The World' Frees Slaves in Yucatan," *World*, 1.

69. Alice D. Le Plongeon, "The New and Old in Yucatan," *Harper's New Monthly*, February 1885, p. 372, in CUL: MOA database (accessed July 5, 2011).

70. "Threatened the Consul," *World*, 12.

71. "'The World' Frees Slaves in Yucatan," *World*, 1.

72. Ibid., 2.

73. Ibid.

74. Ibid., 1, 2.

75. Ibid., 2.

76. Ibid.

77. Ibid., 1; "Now, 'Liverpool Jack,'" *World*, 3.

78. "They May Be Shanghaied: Witnesses Against 'Liverpool Jack' in Fear of Bodily Harm," *World*, June 17, 1889, p. 3, in NA database (accessed October 21, 2010).

79. Charles Sutton, *The New York Tombs: Its Secrets and Mysteries, Being a History of the Noted Criminals with Narratives of Their Crimes* (San Francisco: A. Roman, 1874), 42, 48, 52.

80. Sante, *Lures and Snares, Low of Life*, 245.

81. "Now, 'Liverpool Jack,'" *World*, September 25, 1889, p. 3; "Crime's Reward Deferred: The Trial of 'Liverpool Jack' Postponed Indefinitely," *World*, June 26, 1889, p. 12, in NA database (accessed October 21, 2010).

82. "Threatened the Consul," *World*, 12.

83. "They May Be Shanghaied," *World*, 3; "Crime's Reward Deferred," *World*, 12.

84. "They May Be Shanghaied," *World*, 3.

85. Ibid.

86. "Now, 'Liverpool Jack,'" *World,* 3; "Quickly Convicted: 'Liverpool Jack' Pronounced Guilty After Eight Minutes Deliberation," *World,* October 2, 1889, p. 1, and "Sent Up to Join De Leon: 'Liverpool Jack' Sentenced to Sing Sing for Nine Years," *World,* October 8, 1889, p. 5, both in NA database (accessed October 21, 2010); Norval Morris and David J. Rothman, eds., *The Oxford History of the Prison: The Practice of Punishment in Western Society* (New York: Oxford University Press, 1995), 117, 121.

Chapter 7

1. "Middlesex Sessions, Oct. 29," *British Press,* October 30, 1810, p. 3, in NA database (accessed September 16, 2011).

2. Ibid.

3. Bolster, *Black Jacks,* 72.

4. Jesse Lemisch, *Jack Tar vs. John Bull: The Role of New York's Seamen in Precipitating the Revolution* (New York: Garland, 1997), 16.

5. Ibid., 17; Denver Brunsman, "The Knowles Atlantic Impressment Riots of the 1740s," *Early American Studies* 5:2 (Fall 2007): 329, in ProQuest: HM database (accessed December 15, 2010); Lemisch, *Jack Tar vs. John Bull,* 17.

6. James Edward Oglethorpe, "The Sailor's Advocate," in *The Manning of the Royal Navy: Selected Pamphlets, 1693–1873,* ed. J.S. Bromley (London: William Clowes & Sons, 1976), 72.

7. Ibid., 72–74.

8. Frank Mabee, "The Spithead Mutiny and Urban Radicalism in the 1790s," *Romanticism* 13:2 (2007): 135, in ESBCO: ASP database (accessed June 14, 2011).

9. Ibid., 133, 135–137, 143.

10. Denver Brunsman, "Subjects vs. Citizens," *Journal of the Early Republic* 30:4 (Winter 2010): 562, 567, in ESBCO: *ASC* database (accessed November 14, 2010).

11. Jesse Lemisch, "Jack Tar in the Streets: Merchant Seamen in the Politics of Revolutionary America," *William and Mary Quarterly* 25:3, 3rd series (July 1968): 386, in JSTOR database (accessed November 30, 2010).

12. Ibid., 383.

13. Brunsman, "The Knowles Atlantic Impressment Riots of the 1740s," 330.

14. Lemisch, "Jack Tar in the Streets," 388.

15. Brunsman, "Subjects vs. Citizens," 559.

16. William M. Fowler, Jr., "The Non-Volunteer Navy," *U.S. Naval Institute Proceedings* 100:8 (August 1974): 75–76.

17. Ibid., 76–78.

18. *Encyclopedia of North American Conflicts to 1775: A Political, Social, and Military History: A–K,* vol. 1 (Santa Barbara: ABC-CLIO, 2008), 16–17.

19. Lemisch, "Jack Tar in the Streets," 391.

20. Pauline Maier, "Popular Uprisings and Civil Authority in Eighteenth-Century America," *William and Mary Quarterly* 27:1, 3rd series (January 1970): 9, in JSTOR database (accessed November 30, 2010).

21. Justin Windsor, ed., *The Memorial of Boston, Including Suffolk County, Massachusetts, 1630–1880: The Provincial Period,* vol. 2 (Boston: James R. Osgood, 1881), 488.

22. *Encyclopedia of North American Conflicts to 1775,* 33.

23. Ibid., 1.

24. Brunsman, "The Knowles Atlantic Impressment Riots of the 1740s," 355–356.

25. Windsor, ed., *The Memorial of Boston,* 488–489; Lemisch, "Jack Tar in the Streets," 391.

26. Lemisch, "Jack Tar in the Streets," 391; Brunsman, "The Knowles Atlantic Impressment Riots of the 1740s," 359–360.

27. "Sir Charles Knowles," *Oxford Dictionary of National Biography: From the Earliest Times to the Year 2000,* vol. 31, ed. H.G.G. Matthew and Brian Harrison (New York: Oxford University Press, 2004), 978–979.

28. Joseph Phillip Reid, *In a Rebellious Spirit: The Argument of Facts, the Liberty Riot, and the Coming of the American Revolution* (University Park: Pennsylvania State University Press, 1979), 86–88; William Senhouse, "Memoirs of a British Naval Officer at Boston, 1768–1769: Extracts from the Autobiography of William Senhouse," ed. James C. Brandow, *Proceedings of the Massachusetts Historical Society* 105, 3rd series (1993): 74, 80, in JSTOR database (accessed October 6, 2011.

29. Reid, *In a Rebellious Spirit,* 93, 95; Senhouse, "Memoirs of a British Naval Officer at Boston, 1768–1769," 80–81.

30. Brunsman, "Subjects vs. Citizens," 567.

31. Lemisch, *Jack Tar vs. John Bull,* 17, 382; Alexander Tabarrok, "The Rise, Fall, and Rise Again of Privateers," *Independent Review* 11:4 (Spring 2007): 566, 571, in EBSCO: MFP database (accessed March 25, 2011).

32. Lemisch, *Jack Tar vs. John Bull,* 382; Angus Konstam, *Scourge of the Seas: Buccaneers, Pirates and Privateers* (Oxford, UK: Osprey, 2007), 181–183.

33. Edwin G. Burrows and Mike Wallace, *Gotham: A History of New York City to 1898* (New York: Oxford University Press, 1999), 182; Konstam, *Scourge of the Seas,* 181–183.

34. J.L. Anderson, "Piracy and World History: An Economic Perspective on Maritime Predation," *Journal of World History* 6:2 (Fall 1995): 186, in JSTOR database (accessed October 27, 2011).

35. Burrows and Wallace, *Gotham,* 182; Konstam, *Scourge of the Seas,* 180; "St. George, Private Ship of War," "The Middleton, Private Ship of War," *Public Advertiser,* March 3, 1757, p. 3, in NA database (accessed July 3, 2011).

36. Burrows and Wallace, *Gotham,* 182; Lemisch, *Jack Tar vs. John Bull,* 13, 14–15, 21.

37. Letter from Cadwallader Colden to the Lords Commissioners for Trade and Plantations, August 30, 1760, in *Documents Relative to the Colonial History of the State of New-York; Procured in Holland, England and France,* vol. 7, ed. John Romeyn Brodhead (Albany: Weed, Parsons, 1856), 446.

38. Ibid.

39. Lemisch, *Jack Tar vs. John Bull,* 15–16.

40. Aaron Smith, *The Atrocities of Pirates: Being a Faithful Narrative of the Unparalleled Sufferings Enduring by the Author During His Captivity Among the Pirates of the Island of Cuba, with an Account of the Excesses and Barbarities of Those Inhuman Freebooters* (London: G. and W.B. Whittaker, 1824), 1–2, 4, 6, 8.

41. Ibid., 9–10.

42. Ibid., 14–17, 107; "Admiralty Sessions, Friday, Dec. 19," *New Times,* December 20, 1823, p. 2, in NA database, and "High Court of Admiralty—Friday: Piracy," *Courier,* December 20, 1823, p. 3 (accessed May 28, 2011), both in NA database; Cordingly, *Under the Black Flag,* 122.

43. Smith, *The Atrocities of Pirates,* 87–89, 143.

44. Ibid., 34, 60, 72, 75, 77.

45. Ibid., 81–83.

46. "Admiralty Sessions, Friday, Dec. 19," *New Times,* 2.

47. Smith, *The Atrocities of Pirates,* 147–149.

48. "Admiralty Sessions, Friday, December 19," *British Press,* London, 4, in NA database (accessed May 28, 2011); "Admiralty Sessions, Friday, Dec. 19," *New Times,* 2.

49. Smith, *The Atrocities of Pirates,* 160–161.

50. Ibid., v, 60, 191–192.

51. Ibid., 193–195.

52. Dick Cluster and Rafael Hernández, *The History of Havana* (New York: Palgrave Macmillan, 2006), 3, 36–38.

53. Smith, *The Atrocities of Pirates,* 195–197.

54. Ibid., 201, 204–207, 209.

55. Anthony Babington, *The English Bastille: A History of Newgate Gaol and Prison Conditions in Britain, 1188–1902* (New York: St. Martin's, 1971), 5, 161–162, 169.

56. "Admiralty Sessions, Friday, Dec. 19," *New Times,* 2; "High Court of Admiralty," *Courier,* 3.

57. Ibid., 2.

58. Brunsman, "Subjects vs. Citizens," 559, 573.

59. Burns, *Skin and Bones,* 25; Ira Dye, "Early American Merchant Seafarers," *Proceedings of the American Philosophical Society* 120:5 (October 15, 1976): 331, in JSTOR database (accessed January 10, 2011).

60. Christopher McKee, "Foreign Seamen in the United States Navy: A Census of 1808," *William and Mary Quarterly* 42:3, 3rd series (July 1985): 388, in JSTOR database (accessed February 16, 2011).

61. "Flagrant Outrage!" *Centinel,* July 1, 1807, p. 38, in NA database (accessed February 17, 2011); Robert E. Cray, Jr., "Remembering the USS *Chesapeake*: The Politics of Maritime Death and Impressment," *Journal of the Early Republic* 25:3 (Fall 2005): 453, in JSTOR database (accessed February 16, 2011).

62. Cray, Jr., "Remembering the USS *Chesapeake*," 454: "ten miles off ..."; "Flagrant Outrage!" *Centinel,* 38.

63. Cray, Jr., "Remembering the USS *Chesapeake*," 454, 458.

64. Account by Josiah Penny, in *At Sea Under Impressment: Accounts of Involuntary Service Aboard Navy and Pirate Vessels, 1700–1820,* ed. Jean Choate (Jefferson, NC: McFarland, 2010), 50–51.

65. Ibid., 53–55.

66. Ibid., 56–57.

67. Ibid., 57–58.

68. "The Cape of Storms," in *Macmillan's,* May 1894 to October 1894, vol. 70 (London: Macmillan, 1894), 143.

69. Carolyn Hamilton, ed., *The Cambridge History of South Africa: From Early Times to 1885,* vol. 1 (New York: Cambridge University Press, 2010), 173–174.

70. David Mason, *A Traveller's History of South Africa* (New York: Interlink, 2004), 23, 48; Hamilton, ed., *The Cambridge History of South Africa,* 175; Sir Thomas Herbert, "The Road Worthily Cald Good Hope," in *The Cape of Adventure: Being Strange and Notable Discoveries, Perils, Shipwrecks, Battles Upon Sea and Land, with Pleasant and Interesting Observations Upon the Country and the Natives of the Cape of Good Hope,* ed. Ian D. Colvin (New York: AMS, 1969), 206.

71. Frank Welsh, *South Africa: A Narrative History* (New York: Kodansha International, 1999), 88–89; Duncan Campbell Francis Moodie, *The History of the Battles and Adventures of the British, the Boers, and the Zulus, &c., in Southern Africa from the Time of Pharaoh Necho, to 1880, with Copious Chronology,* vol. 1 (Cape Town: Murray & St. Leger, 1888), 174; Account by Penny, in *At Sea Under Impressment,* 58.

72. Christopher Saunders and Nicholas Southey, *Historical Dictionary of South Africa,* 2nd ed. (Lanham, MD: Scarecrow, 2000), 228; Moodie, *The History of the Battles and Adventures of the British, the Boers, and the Zulus, &c.,* 175; Account by Penny, in *At Sea Under Impressment,* 58.

73. Ibid., 175; Saunders and Southey, *Historical Dictionary of South Africa,* 228; Acount by Penny, in *At Sea Under Impressment,* 59–60.

74. Account by Penny, in *At Sea Under Impressment,* 60–62; Moodie, *The History of the Battles and Adventures of the British, the Boers, and the Zulus, &c.,* 176.

75. Account by Penny, in *At Sea Under Impressment,* 62–63.

76. Ibid., 63; Funso S. AfoÚlayan, *Culture and Customs of South Africa* (Westport, CT: Greenwood, 2004), 12.

77. Account by Penny, in *At Sea Under Impressment,* 64–66.

78. Ibid., 66–67.

79. Richard Grove, "Conserving Eden: The (European) East India Companies and Their Environmental Policies on St. Helena, Mauritius and in Western India, 1660 to 1854," *Comparative Studies in Society and History* 35:2 (April 1993): 327–328, in JSTOR database (accessed July 3, 2011).

80. Account by Penny, in *At Sea Under Impressment,* 67–68.

81. Ibid., 68–70.

82. Ibid., 71.

83. Ibid., 72–75.

84. Ibid., 75–76.

85. Account by Penny, in *At Sea Under Impressment,* 76–77, 185.

86. Ibid., 185–186, 188–190, 196–197.

Chapter 8

1. F.C.P., "Two Weeks as a Shanghaied," *Washington Times,* magazine section, December 3, 1905, p. 6, in LOC: CA: HAN database (accessed March 24, 2011); Harry Snowden Stabler, "His Succulency—the Oyster: What the Chesapeake Might Add to the World's Food Supply," *Saturday Evening Post,* April 22, 1911, p. 25.

2. Ibid.

3. Ibid.

4. Mitchell Postel, "A Lost Resource Shellfish in San Francisco Bay," *California History* 67:1 (March 1988): 27, in JSTOR database (accessed February 16, 2011); Clyde L. MacKenzie Jr., "History of Oystering in the United States and Canada, Featuring the Eight Greatest Oyster Estuaries," *Marine Fisheries Review* 58:4 (1996): html document, no page numbers, in EBSCO: ASP database (accessed December 7, 2010).

5. Mark Kurlansky, *The Big Oyster: History on the Half-Shell* (New York: Ballantine, 2006), 28–30.

6. John R. Philpots, *Oysters, and All About Them: Being a Complete History of the Subject, Exhaustive on All Points of Necessary and Curious Information from the Earliest Writers to Those of the Present Time, with Numerous Additions, Facts, and Notes* (London: John Richardson, 1890), 313, 316–318, 321, 323.

7. MacKenzie Jr., "History of Oystering in the United States and Canada," no page numbers; John R. Wennersten, *The Oyster Wars of Chesapeake Bay* (Centreville, MD: Tidewater, 1981), 14, 16.

8. Postel, "A Lost Resource Shellfish in San Francisco Bay," 27; Booker, "Oyster Growers and Oyster Pirates in San Francisco Bay," 30, 73.

9. Postel, "A Lost Resource Shellfish in San Francisco Bay," 30–31, 79; Matthew Morse Booker, "Oyster Growers and Oyster Pirates in San Francisco Bay," *Pacific Historical Review* 75:1 (February 2006): 76, 79, in JSTOR database (accessed February 16, 2011).

10. "A Stingray Hunt: Slaughtering Iron-jawed Fishes That Feed on Oysters," *Daily Alta California,* May 8, 1886, p. 1, in CDNC database (accessed September 26, 2012).

11. Ibid; David A. Ebert, *Sharks, Rays, and Chimaeras of California* (Berkeley: University of California Press, 2003), 228.

12. John J. Alford, "The Chesapeake Oyster Fishery," *Annals of the Association of American Geographers* 65:2 (June 1975): 229–230, in EBSCO: ASP database (accessed December 7, 2010); Wennersten, *The Oyster Wars of Chesapeake Bay,* 5; Philippe Goulletquer and Catherine Goulletquer, "The Chesapeake Bay Skipjacks," *Maritime Life and Traditions* (Fall 2005), 14, in EBSCO: MFP database (accessed June 15, 2011).

13. Wennersten, *The Oyster Wars of Chesapeake Bay,* 17; Howard Pyle, "A Peninsular Canaan," *Harper's New Monthly,* June 1879, p. 63, in CUL: MOA database (accessed December 11, 2010).

14. Pyle, "A Peninsular Canaan," 63–64.

15. Wennersten, *The Oyster Wars of Chesapeake Bay,* 25.

16. Ibid., 11, 23, 32.

17. "The Hygiene of Sailors," *Cincinnati Lancet and Clinic: A Weekly Journal of Medicine and Surgery* 13, ed. J.C. Culbertson and A.B. Thrasher (Cincinnati: Dr. J.C. Culbertson, 1884), 524–525.

18. Ibid., 525.

19. Goulletquer and Goulletquer, "The Chesapeake Bay Skipjacks," 15–16; MacKenzie Jr., "History of Oystering in the United States and Canada, Featuring the Eight Greatest Oyster Estuaries," no page numbers.

20. "Wickedness of the Frozen Oysterman: And the Wickedest Man Who Thrived on It Until He Became a Trust," *Sun,* February 19, 1905, p. 8, in LOC: CA: HAN database (accessed September 26, 2012).

21. "Doctor and Parson Carried by Apache to Islanders' Aid: Revenue Cutter Attempts Second Relief Trip—Fishermen Have Food," *Washington Times,* February 8, 1912, p. 7 (accessed September 27, 2012), and "Fear Oystermen Are in Distress," *Washington Herald,* February 6, 1912, p. 1 (accessed September 26, 2012, both in LOC: CA: HAN database.

22. "Barrier of Ice Separates Apache and Stricken Isle: Vessel Sighted Solitary Island Early Today but Is Unable to Get in Communication with Marooned Oystermen," *Washington Times,* February 7, 1912, p. 1, in LOC: CA: HAN database (accessed September 27, 2012).

23. "Doctor and Parson Carried by Apache to Islanders' Aid," *Washington Times,* 7.

24. Goulletquer and Goulletquer, "The Chesapeake Bay Skipjacks," 15–17; Wennersten, *The Oyster Wars of Chesapeake Bay,* 35; Pyle, "A Peninsular Canaan," 65.

25. "Scarcity of Oysters," *News,* February 13, 1885, p. 2, in NA database (accessed May 28, 2011).

26. Wennersten, *The Oyster Wars of Chesapeake Bay,* 48–49; Stabler, "His Succulency—the Oyster," 25.

27. "Fish and Oyster Notes," *Virginia Citizen,* February 16, 1906, p. 1, LOC: CA: HAN database (accessed March 24, 2011); "Daring Oyster Pirates," *New York Times,* December 8, 1888, p. 2, in ProQuest: HN: TNYT database (accessed February 28, 2011).

28. Pyle, "A Peninsular Canaan," 45; Goulletquer and Goulletquer, "The Chesapeake Bay Skipjacks," 17.

29. "A Campaign of Vengeance: Oyster Pirates Said to Be Gathering in Force to Fight the State Steamers," *Cleveland Plain Dealer,* December 30, 1888, p. 7, in NewsBank: CPDHN database (accessed September 26, 2012).

30. Ibid.

31. "Daring Oyster Pirates," *New York Times,* 1888, p. 2.

32. "Lively Fusillade: Between a Police Boat and an Oyster Pirate—The Latter Surrenders," *Evening Bulletin,* January 14, 1890, p. 4, in LOC: CA: HAN database (accessed September 26, 2012).

33. James L. Haley, *Wolf: The Lives of Jack London* (New York: Basic Books, 2010), 35–38.

34. "Scattered A Pirate Fleet: Battle of the Police with a Number of Oyster Poachers," *Evening Times,* March 24, 1900, p. 5, in LOC: CA: HAN database (accessed September 26, 2012).

35. Ibid.

36. F.C.P., "Two Weeks as a Shanghaied," *Washington Times,* 6.

37. Ibid.

38. Ibid.

39. "Shanghaied at Baltimore: Tricks by Which Sailors for the Oyster Dredgers Are Obtained," *Des Moines Capital,* January 1, 1904, p. 6, in NA database (accessed October 6, 2010).

40. Ibid., 6.

41. "Shanghaied on Oyster Boat," *Tyrone Herald,* February 9, 1905, p. 8, in NA database (accessed October 6, 2010).

42. "The Boys Are Found," *World,* Febru-

ary 5, 1889, pp. 1, 3, in NA database (accessed March 2, 2011).

43. "Squeers on the Sea," *World,* February 4, 1889, p. 1 (accessed March 2, 2011), and "Capture of the Oyster Pirates," *World,* May 5, 1889, p. 5 (accessed October 6, 2010), both in NA database; "The Boys Are Found," *World,* February 5, 1889, p. 1; Davis, "Reporters To-day," *Everybody's Magazine,* 69;

44. F.C.P., "Two Weeks as a Shanghaied," *Washington Times,* 6; Henry Gannett, *A Gazetteer of Maryland* (Washington, D.C.: Government Printing Office, 1904), 28.

45. "Widow Demands Justice," *Washington Post,* December 6, 1905, p. 2, in NA database (accessed October 6, 2010).

46. "Shanghai Indictment Found: Persistent Efforts of Wife of Dead Oysterman Bear Fruit," *New-York Tribune,* December 8, 1905, p. 11, in LOC: CA: HAN database (accessed October 19, 2012).

47. "Barbarities of Oyster Dredgers: An Investigation by a United States Grand Jury," *Cleveland Plain Dealer,* June 10, 1888, p. 9, in NewsBank: CPDHN database (accessed December 23, 2010).

48. Wennersten, *The Oyster Wars of Chesapeake Bay,* 61; "Brutal Oyster Dredgers," *New York Times,* March 13, 1893, p. 8, in ProQuest: HN: TNYT database (accessed February 28, 2011).

49. Wennersten, *The Oyster Wars of Chesapeake Bay,* 62.

50. "Secret Service Officers May Go After Dredgers: United States Authorities Worked Up Over Alleged Outrages on Chesapeake Bay and Its Tributaries," *Washington Times,* November 26, 1905, p. 9, in LOC: CA: HAN database (accessed September 26, 2012).

51. "Untitled," *New York Times,* December 4, 1905, p. 2, in ProQuest: HN: TNYT database (accessed March 2, 2011).

52. "White Slaves in Virginia," *Times Dispatch,* February 10, 1906, p. 1, in LOC: CA: HAN database (accessed March 25, 2011); "Oyster Boat Slaves," *Washington Post,* February 12, 1906, p. 20, in NA database (accessed October 6, 2010).

53. "White Slaves in Virginia," *Times Dispatch,* 1; "Oyster Boat Slaves," *Washington Post,* 20.

54. "Shanghaiing Stopped: Oystermen Quit the Business for Lack of Workmen," *Daily Press,* November 22, 1906, p. 6, in LOC: CA: HAN database (accessed September 26, 2012).

55. "Shanghaied a Bluejacket," *New York* *Times,* January 19, 1908, p. 6, in ProQuest: HN: TNYT database (accessed March 2, 2011).

56. "Nagel in War on Oyster Boats in Chesapeake," *Washington Herald,* November 28, 1911, p. 1, in LOC: CA: HAN database (accessed March 25, 2011); "Cruelty on Oyster Fleet," *Evening Post,* December 15, 1911, p. 1, in NA database (accessed October 6, 2010).

57. Ibid.

58. Goulletquer and Goulletquer, "The Chesapeake Bay Skipjacks," 17; New Jersey, *State of New Jersey Report of the Bureau of Shell Fisheries for the Year Ending October 31st, 1905: Embracing the Annual Reports of the State Oyster Commission, the State Commission for the District of Ocean County, the Oyster Commission for the District of Atlantic County* (Trenton, NJ: MacCrellish & Quigley, 1905), 63–64.

59. Stabler, "His Succulency—the Oyster," 24

60. "With Rapid-Fire Guns to Round Up Oystermen," *New York Times,* December 4, 1905, p. 2, in ProQuest: HN: TNYT database (accessed March 2, 2011).

61. Goulletquer and Goulletquer, "The Chesapeake Bay Skipjacks," 17; Wennersten, *The Oyster Wars of Chesapeake Bay,* 63–64.

Chapter 9

1. "A Pitiful Story: Bernard Morrison's Cruise on the Whaler Bound Billow," *Daily Alta California,* April 26, 1889, p. 1, in CDNC database (accessed May 23, 2011).

2. Ibid; Gerald A. Waring, *Thermal Springs of the United States and Other Countries of the World: A Summary,* revised by Reginald R. Blankenship and Ray Bentall (Washington, D.C.: Government Printing Office, 1965), 105; Robert Francis Scharf, *Distribution and Origin of Life in America* (New York: Macmillan, 1912), 386.

3. "A Pitiful Story," *Daily Alta California,* 1.

4. Gerald O. Williams, "Share Croppers at Sea: The Whaler's 'Lay' and Events in the Arctic, 1905–1907," *Labor History* 29:1 (Winter 1988): 34, in EBSCO: A: H&L database (accessed June 16, 2011).

5. David Moment, "The Business of Whaling in America in the 1850's [sic]," *Business History Review* 31:3 (Autumn 1957): 263–264, in JSTOR database (accessed De-

cember 27, 2010); Eric Jay Dolin, *Leviathan: The History of Whaling in America* (New York: W.W. Norton, 2007), 41.

6. Ellis, *Men and Whales,* 99.
7. Dolin, *Leviathan,* 41–43.
8. Walter S. Tower, *A History of the American Whale Fishery* (Philadelphia: University of Philadelphia Press, 1907), 22–23.
9. Phil Clapham, *Whales of the World* (Stillwater, MN: Voyageur, 1997), 73, 76; Ellis, *Men and Whales,* 141, 143; Tower, *A History of the American Whale Fishery,* 26.
10. Ellis, *Men and Whales,* 141–143; Dolin, *Leviathan,* 64–65, 91; Callum Roberts, *The Unnatural History of the Sea* (Washington, D.C.: Island/Shearwater, 2007), 91; Tower, *A History of the American Whale Fishery,* 26, 28.
11. Clapham, *Whales of the World,* 93; Dolin, *Leviathan,* 77–78; Moment, "The Business of Whaling in America in the 1850's [*sic*]," 266.
12. Clapham, *Whales of the World,* 94, 97–98; Ellis, *Men and Whales,* 144; Moment, "The Business of Whaling in America in the 1850's [*sic*]," 264.
13. W.C. Pich, "The Whale's Pearl: The Story of Ambergris," *Oceans,* May/June 1985, 23–25; Dolin, *Leviathan,* 86.
14. Clapham, *Whales of the World,* 98; Karl H. Dannenfeldt, "Ambergris: The Search for Its Origin," *Isis* 73:3 (September 1982): 395, in JSTOR database (accessed January 10, 2011); Pich, "The Whale's Pearl," 25.
15. Pich, "The Whale's Pearl," 24.
16. Daniel Vickers, "Nantucket Whalemen in the Deep-Sea Fishery: The Changing Anatomy of an Early American Labor Force," *Journal of American History* 72:2 (September 1985): 286–287, 291, 295–296, in JSTOR database (accessed November 4, 2012).
17. Tower, *A History of the American Whale Fishery,* 40; Dolin, *Leviathan,* 122–123.
18. James M. Lindgren, "'Let Us Idealize Old Types of Manhood': The New Bedford Whaling Museum, 1903–1941," *New England Quarterly* 72:2 (June 1999): 166–167, in JSTOR database (accessed December 26, 2010); Dolin, *Leviathan,* 67; Moment, "The Business of Whaling in America in the 1850's [*sic*]," 262–263.
19. Lindgren, "'Let Us Idealize Old Types of Manhood,'" 167.
20. Roberts, *The Unnatural History of the Sea,* 89, 91, 96; Lindgren, "'Let Us Idealize Old Types of Manhood,'" 167.

21. Gordon Grant, *Greasy Luck: A Whaling Sketch Book* (New York: William Farquhar Payson, 2004), 56; Manning, "The Model of a Mutiny, 3–4.
22. Browne, *Etchings of a Whaling Cruise,* 51–52, 54, 60–61; Grant, *Greasy Luck,* 6.
23. Kaplan, "Lewis Temple and the Hunting of the Whale," 78–81, 85.
24. Grant, *Greasy Luck,* 68, 70, 72, 74.
25. Tower, *A History of the American Whale Fishery,* 81–84.
26. Browne, *Etchings of a Whaling Cruise,* 53–54.
27. Ellis, *Men and Whales,* 143; Grant, *Greasy Luck,* 80, 94.
28. "Thrilling Account of the Destruction of a Whale Ship by a Sperm Whale—Sinking of the Ship—Loss of the Boats and Miraculous Escape of the Crew," *New-York Daily Times,* November 5, 1851, p. 4, in ProQuest: HN: TNYT database (accessed October 1, 2012).
29. Ibid.
30. Ibid.
31. Ibid.
32. "The *Eliza's* Crew: Four of Them Sent Out to the Marine Hospital," *Morning Call,* November 24, 1890, p. 1 (accessed May 23, 2011), and "Frost-Bitten Whalemen," *Morning Call,* November 23, 1890, p. 2 (accessed May 23, 2011), both in CDNC database.
33. Ibid.
34. Julie Baker, "The Great Whaleship Disaster of 1871," *American History,* (October 2005), 52, 54–55, in EBSCO: MFP database (accessed June 15, 2011).
35. Ibid., 56–58.
36. Creighton, *Dogwatch and Liberty Days,* 67.
37. "A Countryman Shanghaied," *San Francisco Call,* March 30, 1898, p. 10, in LOC: CA: HAN database (accessed May 28, 2011).
38. Burns, *A Year with a Whaler,* 21–22.
39. "A Countryman Shanghaied," *San Francisco Call,* 10.
40. Manning, "The Model of a Mutiny," 2–4; Ellis, *Men and Whales,* 171.
41. Tilton, *"Cap'n George Fred" Himself,* 47–49.
42. Ibid., 47; Creighton, *Rites and Passages,* 87–89.
43. Creighton, *Rites and Passages,* 88–89.
44. Ibid., 87–89; Ellis, *Men and Whales,* 174.
45. "Whalers Are Fined for Debauching Eskimo Girls," *Oakland Tribune,* November

25, 1906, pp. 9, 12, in NA database (accessed May 28, 2011).

46. "Whalers to Face Grave Charges," *San Francisco Call,* October 24, 1906, p. 7, in CDNC database (accessed October 1, 2012); Truman R. Strobridge and Dennis L Noble, *Alaska and the U.S. Revenue Cutter Service, 1867–1915* (Annapolis, MD: Naval Institute Press, 1999), 157.

47. "Captain Hears Victim Tell of His Cruelty: Sailor Says That Master of Jeanette Triced Him Up," *San Francisco Call,* September 19, 1907, p. 9, and "Sailor Takes Pity on Captain He Accused: Moves for Dismissal of Man He Charged with Cruelty to the Crew," *San Francisco Call,* September 22, 1907, p. 44, both in CDNC database (accessed October 1, 2012).

48. "Sailor Takes Pity on Captain He Accused," *San Francisco Call,* 44.

49. R.T.F. Harding, "Shanghaied: This Young Man Reaches Cleveland After a Series of Scarcely Credible Adventures and Experiences," *Cleveland Plain Dealer,* February 12, 1911, p. 60, in NewsBank: CPDHN database (accessed October 4, 2012).

50. Ibid.

51. Fred R. Bechdolt, "Shanghaiing Today," *San Francisco Call,* April 23, 1911, p. 4, in LOC: CA: HAN database (accessed May 28, 2011).

52. Williams, "Share Croppers at Sea," 35; Ellis, *Men and Whales,* 172.

53. Williams, "Share Croppers at Sea," 35, 38.

54. Harding, "Shanghaied: This Young Man Reaches Cleveland After a Series of Scarcely Credible Adventures and Experiences," *Cleveland Plain Dealer,* 60.

55. "Starved and Frozen," *Oakland Tribune,* November 9, 1897, p. 5, in NA database (accessed April 18, 2011).

56. Ibid.

57. Florence Thrale, "Millionaire[']s Son Works Seven Months for One Dollar," *San Francisco Call,* November 19, 1905, p. 7, in LOC: CA: HAN database (accessed October 4, 2012); "G.H. Hammond Company Sold: Former Owners Buy Packing Plant from the English Syndicate" *New York Times,* September 16, 1900, p. 25, ProQuest: HN: TNYT database (accessed October 5, 2012).

58. Thrale, "Millionaire[']s Son Works Seven Months for One Dollar," *San Francisco Call,* 7.

59. Ibid.

60. Ibid.

61. Henry A. Clock, "A Narrative of a Shanghaied Whaleman, Part V," *Pacific Monthly,* January 1911, pp. 315–316.

62. "Shanghaied Youth's Death," *Naugatuck Daily News,* September 25, 1902, p. 3, in NA database (accessed April 10, 2011).

63. Williams, "Share Croppers at Sea," 32, 34.

64. Clock, "A Narrative of a Shanghaied Whaleman, Part V," 317.

65. Tilton, *"Cap'n George Fred" Himself,* 1–2, 7, 9–10.

66. Ibid., 10–15, 21.

67. Dorothy Harley Eber, *When Whalers Were Up North: Inuit Memories from the Eastern Arctic* (Kingston, ON: Migill-Queen's University Press, 1989), 124; Peter Freuchen, *Peter Freuchen's Men of the Frozen North,* ed. Dagmar Freuchen (Cleveland: World, 1962), 287.

68. Eber, *When Whalers Were Up North,* 124.

69. Nancy Wachowich Apphia in collaboration with Agalakti Awa, *Saqiyuq: Stories from the Lives of Three Inuit Women* (Kingston, ON: McGill-Queen's University Press), 118.

70. Freuchen, *Peter Freuchen's Men of the Frozen North,* 290–291, 293, 295: "for medicinal purposes," 291, "three of everything ... " 293; Eber, *When Whalers Were Up North,* 124.

71. Eber, *When Whalers Were Up North,* 125, 127.

72. Ibid., 124; Freuchen, *Peter Freuchen's Men of the Frozen North,* 289; Minna Littmann and George C. Cleveland, "A White Man Alone in the Arctic When His Supplies Failed to Arrive," *Sunday Standard,* April 13, 1924, p. 23.

73. Eber, *When Whalers Were Up North,* 124; Freuchen, *Peter Freuchen's Men of the Frozen North,* 289–290; Littmann and Cleveland, "A White Man Alone in the Arctic When His Supplies Failed to Arrive," *Sunday Standard,* 23.

74. Minna Littmann and George C. Cleveland, "Spending a Winter Among the Eskimos—Adrift on a Big Floating Island of Ice," *Sunday Standard,* April 20, 1924, p. 34, and "A White Man Alone in the Arctic When His Supplies Failed to Arrive," *Sunday Standard,* 24; Eber, *When Whalers Were Up North,* 124; Freuchen, *Peter Freuchen's Men of the Frozen North,* 288–289.

75. Creighton, *Rites and Passages,* 26; Clapham, *Whales of the World,* 83; W. Gillies

Ross, "Distribution, Migration, and Depletion of Bowhead Whales in Hudson Bay, 1860 to 1915," *Arctic and Alpine Research* 6:1 (Winter 1974): 94, in JSTOR database (accessed December 15, 2010).

76. Littmann and Cleveland, "A White Man Alone in the Arctic When His Supplies Failed to Arrive," *Sunday Standard,* 24.

77. Ibid; W. Gillies Ross, "Whaling and the Decline of Native Populations," *Arctic Anthropology* 14:2 (1977): 5, in JSTOR database (accessed October 3, 2012).

78. Eber, *When Whalers Were Up North,* 124.

79. Minna Littmann and George C. Cleveland, "Post Sacked—Lone White Man Turns Eskimo—He Becomes a Witch Doctor," *Sunday Standard,* April 27, 1924, p. 35; Freuchen, *Peter Freuchen's Men of the Frozen North,* 291.

80. William C. Sturtevant and David Damas, eds., *Handbook of North American Indians: Arctic,* vol. 5 (Washington: Smithsonian Institution, 1984), 441–442.

81. Littmann and Cleveland, "Post Sacked—Lone White Man Turns Eskimo—He Becomes a Witch Doctor," *Sunday Standard,* 36; Eber, *When Whalers Were Up North,* 124; Ross, "Whaling and the Decline of Native Populations," 3–4.

82. *Encyclopedia of World Geography: Canada and the Arctic,* vol. 3 (New York: Marshall Cavendish, 1994), 350–351.

83. Minna Littmann and George C. Cleveland, "New Bedford Captain He Knew as a Boy Confiscated Cleveland's Stock of Furs," *Sunday Standard,* May 4, 1924, p. 35.

84. Entries of August 8, September 11, and September 14, 1904, George Comer, *The Journal of Captain George Comer in Hudson Bay: 1903–1905,* ed. W. Gillies Ross (Toronto: University of Toronto Press, 1984), 133, 139–140.

85. Ibid., entry for September 14, 140; Littmann and Cleveland, "New Bedford Captain He Knew as a Boy Confiscated Cleveland's Stock of Furs," *Sunday Standard,* 35; Eber, *When Whalers Were Up North,* 124.

86. Littmann and Cleveland, "New Bedford Captain He Knew as a Boy Confiscated Cleveland's Stock of Furs," *Sunday Standard,* 35; "Stranded in the Arctic for Seven Long Years," *Anaconda Standard,* December 26, 1905, p. 2, in NA database (accessed December 12, 2010).

87. Minna Littmann and George C. Cleveland, "A Floating Trading Post in the Far North—Hunting Seals in the Company of It," *Sunday Standard,* May 11, 1924, p. 35.

88. Ibid; Kiple, ed., *The Cambridge Historical Dictionary of Disease,* 43.

89. Littmann and Cleveland, "A Floating Trading Post in the Far North," *Sunday Standard,* 35.

90. Eber, *When Whalers Were Up North,* 124.

91. Freuchen, *Peter Freuchen's Men of the Frozen North,* 290–291.

92. Eber, *When Whalers Were Up North,* 127.

Chapter 10

1. "No Shanghai for Him," *Independent,* March 19, 1904, p. 1, in LOC: CA: HAN database (accessed May 28, 2011).

2. Raffety, "Discipline But Not Punish," 184.

3. John R. Brown, "Admiralty Judges: Flotsam on the Sea of Maritime Law?" *Houston Journal of International Law* 25:2 (Winter 2003): 257–299, in EBSCO: LC database (accessed May 28, 2011).

4. Martin J. Norris, "The Seaman as Ward of the Admiralty," *Michigan Law Review* 52:4 (February 1954): 480–481, in JSTOR database (accessed March 17, 2011); Creighton, *Dogwatch and Liberty Days,* 93.

5. Norris, "The Seaman as Ward of the Admiralty," 481–482.

6. Raffety, "Discipline But Not Punish," 185; United States, "An Act for the Government and Regulation of Seamen in the Merchants Service," *Statutes at Large,* vol. 1 (1789–1799), 131.

7. Gautham Rao, "Sailors' Health and National Wealth: Marine Hospitals in the Early Republic," *Common-Place* (online journal) 9:1 (October 2008), http://www.common-place.org/vol-09/no-01/rao (accessed February 5, 2011), html, no page numbers.

8. Norris, "The Seaman as Ward of the Admiralty," 485–486; United States, *The Federal Cases Comprising Cases Argued and Determined in the Circuit and District Courts of the United States: From the Earliest Times to the Beginning of the Federal Reporter, Arranged Alphabetically by the Titles of the Cases and Numbered Consecutively,* book 11 (St. Paul: West, 1895), 480; Brown, "Admiralty Judges," 264.

9. Norris, "The Seaman as Ward of the Admiralty," 483–484, 486; United States,

The Federal Cases Comprising Cases Argued and Determined in the Circuit and District Courts of the United States, 483; Brown, "Admiralty Judges," 266–267.

10. Gerald J. Barry, "Philanthropic Privateers—The Story of Sailor's Snug Harbor," *Maritime Life and Traditions* (Summer 2005): 26–27, in EBSCO: MFP database (accessed January 10, 2011), 27.

11. Ibid., 26–28.

12. Ibid., 29.

13. Ibid., 30–32.

14. G.J.B., "Up, Down, Up with the Harbor," *Maritime Life and Traditions* (Summer 2005), 34, in EBSCO: MFP database (accessed January 11, 2011).

15. Bolster, *Black Jacks,* 73–74.

16. Johnson, *A General History of the Robberies and Murderers of the Most Notorious Pirates,* 50; Robert E. Lee, *Blackbeard the Pirate: A Reappraisal of His Life and Times* (Winston-Salem, NC: John F. Blair, 1974), 99.

17. Lee, *Blackbeard the Pirate,* 100–101, 104–105; Johnson, *A General History of the Robberies and Murderers of the Most Notorious Pirates,* 57.

18. United States, "An Act for the Government and Regulation of Seamen in the Merchants Service," *Statutes at Large*, vol. 1 (1789–1799), 133–134.

19. United States, "An Act for the Punishment of Certain Crimes Against the United States," 113–115, and "An Act in Amendment of the Acts for Punishment and Offense against the United States," 776–777, both in *Statutes at Large*, vol. 1. (1789–1799).

20. United States, "An Act to Authorize the Appointment of Shipping-Commissioners by the Several Circuit Courts of the United States to Superintend the Shipping and Discharge of Seamen Engaged in Merchant Ships Belonging to the United States, and for the Further Protection of Seamen," in *Statutes at Large*, vol. 17 (1871–1873) (Boston: Little, Brown, 1873), 262–263, 273–274; Craig J. Forsyth, *The American Merchant Seaman and His Industry: Struggle and Stigma* (New York: Taylor & Francis, 1989), 8–9.

21. William L. Standard, *Merchant Seamen: A Short History of Their Struggles* (Standfordville, NY: Earl M. Coleman, 1979), 13.

22. Merchant Marine Commission, *Report of the Merchant Marine Commission,* xii, 55–57.

23. Russell, "The Life of The Merchant Sailor," 122–123, 134.

24. Foulke, "Life in the Dying World of Sail, 1870–1910," 134–135.

25. Sidney Kaplan, "The American Seamen's Protective Union Association of 1863: A Pioneer Organization of Negro Seamen in the Port of New York," *Science and Society* 21:2 (Spring 1957): 155–158, 155, in JSTOR database (accessed December 27, 2010); Bolster, *Black Jacks,* 182.

26. Ibid., 158.

27. David Goldfield, *America Aflame: How the Civil War Created a Nation* (New York: Bloomsbury, 2011), 291.

28. "The Draft: The Riot in the Ninth Congressional District," *New-York Daily Tribune,* July 14, 1863, pp. 1, 5, in LOC: CA: HAN database (accessed May 29, 2011).

29. Kaplan, "The American Seamen's Protective Union Association of 1863," 158–159.

30. Schwartz, *Brotherhood of the Sea,* x, xii, 1, 6.

31. Ibid., 1, 7; "Coast Seamen's Union: A Powerful Labor Organization and Its Work on the Pacific," *Daily Evening Bulletin,* September 14, 1886, p. 1, and "Latest Foreign News! American," *Hawaiian Gazette,* September 21, 1886, p. 9, both in LOC: CA: HAN database (accessed May 29, 2011).

32. Schwartz, *Brotherhood of the Sea,* 15.

33. "The Great Labor Lockout," *Daily Alta California,* August 27, 1886, p. 1, in CDNC database (accessed May 29, 2011).

34. Ibid; "River Front Troubles," *Daily Alta California,* August 31, 1886, p. 1, in CDNC database (accessed May 29, 2011).

35. Standard, *Merchant Seamen,* 15; Schwartz, *Brotherhood of the Sea,* 15.

36. Pickelhaupt, *Shanghaied in San Francisco,* 38–39.

37. "Dynamite Used in San Francisco," *Weekly Gazette and Stockman,* September 28, 1893, p. 7, in NA database (accessed November 16, 2010).

38. "A Dynamite Bomb," *Iowa Postal Card,* September 29, 1893, p. 2, in NA database (accessed November 16, 2010).

39. Ibid; "Dynamite Used in San Francisco," *Weekly Gazette and Stockman,* 7: ; Pickelhaupt, *Shanghaied in San Francisco,* 39.

40. Schwartz, *Brotherhood of the Sea,* 24.

41. Brotherhood of the Sea, "In Memory of the Emancipator of the Sea: Andrew Furuseth 150th Anniversary," *West Coast Sailors,* March 12, 2004, pp. 1, 3; Bechdolt, "Shanghaiing Today," 4.

42. Brotherhood of the Sea, "In Memory of the Emancipator of the Sea," 1–2.

43. Ibid., 2–3.

44. Forsyth, *The American Merchant Seaman and His Industry,* 10; United States, U.S. Congress, Committee on the Merchant Marine and Fisheries, *Hearings Held Before the Committee on the Merchant Marine and Fisheries on House Bill 11372,* Thursday, December 14, 1911 (Washington, D.C.: Government Printing Office, 1912), 28.

45. Forsyth, *The American Merchant Seaman and His Industry,* 12.

46. Merchant Marine Commission, *Report of the Merchant Marine Commission,* i–iii.

47. Ibid., iv–vi.

48. Ibid., 21–22.

49. Ibid., vi–xiii, xv–xvi; Forsyth, *The American Merchant Seaman and His Industry,* 7.

50. Broughton Brandenburg, "The Deep Sea Sailor: The Ocean Tramp," *Frank Leslie's Popular Monthly,* May 1903, pp. 276–277.

51. Interview with Otto Parsons, Merchant Marine Commission, *Report of the Merchant Marine Commission,* 44, 50–51–52, 54.

52. United States, Supreme Court, *United States Reports: Cases Adjudged in the Supreme Court,* vols. 165–168 (Washington, D.C.: U.S. Government Printing Office, 1896–1897), 275–276; Brotherhood of the Sea, "In Memory of the Emancipator of the Sea," 4.

53. Supreme Court, *United States Reports,* 275–276, 280, 282.

54. Ibid., 282–283; "Henry Billings Brown," in *American National Biography,* vol. 3, ed. John A. Garraty and Mark C. Carnes (New York: Oxford University Press, 1999), 680–681; Forsyth, *The American Merchant Seaman and His Industry,* 10.

55. "An Important Decision," *Broad Ax,* February 20, 1897, p. 1, in NA database (accessed November 1, 2010).

56. Nancy C. Unger, *Fighting Bob La Follette: The Righteous Reformer* (Chapel Hill: University of North Carolina Press, 2000), 226.

57. "Robert La Follett," in *American National Biography,* vols. 13, 46–47; Unger, *Fighting Bob La Follette,* 227.

58. Wyn Craig Wade, *The Titanic: End of a Dream* (New York: Penguin, 1986), 24, 30–31, 40–41.

59. Tom Kuntz, ed., *The Titanic Disaster Hearings: The Official Transcripts of the 1912 Senate Investigation* (New York: Pocket Books, 1998), 554–555.

60. Unger, *Fighting Bob La Follette,* 227; Wade, *The Titanic: End of a Dream,* 307–308.

61. "Ship Owners Fear Labor Union Trust," *New York Times,* January 26, 1913, p. 18, in ProQuest: HN: TNYT database (accessed March 2, 2011).

62. Ibid.

63. Ibid.

64. Ibid.

65. United States, Congress, *Congressional Record: Containing the Proceedings and Debates of the Sixty-Third Congress,* Second Session, vol. 51 (Washington, D.C.: Government Printing Office, 1914), 14358–14359.

66. Unger, *Fighting Bob La Follette,* 227.

67. "Petition Wilson to Suspend Act," *Fairbanks Daily News-Miner,* October 27, 1915, p. 11, in NA database (accessed November 1, 2010).

68. E. Mowbray Tate, *Transpacific Steam: The Story of Steam Navigation from the Pacific Coast of North America to the Far East and Antipodes, 1867–1941* (New York: Cornwall, 1986), 37; "Stockholders Will Decide Pacific Mail Case," *Mason City Globe-Gazette,* October 14, 1915, p. 5, in NA database (accessed November 1, 2010).

69. John Haskell Kemble, "The Genesis of the Pacific Mail Steamship Company," *California Historical Society Quarterly* 13:3 (September 1934): 240–241, in JSTOR database (accessed December 25, 2010)

70. Ibid., 21, 26.

71. A.C.W. Bethel, "The Golden Skein: California's Gold-Rush Transportation Network," *California History* 77:4 (Winter 1998/1999): 252, in JSTOR database (accessed December 26, 2010).

72. Tate, *Transpacific Steam,* 23, 26–27.

73. Ibid., 28, 37.

74. Schwendinger, "Chinese Sailors," 65–66.

75. Ibid., 66; "Chinese Sailors Pass Examination," *Salt Lake Tribune,* December 30, 1915, p. 2, in NA database (accessed November 1, 2010).

76. "Seamen's Act Goes into Effect Today," *Boston Daily Globe,* November 4, 1915, p. 11, in NA database (accessed November 1, 2010).

77. Tate, *Transpacific Steam,* 37–39.

78. Forsyth, *The American Merchant Seaman and His Industry,* 13.

Bibliography

Newspapers

Anaconda (MT) *Standard*
The Atlanta Constitution
Bangor (MN) *Daily Whig and Courier*
The Boston Daily Globe
The British Press (London)
The Broad Ax (Salt Lake City, UT)
The Centinel (Gettysburg, PA)
Cleveland Plain Dealer
The Courier (London)
Daily Alta California (San Francisco, CA)
Daily Capital Journal (Salem, OR)
Daily Evening Bulletin/Evening Bulletin
   (Maysville, KY)
The Daily Gazette (Janesville, WI)
The Daily Herald (Delphos, OH)
The Daily Morning Astorian (Astoria, OR)
Daily Press (Newport News, VA)
Des Moines (IA) *Capital*
Evening Bulletin (Honolulu, HI)
Evening Express (Lock Haven, PA)
The Evening Post (Frederick, MD)
The Evening Times (Washington, D.C.)
Fairbanks (AK) *Daily News-Miner*
The Grenville (PA) *Advance*
The Independent (Honolulu, HI)
The Hawaiian Gazette (Honolulu, HI)
The Hawaiian Star (Honolulu, HI)
Iowa Postal Card (Fayette, IA)
Janesville (WI) *Daily Gazette*
Mason City (IA) *Globe-Gazette*
The Mathews Journal (Mathews Court
   House, VA)
Middletown (NY) *Times-Press*
The Milwaukee Sentinel
The Morning Call/The San Francisco Call

*The Morning Oregonian/The Sunday Ore-
   gonian* (Portland, OR)
Naugatuck (CT) *Daily News*
The Nautical Standard (London)
*The New-York Daily Times/The New York
   Times*
New-York Daily Tribune/New-York Tribune
The New Times (London)
The News (Frederick, MD)
North-China Herald (Shanghai, China)
Oakland Tribune
The Olean (NY) *Democrat*
The Public Advertiser (London)
The Record-Union (Sacramento, CA)
The Reno Evening Gazette
The Salt Lake Tribune
The Star and Banner (Gettysburg, PA)
The Sun (New York)
The Sunday Standard (New Bedford, MA)
The Syracuse (NY) *Herald*
The Times Dispatch (Richmond, VA)
The Titusville (PA) *Morning Herald*
Tyrone (PA) *Herald*
Virginia Citizen (Irvington, VA)
The Washington Herald (Washington, D.C.)
The Washington Post (Washington, D.C.)
Washington Times (Washington, D.C.)
Waterloo (IA) *Daily Courier*
The Weekly Gazette and Stockman (Reno,
   NV)
The World/The Evening World (New York)

Magazines

American History
Antiques
The Atlantic Monthly

225

The Bellman
The Century
Everybody's Magazine
Frank Leslie's Popular Monthly
The Friend
Harper's New Monthly Magazine
Macmillan's Magazine
The New-York Organ
The Pacific Monthly
The Saturday Evening Post
Scribner's Magazine
Smithsonian Magazine
West Coast Sailors

Manuscripts and Collections

Bugbee, George C. George C. Bugbee Collection, 1866–1917. G.W. Blunt White Library. Manuscripts Division. Mystic Seaport: Museum of America and the Sea.

Diomede, Adonis Johnson Aloysius. "Reminiscence, 1837–1864." Journal, 1864. Typescript copy. G.W. Blunt White Library. Manuscripts Division. Mystic Seaport: Museum of America and the Sea.

Freeman, Albert L. Albert L. Freeman Papers. G.W. Blunt White Library. Manuscripts Division. Mystic Seaport: Museum of America and the Sea.

Manning, Lisa. "The Model of a Mutiny: An Examination of Insurrection Aboard American Whaleships from 1820–1860." Research Paper. G.W. Blunt White Library. Manuscripts Division. Mystic Seaport: Museum of America and the Sea.

"Scrimshaw." *Voyages: Stories of America and the Sea.* Exhibit. Stillman Building. Mystic Seaport: Museum of America and the Sea.

Steers, MacDonald. "Research Notes." G.W. Blunt White Library. Manuscripts Division. Mystic Seaport: Museum of America and the Sea.

"Whitehall Boats." *Our Grandfather's Boats.* Exhibit. North Boat Shed. Mystic Seaport: Museum of America and the Sea.

Personal Correspondence

Bardi, Gina. J. Porter Shaw Library. E-mail to author. March 21, 2011.

Dean, Clarissa. National Museum of the U.S. Navy. E-mail to Author. June 9, 2012.

Government Documents

Brodhead, John Romeyn, ed. *Documents Relative to the Colonial History of the State of New-York; Procured in Holland, England and France.* Vol. 7. Albany: Weed, Parsons, 1856.

Canada, Legislature, Legislative Assembly. *Appendix to the Fifteenth Volume of the Journals of the Legislative Assembly of the Province of Canada, from the 26th February of the 10th June, 1857, both Days Inclusive, in the Twentieth Year of the Reign of Our Sovereign Lady Queen Victory, Being the 3rd Session of the 5th Provincial Parliament of Canada.* Session, 1857. Toronto: John Lovell, 1857.

Dean, Clarissa. National Museum of the U.S. Navy. E-mail to Author. June 9, 2012.

Gannett, Henry. *A Gazetteer of Maryland.* Washington, D.C.: Government Printing Office, 1904.

Kuntz, Tom, ed. *The* Titanic *Disaster Hearings: The Official Transcripts of the 1912 Senate Investigation.* New York: Pocket Books, 1998.

New Jersey. *State of New Jersey Report of the Bureau of Shell Fisheries for the Year Ending October 31st, 1905: Embracing the Annual Reports of the State Oyster Commission, the State Commission for the District of Ocean County, the Oyster Commission for the District of Atlantic County.* Trenton, NJ: MacCrellish & Quigley, 1905.

Shindler, Henry. *History of the United States Military Prison.* Fort Leavenworth, KS: Army Service School Press, 1911.

Svejda, Dr. George J. *Castle Garden as an Immigrant Depot, 1855–1890.* Washington, D.C.: National Park Service. Division of History. Office of Archaeology and Historic Preservation, 1968.

United States Government. Committee on the Merchant Marine and Fisheries. *Hearings Held Before the Committee on the Merchant Marine and Fisheries on House Bill 11372, Thursday, December 14,*

1911. Washington, D.C.: Government Printing Office, 1912.

_____. *The Federal Cases Comprising Cases Argued and Determined in the Circuit and District Courts of the United States: From the Earliest Times to the Beginning of the Federal Reporter, Arranged Alphabetically by the Titles of the Cases and Numbered Consecutively.* Book 11. St. Paul: West, 1895.

_____. Merchant Marine Commission. *Report of the Merchant Marine Commission, Together with the Testimony Taken at the Hearings; Report and Recommendations of the Commission (Including the Views of the Minority) and Hearings on the North Atlantic Coast.* Vol. 1. Washington, D.C.: Government Printing Office, 1905.

_____. *Statutes at Large.* Vol. 1 (1789–1799). Washington, D.C.: Microcard Editions, 1972.

_____. *Statutes at Large.* Vol. 4 (1824–1835) Boston: Little, Brown, 1846.

_____. *Statutes at Large.* Vol. 17 (1871–1873). Boston: Little, Brown, 1873.

_____. Supreme Court. *United States Reports: Cases Adjudged in the Supreme Court.* Vols. 165–168. Washington, D.C.: U.S. Government Printing Office, 1896–1897.

_____. U.S. Congress. *Congressional Record: Containing the Proceedings and Debates of the Sixty-Third Congress.* Second Session. Vol. 51. Washington, D.C.: Government Printing Office, 1914.

_____. U.S. Department of the Interior. *Historical American Landscapes Survey: Fort Shafter Military Reservation, N.C.O. Housing Area (Fort Shafter Military Reservation, Rice Manor Housing Area).* Oakland, CA: National Park Service, 2011.

Waring, Gerald A. *Thermal Springs of the United States and Other Countries of the World: A Summary.* Revised by Reginald R. Blankenship and Ray Bentall. Washington, D.C.: Government Printing Office, 1965.

Journals

"Agriculture and Livestock." *Mountain Research and Development* 4:2 (May, 1984): 150–162.

Alborn, Denise M. "Crimping and Shanghaiing on the Columbia River." *Oregon Historical Quarterly* 93:3 (Fall 1992): 262–291.

Alcorn, Rowena L.D., and Gordon D. Alcorn. "Tacoma Seamen's Rest: Waterfront Mission, 1897–1903." *Oregon Historical Quarterly* 66:2 (June 1965): 101–131.

Alford, John J. "The Chesapeake Oyster Fishery." *Annals of the Association of American Geographers* 65:2 (June 1975): 229–239.

Altrocchi, Julia Cooley. "Paradox Town: San Francisco in 1851." *California Historical Society Quarterly* 28:1 (March 1949): 31–46.

Anderson, Godfrey T. "The Captain Lays Down the Law." *New England Quarterly* 44:2 (June 1971): 305–309.

Anderson, J.L. "Piracy and World History: An Economic Perspective on Maritime Predation." *Journal of World History* 6:2 (Fall 1995): 175–199.

Barry, Gerald J. "Philanthropic Privateers: The Story of Sailor's Snug Harbor." *Maritime Life and Traditions* (Summer 2005): 26–35.

Bethel, A.C.W. "The Golden Skein: California's Gold-Rush Transportation Network." *California History* 77:4 (Winter 1998/1999): 250–275.

Bloch, Kurt. "The Basic Conflict Over Foreign Concessions in China." *Far Eastern Survey* 8:10 (May 10, 1939): 111–116.

Booker, Matthew Morse. "Oyster Growers and Oyster Pirates in San Francisco Bay." *Pacific Historical Review* 75:1 (February 2006): 63–88.

Bowen, Huw V. "400 Years of the East India Company." *History Today* 50:7 (July 2000): 47–53.

Brown, John R. "Admiralty Judges: Flotsam on the Sea of Maritime Law?" *Houston Journal of International Law* 25:2 (Winter 2003): 257–299.

Brunsman, Denver. "The Knowles Atlantic Impressment Riots of the 1740s." *Early American Studies* 5:2 (Fall 2007): 324–366.

_____. "Subjects vs. Citizens." *Journal of the Early Republic* 30:4 (Winter 2010): 557–586.

Buck, Pearl S. "China and the West." *Annals of the American Academy of Political and Social Science* 168 (July 1933): 118–131.

Cavendish, Richard. "The Australian Gold Rush Begins." *History Today* (February 2001): 50–51.

"China and the Foreign Devils." *Bulletin of the Business Historical Society* 3:6 (November 1929): 9–19.

Cooper, Malcolm. "Maritime Labour and Crew List Analysis: Problems, Prospects, and Methodologies." *Labour/Le Travail* 23 (Spring 1989): 179–194.

Cranston, Earl. "Shanghai in the Taiping Period." *Pacific Historical Review* 5:2 (June 1936): 147–160.

Cray, Jr., Robert E. "Remembering the USS *Chesapeake*: The Politics of Maritime Death and Impressment." *Journal of the Early Republic* 25:3 (Fall 2005): 445–474.

Culbertson, J.C., and A.B. Thrasher, eds. *Cincinnati Lancet and Clinic* 13. Cincinnati: (Dr.) J.C. Culbertson, 1884.

Czitrom, Daniel. "Underworlds and Underdogs: 'Big' Tim Sullivan and Metropolitan Politics in New York, 1889–1913." *Journal of American History* 78:2 (September 1991): 536–558.

Dannenfeldt, Karl H. "Ambergris: The Search for Its Origin." *Isis* 73:3 (September 1982): 382–397.

Davidson, Lance S. "Shanghaied! The Systematic Kidnapping of Sailors in Early San Francisco." *California History* 64:1 (Winter 1985): 10–17.

Downs, Jacques M. "American Merchants and the China Opium Trade, 1800–1840." *Business History Review* 42:4 (Winter, 1968): 418–442.

Dye, Ira. "Early American Merchant Seafarers." *Proceedings of the American Philosophical Society* 120:5 (October 15, 1976): 331–360.

_____. "The Tattoos of Early American Seafarers, 1796–1818." *Proceedings of the American Philosophical Society* 133:4 (December 1989): 520–554.

"Exclusion in Washington," *Chinese American Forum* 26:4 (April 2011): 18.

Fairbank, J.K. "Chinese Diplomacy and the Treaty of Nanking, 1842." *Journal of Modern History* 12:1 (March 1940): 1–30.

Farr, James. "A Slow Boat to Nowhere: The Multi-Racial Crews of the American Whaling Industry." *Journal of Negro History* 68:2 (Spring 1983): 159–170.

Fingard, Judith. "The Decline of the Sailor as a Ship Labourer in 19th Century Timber Ports." *Labour/Le Travail* 2 (1977): 35–53.

Fletcher, Max E. "The Suez Canal and World Shipping, 1869–1914." *Journal of Economic History* 18:4 (December 1958): 556–573.

Foulke, Robert D. "Life in the Dying World of Sail, 1870–1910." *Journal of British Studies* 3:1 (November 1963): 105–136.

Fowler, Jr., William M. "The Non-Volunteer Navy." *U.S. Naval Institute Proceedings* 100:8 (August 1974): 74–78.

Gibbons, Michelle G. "'Voices from the People': Letters to the *American Phrenological Journal,* 1854–64." *Journalism History* 35:2 (Summer 2009): 72–81.

G.J.B. "Up, Down, Up with the Harbor." *Maritime Life and Traditions* (Summer 2005), 34.

Glenn, Myra C. "The Naval Reform Campaign Against Flogging: A Case Study in Changing Attitudes Toward Corporal Punishment, 1830–1850." *American Quarterly* 35:4 (Autumn 1983): 408–425.

_____. "Troubled Manhood in the Early Republic: The Life and Autobiography of Sailor Horace." *Journal of the Early Republic* 26:1 (Spring 2006): 59–93.

Goulletquer, Philippe, and Catherine Simon-Goulletquer. "The Chesapeake Bay Skipjacks." *Maritime Life and Traditions* (Fall 2005): 14–29.

Graham, Gerald S. "The Ascendancy of the Sailing Ship, 1850–85." *Economic History Review.* New Series 9:1 (1956): 74–88.

Grove, Richard. "Conserving Eden: The (European) East India Companies and Their Environmental Policies on St. Helena, Mauritius and in Western India, 1660 to 1854." *Comparative Studies in Society and History* 35:2 (April 1993): 318–351.

Heyningen, van, Elizabeth B. "The Social Evil in the Cape Colony, 1868–1902: Prostitution and the Contagious Diseases Acts." *Journal of Southern African Studies* 10:2 (April 1984): 170–197.

Hovde, David M. "Sea Colportage: The Loan Library System of the American Seamen's Friend Society, 1859–1967." *Libraries and Culture* 29:4 (Fall 1994): 389–414.

Kaplan, Sidney. "The American Seamen's Protective Union Association of 1863: A Pioneer Organization of Negro Seamen in the Port of New York." *Science and Society* 21:2 (Spring 1957): 154–159.

_____. "Lewis Temple and the Hunting of the Whale." *New England Quarterly* 26:1 (March 1953): 78–88.

Keire, Mara L. "Dope Fiends and Degenerates: The Gendering of Addiction in the Early Twentieth Century." *Journal of Social History* 31:4 (Summer 1998): 809–822.

Kemble, John Haskell. "The Genesis of the Pacific Mail Steamship Company." *California Historical Society Quarterly* 13:3 (September 1934): 240–254.

Lafeber, Walter. "United States Depression Diplomacy and the Brazilian Revolution, 1893–1894." *Hispanic American Historical Review* 40:1 (February 1960): 107–118.

Lemisch, Jesse. "Jack Tar in the Streets: Merchant Seamen in the Politics of Revolutionary America." *William and Mary Quarterly* 25:3, Third Series (July 1968): 371–407.

Light, Ivan. "From Vice District to Tourist Attraction: The Moral Career of American Chinatowns, 1880–1940." *Pacific Historical Review* 43:3 (August 1974): 367–394.

Lindgren, James M. "'Let Us Idealize Old Types of Manhood': The New Bedford Whaling Museum, 1903–1941." *New England Quarterly* 72:2 (June 1999): 163–206.

Mabee, Frank. "The Spithead Mutiny and Urban Radicalism in the 1790s." *Romanticism* 13:2 (2007): 133–144.

MacKenzie Jr., Clyde L. "History of Oystering in the United States and Canada, Featuring the Eight Greatest Oyster Estuaries." *Marine Fisheries Review* 58:4 (1996): html document, no page numbers.

Madancy, Joyce. "Unearthing Popular Attitudes Toward the Opium Trade and Opium Suppression in Late Qing and Early Republican Fujian." *Modern China* 27:4 (October 2001): 436–483.

Maier, Pauline. "Popular Uprisings and Civil Authority in Eighteenth-Century America." *William and Mary Quarterly* 27:1, Third Series (January 1970): 3–35.

McArthur, Judith N. "Demon Rum on the Boards: Temperance, Melodrama and the Tradition of Antebellum Reform." *Journal of the Early Republic* 9:4 (Winter 1989): 517–540.

McKee, Christopher. "Foreign Seamen in the United States Navy: A Census of 1808." *William and Mary Quarterly* 42:3, Third Series (July 1985): 383–393.

Melancon, Glenn. "Peaceful Intentions: The First British Trade Commission in China, 1833–5." *Historical Research* 73:180 (February 2000): 33–47.

Merriam, Paul G. "Riding the Wind: Cape Horn Passage to Oregon, 1840s–1850s." *Oregon Historical Quarterly* 77:1 (March 1976): 36–60.

Michael, Franz. "Revolution and Renaissance in Nineteenth-Century China: The Age of Tseng Kuo-fan." *Pacific Historical Review* 16:2 (May 1947): 144–151.

Moment, David. "The Business of Whaling in America in the 1850's." *Business History Review* 31:3 (Autumn 1957): 261–291.

Newman, Simon P. "Reading the Bodies of Early American Seafarers." *William and Mary Quarterly* 55:1, Third Series (January 1998): 59–82.

Norris, Martin J. "The Seaman as Ward of the Admiralty." *Michigan Law Review* 52:4 (February 1954): 479–504.

Pich, W.C. "The Whale's Pearl: The Story of Ambergris." *Oceans* 18 (May/June 1985): 23–5.

Postel, Mitchell. "A Lost Resource: Shellfish in San Francisco Bay." *California History* 67:1 (March 1988): 26–41.

Prichard, Earl H. "The Origins of the Most-Favored-Nation and the Open Door Policies in China." *Far Eastern Quarterly* 1:2 (February 1942): 161–172.

Rao, Gautham. "Sailors' Health and National Wealth: Marine Hospitals in the Early Republic." *Common-Place* (online journal) 9:1 (October 2008), no page numbers. www.common-place.org (accessed February 5, 2011).

Rediker, Marcus. "'Under the Banner of King Death': The Social World of Anglo-American Pirates, 1716 to 1726." *William and Mary Quarterly* 38:2, Third Series (April 1981): 203–227.

Ripp-Shucha, Bonnie. "'This Naughty, Naughty City': Prostitution in Eau Claire from the Frontier to the Progressive Era." *Wisconsin Magazine of History* 81:1 (Autumn 1997): 30–54.

Rockhill, William W. "Korea in Its Relations with China." *Journal of the American Oriental Society* 13 (1889): 1–33.

Rohrbough, Malcolm J. "The California Gold Rush as a National Experience." *California History* 77:1 (Spring 1998): 16–29.

Roske, Ralph J. "The World Impact of the California Gold Rush, 1849–1857." *Arizona and the West* 5:3 (Autumn 1963): 187–232.

Ross, W. Gillies. "Distribution, Migration, and Depletion of Bowhead Whales in Hudson Bay, 1860 to 1915." *Arctic and Alpine Research* 6:1 (Winter 1974): 85–98.

_____. "Whaling and the Decline of Native Populations." *Arctic Anthropology* 14:2 (1977): 1–8.

Rouleau, Brian J. "Dead Men Do Tell Tales: Folklore, Fraternity, and the Forecastle." *Early American Studies* 5:1 (Spring 2007): 30–62.

Ruskola, Teemu. "Canton Is Not Boston: The Invention of American Imperial Sovereignty." *American Quarterly* 57:3 (September 2005): 859–884.

Sawers, Larry. "The Navigation Acts Revisited." *Economic History Review* 45:2 (May 1992): 262–284.

Scally, Robert. "Liverpool Ships and Irish Emigrants in the Age of Sail." *Journal of Social History* 17:1 (Autumn 1983): 5–30.

Schwendinger, Robert J. "Chinese Sailors: America's Invisible Merchant Marine, 1876–1905." *California History* 57:1 (Spring 1978): 58–69.

Senhouse, William. "Memoirs of a British Naval Officer at Boston, 1768–1769: Extracts from the Autobiography of William Senhouse." Edited by James C. Brandow. *Proceedings of the Massachusetts Historical Society* 105, Third Series (1993): 74–93.

Shijie Guan. "Chartism and the First Opium War." *History Workshop* 24 (Autumn 1987): 17–31. In *JSTOR* database (accessed December 25, 2010).

Smart, William. "Notes on Sea-Scurvy." *British Medical Journal* 2:879 (November 3, 1877): 617–620.

Smith, Joseph. "Britain and the Brazilian Naval Revolt of 1893–4." *Journal of Latin American Studies* 2:2 (November 1970): 175–198.

Swisher, Earl. "The Adventure of Four Americans in Korea and Peking in 1855." *Pacific Historical Review* 21:3 (August 1952): 237–241.

Tabarrok, Alexander. "The Rise, Fall, and Rise Again of Privateers." *Independent Review* 11:4 (Spring 2007): 565–577.

Tamony, Peter. "Shanghai." *Western Folklore* 25:1 (January 1966): 41–45.

Vickers, Daniel. "Nantucket Whalemen in the Deep-Sea Fishery: The Changing Anatomy of an Early American Labor Force." *Journal of American History* 72:2 (September 1985): 277–296.

Williams, Gerald O. "Share Croppers at Sea: The Whaler's 'Lay' and Events in the Arctic, 1905–1907." *Labor History* 29:1 (Winter 1988): 32–55.

Yangwen Zheng. "The Social Life of Opium in China, 1483–1999." *Modern Asian Studies* 37:1 (February 2003): 1–39.

Books

Afọlayan, Funso S. *Culture and Customs of South Africa*. Westport, CT: Greenwood, 2004.

Asbury, Herbert. *The Barbary Coast: An Informal History of the San Francisco Underworld*. New York: Garden City, 1933.

Association for the Prevention of Torture (APT) and Center for Justice and International Law. *Torture in International Law: A Guide to Jurisprudence*. Geneva: SRO-Kunding, 2008.

Babington, Anthony. *The English Bastille:*

A History of Newgate Gaol and Prison Conditions in Britain, 1188–1902. New York: St. Martin's, 1971.

Bailey, Hiram P. *Shanghaied Out of 'Frisco in the Nineties.* Boston: Charles E. Lauriat, 1925.

Barnes, William Morris. *When Ships Were Ships and Not Tin Pots: The Seafaring Adventures of Captain William Morris Barnes.* New York: Albert & Charles Boni, 1930.

Bender, Daniel E. *American Abyss: Savagery and Civilization in the Age of Industry.* Ithaca, NY: Cornell University Press, 2009.

Bernstein, William J. *A Splendid Exchange: How Trade Shaped the World.* New York: Atlantic Monthly Press, 2008.

Bligh, William. *Narrative of the Mutiny of the Bounty, on a Voyage to the South Seas to Which Are Added Some Additional Particulars, and a Relation to the Subsequent Fate of the Mutineers, and of the Settlement in Pitcairn's Island.* London: William Smith, 1853.

Bolster, W. Jeffrey. *Black Jacks: African American Seamen in the Age of Sail.* Cambridge, MA: Harvard University Press, 1997.

The Book of the Ocean and Life on the Sea: Containing Thrilling Narratives and Adventures of Ocean Life in All Countries, from the Earliest Period to the Present Time. Auburn, NY: John E. Beardsley, ca. 1835.

Booth, Martin. *Opium: A History.* New York: St. Martin's, 1996.

Bradford, Richard H. *The Virginius Affair.* Boulder: Colorado Associated University Press, 1980.

Brand, H.W. *The California Gold Rush and the New American Dream.* New York: Doubleday, 2002.

Breverton, Terry. *Breverton's Nautical Curiosities.* Guilford, CT: Lyons Press, 2010.

Bromley, J.S., ed. *The Manning of the Royal Navy: Selected Pamphlets, 1693–1873.* London: William Clowes & Sons, 1976.

Browne, J. Ross. *Etchings of a Whaling Cruise, with Notes of a Sojourn on the Island of Zanzibar: To Which Is Appended a Brief History of the Whale Fishery, Its Past and Present Condition.* New York: Harper & Brothers, 1846.

Burns, Craig. *Skin and Bones: Tattoos in the Life of the American Sailor.* Philadelphia: Independence Seaport Museum, 2011.

Burns, Walter Noble. *A Year with a Whaler.* New York: Outing, 1913.

Burrows, Edwin G., and Mike Wallace. *Gotham: A History of New York City to 1898.* New York: Oxford University Press, 1999.

Caughey, John Walton. *The California Gold Rush with Vignettes by W.R. Cameron.* Berkeley: University of California Press, 1975.

Chapuis, Oscar. *A History of Vietnam: From Hong Bang to Tu Duc.* Westport, CT: Greenwood, 1995.

Choate, Jean, ed. *At Sea Under Impressment: Accounts of Involuntary Service Aboard Navy and Pirate Vessels, 1700–1820.* Jefferson, NC: McFarland, 2010.

Clapham, Phil. *Whales of the World.* Stillwater, MN: Voyageur, 1997.

Clennell, W.J. *The Historical Development of Religion in China.* New York: E.P. Dutton, 1917.

Cluster, Dick, and Rafael Hernández. *The History of Havana.* New York: Palgrave Macmillan, 2006.

Colvin, Ian D., ed. *The Cape of Adventure: Being Strange and Notable Discoveries, Perils, Shipwrecks, Battles Upon Sea and Land, with Pleasant and Interesting Observations Upon the Country and the Natives of the Cape of Good Hope.* New York: AMS, 1969

Comer, George. *The Journal of Captain George Comer in Hudson Bay, 1903–1905.* Edited by W. Gillies Ross. Toronto: University of Toronto Press, 1984.

Cordingly, David. *Under the Black Flag: The Romance and Reality of Life Among the Pirates.* San Diego: Harcourt, Brace, 1995.

_____. *Women Sailors and Sailors' Women: An Untold Maritime History.* New York: Random House, 2001.

Creighton, Margaret S. *Dogwatch and Liberty Days: Seafaring Life in the Nineteenth Century.* Worchester, MA: Peabody Museum of Salem, 1982.

_____. *Rites and Passages: The Experience of Whaling, 1830–1870.* New York: Cambridge University Press, 1995.

Cruickshank, Dan. *London's Sinful Secret: The Bawdy History and Very Public Passions of London's Georgian Age.* New York: St. Martin's, 2009.

Cutler, Carl C. *Greyhounds of the Sea: The Story of the American Clipper Ship.* 3rd ed. Annapolis, MD: Naval Institute Press, 1984.

Dana, Richard Henry. *Two Years Before the Mast: Twenty-Four Years After.* London: Everyman's Library, 1969.

Dear, Ian, and Peter Kemp, eds. *An A–Z of Sailing Terms.* New York: Oxford University Press, 1992.

Delgado, James P. *To California by Sea: A Maritime History of the California Gold Rush.* Columbia: University of South Carolina, 1990.

Dennis, Donna. *Licentious Gotham: Erotic Publishing and Its Prosecution in Nineteenth-Century New York.* Cambridge, MA: Harvard University Press, 2009.

de Villiers, Marq. *Windswept: The Story of Wind and Weather.* New York: Walker, 2006.

Dillon, Richard H. *Shanghaiing Days.* New York: Coward-McCann, 1961.

Djun Kil Kim. *The History of Korea.* Westport, CT: Greenwood, 2005.

Dolin, Eric Jay. *Leviathan: The History of Whaling in America.* New York: W.W. Norton, 2007.

Douglas, Walter A. *Let the Sea Make a Noise: A History of the North Pacific from Magellan to MacArthur.* New York: Perennial, 1993.

Douglass, Frederick. *Autobiographies: Narrative of the Life of Frederick Douglass, an American Slave; My Bondage and My Freedom; Life and Times of Frederick Douglass.* New York: Library of America, 1994.

Druett, Joan. *She Captains: Heroines and Hellions of the Sea.* New York: Simon & Schuster, 2000.

Eber, Dorothy Harley. *When Whalers Were Up North: Inuit Memories from the Eastern Arctic.* Kingston, ON: Migill-Queen's University Press, 1989.

Ebert, David A. *Sharks, Rays, and Chimaeras of California.* Berkeley: University of California Press, 2003.

Ellis, Richard. *Men and Whales.* New York: Lyons, 1991.

Ellms, Charles. *The Pirates Own Book; or, Authentic Narratives of the Lives, Exploits, and Executions of the Most Celebrated Sea Robbers, with Historical Sketches of the Joassamee, Spanish, Ladrone, West India, Malay, and Algerian Pirates.* Portland: Sandborn & Carter, 1944.

Encyclopedia of North American Conflicts to 1775: A Political, Social, and Military History: A–K. Vol. 1. Santa Barbara: ABC-CLIO, 2008.

Encyclopedia of World Geography: Canada and the Arctic. Vol. 3. New York: Marshall Cavendish, 1994.

Evans, Albert S. *À la California: Sketches of Life in the Golden State.* San Francisco, A.L. Bancroft, 1873.

Fingard, Judith. *Jack in Port: Sailortowns of Eastern Canada.* Toronto: University of Toronto Press, 1982.

Fischer, Anton Otto. *Focs'le Days: The Story of My Youth.* New York: Charles Scribner's Sons, 1947.

Forsyth, Craig J. *The American Merchant Seaman and His Industry: Struggle and Stigma.* New York: Taylor & Francis, 1989.

Fortune, Robert. *Three Years' Wanderings in the Northern Provinces of China, Including A Visit to the Tea, Silk, and Cotton Countries: With an Account of the Horticulture of the Chinese, New Plants, Etc.* New York: Garland, 1979.

Freeman, Hattie Atwood. *Around the World in 500 Days: The Circumnavigation of the Merchant Bark Charles Stewart, 1883–1884; Recounted with Zest and Detail by the Captain's Daughter, Hattie Atwood Freeman.* Edited by Curtis Dahl. Mystic, CT: Mystic Seaport: Museum of America and the Sea, 1999.

Freeman, Lewis R. *In the Tracks of the Trades: The Account of a Fourteen Thousand Mile Yachting Cruise to the Hawaiis, Marquesas, Societies, Samoas and Fijis.* New York: Dodd, Mead, 1920.

Freuchen, Peter. *Peter Freuchen's Men of the*

Frozen North. Edited by Dagmar Freuchen. Cleveland: World, 1962.

Frey, Richard L. *According to Hoyle: Official Rules of More Than 200 Popular Games of Skill and Chance with Expert Advice on Winning Play*. New York: Fawcett Columbine, 1970.

Frick, John W. *Theater, Culture and Temperance Reform in Nineteenth-Century America*. Cambridge, UK: Cambridge University Press, 2003.

Garraty, John A., and Mark C. Carnes. *American National Biography*. 24 Vols. New York: Oxford University Press, 1999.

Giggal, Kenneth. *Classic Sailing Ships*. Stamford, CT: Longmeadow, 1998.

Gilje, Paul A., and William Pencak, eds. *Pirates, Jack Tar and Memory: New Directions in American Maritime History*. Mystic, CT: Mystic Seaport: Museum of America and the Sea, 2007.

Goldfield, David. *America Aflame: How the Civil War Created a Nation*. New York: Bloomsbury Press, 2011.

Graham, Melissa, and Andrew Benson. *The Rough Guide to Chile*. 4th ed. London: Rough Guides, 2009.

Grant, Gordon. *Greasy Luck: A Whaling Sketch Book*. New York: William Farquhar Payson, 2004.

Green, Hardy. *The Company Town: The Industrial Edens and Satanic Mills That Shaped the American Economy*. New York: Basic Books, 2010.

Haley, James L. *Wolf: The Lives of Jack London*. New York: Basic Books, 2010.

Hamilton, Carolyn, ed. *The Cambridge History of South Africa: From Early Times to 1885*. Vol. 1. New York: Cambridge University Press, 2010.

Hanes, III, W. Travis, and Frank Sanello. *The Opium Wars: The Addiction of One Empire and the Corruption of Another*. Naperville, IL: Sourcebooks, 2002.

Hill, Marilynn Wood. *Their Sisters' Keepers: Prostitution in New York City, 1830–1870*. Berkeley: University of California Press, 1993.

Holbrook, Stewart. *The Columbia*. New York: Holt, Rinehart and Winston, 1956.

Jacobs, Michael. *Andes*. Berkeley: Counterpoint, 2011.

Janin, Hunt. *The India-Opium Trade in the Nineteenth Century*. Jefferson, NC: McFarland, 1999.

Johnson, Captain Charles. *A General History of the Robberies and Murderers of the Most Notorious Pirates*. Guilford, CT: Lyons, 2002.

Johnson, Linda Cooke. *Shanghai: From Market Town to Treaty Port, 1074–1858*. Stanford: Stanford University Press, 1995.

Juergens, George. *Joseph Pulitzer and the New York World*. Princeton: Princeton University Press, 1966.

Karabell, Zachary. *Parting the Desert: The Creation of the Suez Canal*. New York: Alfred A. Knopf, 2003.

Keay, John. *China: A History*. New York: Basic Books, 2009.

Kelley, Frank Bergen, comp. *Historical Guide to New York Compiled by Frank Bergen Kelley from the Original Contributions Made by Members and Friends of the City History Club of New York with Seventy Maps and Diagrams and Forty-six Illustrations*. New York: Frederic A. Stokes, 1909.

Kelley, Joseph. *Thirteen Years in the Oregon Penitentiary*. Portland, OR, 1908.

Kiple, Kenneth F., ed. *The Cambridge Historical Dictionary of Disease*. Cambridge, UK: Cambridge University Press, 2003.

Klein, Shelley. *The Most Evil Pirates in History*. London: Michael O' Mara, 2006.

Konstam, Angus. *Scourge of the Seas: Buccaneers, Pirates and Privateers*. Oxford, UK: Osprey, 2007.

Kowalewski, Michael, ed. *Gold Rush: A Literary Exploration*. Berkeley, CA: Heyday, 1997.

Kuhn, Gabriel. *Life Under the Jolly Roger: Reflections on Golden Age Piracy*. Oakland, CA: PM, 2010.

Kurlansky, Mark. *The Big Oyster: History on the Half-shell*. New York: Ballantine, 2006.

Kurzman, Dan. *Disaster! The Great San Francisco Earthquake and Fire of 1906*. New York: HarperCollins, 2001.

Laing, Alexander. *American Ships*. New York: American Heritage, 1971.

Lane, Horace. *The Wandering Boy, Careless*

Sailor, and Result of Inconsideration: A True Narrative. Skaneateles, NY: Luther A. Pratt, 1837.

Lee, Robert E. *Blackbeard the Pirate: A Reappraisal of His Life and Times.* Winston-Salem, NC: John F. Blair, 1974.

Lees, James. *Dana's Seamen's Friend: Containing a Treatise on Practical Seamanship, with Plates; A Dictionary of Sea Terms; and the Customs and Usages of the Merchant Service; with the British Laws Relating to Shipping, the Duties of Master and Mariners, and the Mercantile Marine.* London: George Philip and Son, 1856.

Lemisch, Jesse. *Jack Tar vs. John Bull: The Role of New York's Seamen in Precipitating the Revolution.* New York: Garland, 1997.

Levine, Robert M. *The History of Brazil.* New York: Palgrave Macmillan, 1999.

Lewis, Colin M. *Argentina: A Short History.* Oxford: Oneworld, 2002.

_____. *British Railways in Argentina, 1857–1914: A Case Study of Foreign Investment.* London: Athlone, 1983.

Lewis, Oscar. *Sea Routes to the Gold Fields: The Migration by Water to California in 1849–1852.* New York: Alfred A. Knopf, 1949.

Little, Benerson. *Pirate Hunting: The Fight Against Pirates, Privateers, and Sea Raiders from Antiquity to the Present.* Washington, D.C.: Potomac, 2010.

Lloyd, B.E. *Lights and Shades in San Francisco.* San Francisco: A.L. Bancroft, 1876.

MacLeod, Donald, ed. *Good Words for 1874.* London: Daldy, Isbister, 1874.

Maddocks, Melvin, and the Editors of Time-Life Books. *The Atlantic Crossing.* Alexandria, VA: Time-Life, 1981.

Mason, David. *A Traveller's History of South Africa.* New York: Interlink, 2004.

Matthew, H.G.G., and Brian Harrison, eds. *Oxford Dictionary of National Biography: From the Earliest Times to the Year 2000.* Vol. 31. New York: Oxford University Press, 2004.

Mayhew, Henry. *London Labour and the London Poor: A Cyclopædia of the Condition and Earnings of Those That Will Work, Those That Cannot Work, and Those That Will Not Work.* Vol. 4. New York: Augustus M. Kelley, 1967.

McGrath, Alister E. *Christianity's Dangerous Idea: The Protestant Revolution; A History from the Sixteenth Century to the Twenty-First.* New York: Harper One, 2007.

McIllwain, Jeffery Scott. *Organizing Crime in Chinatown: Race and Racketeering in New York City, 1890–1910.* Jefferson, NC: McFarland, 2004.

McKenzie, F.A. *The Tragedy of Korea.* London: Hodder and Stoughton, 1908.

Moodie, Duncan Campbell Francis. *The History of the Battles and Adventures of the British, the Boers, and the Zulus, &c., in Southern Africa from the Time of Pharaoh Necho, to 1880, with Copious Chronology.* Vol. 1. Cape Town: Murray & St. Leger, 1888.

Morris, James McGrath. *Pulitzer: A Life in Politics, Print, and Power.* New York: Harper, 2010.

Morris, Norval, and David J. Rothman, eds. *The Oxford History of the Prison: The Practice of Punishment in Western Society.* New York: Oxford University Press, 1995.

Morris, William, and Mary Morris. *Morris Dictionary of Word and Phrase Origins.* Second Edition. New York: Harper-Collins, 1988.

Musick, John R. *Hawaii: Our New Possessions; An Account of Travels and Adventure, with Sketches of the Scenery, Customs and Manners, Mythology and History of Hawaii to the Present, and an Appendix Containing the Treaty of Annexation to the United States.* New York: Funk & Wagalls, 1898.

Nagle, Jacob. *A Diary of the Life of Jacob Nagle, Sailor, from the Year 1775 to 1841.* Edited by John C. Dann. New York: Weidenfeld & Nicolson, 1988.

The Nautical Magazine and Naval Chronicle for 1837: A Journal of Papers on Subjects Connected with Maritime Affair. London: Simpkin, Marshall, 1837.

Nicholson, Paul C., ed. *Abstracts from a Journal Kept Aboard the Ship* Sharon *of Fairhaven on a Whaling Voyage in the South Pacific.* Providence, RI: Private Printing, 1953.

Partridge, Eric. *Origins: A Short Etymolog-*

ical Dictionary of Modern English. New York: Greenwich House, 1983.

Pennell, C.R. *Bandits at Sea: A Pirates Reader*. New York: New York University Press, 2001.

Philpots, John R. *Oysters, and All About Them: Being a Complete History of the Subject, Exhaustive on All Points of Necessary and Curious Information from the Earliest Writers to Those of the Present Time, with Numerous Additions, Facts, and Notes*. London: John Richardson, 1890.

Pickelhaupt, Bill. *Shanghaied in San Francisco*. San Francisco: Flyblister, 1996.

Prager, Ellen J., with Sylvia A. Earle. *The Oceans*. New York: McGraw Hill, 2000.

The Quebec Guide, Comprising an Historical and Descriptive Account of the City and Every Place of Note in the Vicinity with a Plan of the City. Quebec: W. Cowan and Son, 1844.

Radford, Edwin, and Alan Smith. *To Coin A Phrase: A Dictionary of Origins*. London: Hutchinson, 1973.

Rappoport, Angelo S. *Superstitions of Sailors*. Mineola, NY: Dover, 2007.

Reid, Joseph Phillip. *In a Rebellious Spirit: The Argument of Facts, the Liberty Riot, and the Coming of the American Revolution*. University Park: Pennsylvania State University Press, 1979.

Roberts, Callum. *The Unnatural History of the Sea*. Washington, D.C.: Island Press/Shearwater, 2007.

Roberts, J.A.G. *A Concise History of China*. Cambridge, MA: Harvard University Press, 1999.

Rose, Sarah. *For All the Tea in China: How England Stole the World's Favorite Drink and Changed History*. New York: Viking, 2010.

Rosen, Fred. *Gold!: The Story of the 1848 Gold Rush and How It Shaped a Nation*. New York: Thunder's Mouth, 2005.

Rosen, William. *The Most Powerful Idea in the World*. New York: Random House, 2010.

Sante, Luc. *Lures and Snares, Low of Life: Old New York*. New York: Farrar, Straus, and Giroux, 1991.

Sasuly, Richard. *Bookies and Bettors: Two Hundred Years of Gambling*. New York: Holt, Rinehart and Winston, 1982.

Saunders, Christopher, and Nicholas Southey. *Historical Dictionary of South Africa*. 2nd ed. Lanham, MD: Scarecrow, 2000.

Scharf, Robert Francis. *Distribution and Origin of Life in America*. New York: Macmillan, 1912.

Schultz, Charles R. *Forty-Niners 'Round the Horn*. Columbia: University of South Carolina Press, 1999.

Schwartz, David G. *Roll the Bones: The History of Gambling*. New York: Gotham, 2006.

Schwartz, Stephen. *Brotherhood of the Sea: A History of the Sailors' Union of the Pacific, 1895–1985*. New Brunswick: Transaction, 1986.

Shaw, David W. *Flying Cloud: The True Story of America's Most Famous Clipper Ship and the Woman Who Guided Her*. New York: William Morrow, 2000.

Shaw, Frank H., and Ernest H. Robinson, eds. *The Sea and Its Story: From Viking Ship to Submarine*. London: Cassell, 1910.

Sismondo, Christine. *America Walks into a Bar: A Spirited History of Taverns and Saloons, Speakeasies and Grog Shops*. New York: Oxford University Press, 2011.

Smith, Aaron. *The Atrocities of Pirates; Being a Faithful Narrative of the Unparalleled Sufferings Enduring by the Author During His Captivity Among the Pirates of the Island of Cuba; with an Account of the Excesses and Barbarities of Those Inhuman Freebooters*. London: G. and W.B. Whittaker, 1824.

Smith, Philippa Mein. *A Concise History of New Zealand*. New York: Cambridge University Press, 2005.

Smyth, Admiral W.H. *Chapman: The Sailor's Lexicon: The Classic Source for More Than 15,000 Nautical Terms*. New York: Hearst, 1996.

Snyder, Robert W. *The Voice of the City: Vaudeville and Popular Culture in New York*. New York: Oxford University Press, 1989.

Spence, Jonathan D. *The Search for Modern China*. New York: W.W. Norton, 1990.

Standard, William L. *Merchant Seamen: A Short History of Their Struggles*. Standfordville, NY: Earl M. Coleman, 1979.

Stave, Bruce M., and John F. Sutherland with Aldo Salerno, eds. *From the Old Country: An Oral History of European Migration to America*. New York: Twayne, 1994.

Stonehouse, Frederick. *Great Lakes Crime: Murder, Mayhem, Booze and Broads*. Gwinn, MI: Avery Color Studios, 2004.

Strobridge, Truman R., and Dennis L Noble. *Alaska and the U.S. Revenue Cutter Service, 1867–1915*. Annapolis, MD: Naval Institute Press, 1999.

Sturtevant, William C., and David Damas, eds. *Handbook of North American Indians: Arctic*. Vol. 5. Washington: Smithsonian Institution, 1984.

Sutton, Charles. *The New York Tombs: Its Secrets and Mysteries, Being a History of the Noted Criminals with Narratives of Their Crimes*. San Francisco: A. Roman, 1874.

Tate, E. Mowbray. *Transpacific Steam: The Story of Steam Navigation from the Pacific Coast of North America to the Far East and Antipodes, 1867–1941*. New York: Cornwall, 1986.

Taylor, Rev. William. *Seven Years' Street Preaching in San Francisco, California; Embracing Incidents, Triumphant Death Scenes, Etc*. New York: Carlton & Porter, 1857.

Thum, Thos. G., ed. *Hawaiian Almanac and Annual for 1906: The Reference Book of Information and Statistics Relating to the Territory of Hawaii, of Value to Merchants, Tourists and Others*. Honolulu: Thos. G. Thrum, 1905.

Tilton, Captain George Fred. *"Cap'n George Fred" Himself*. Garden City, NY: Doubleday, Doran, 1928.

Tower, Walter S. *A History of the American Whale Fishery*. Philadelphia: University of Philadelphia Press, 1907.

Unger, Nancy C. *Fighting Bob La Follette: The Righteous Reformer*. Chapel Hill: University of North Carolina Press, 2000.

Vandersloot, J. Sam'l. *The True Path; or, Gospel Temperance: Being the Life, Work and Speeches of Francis Murphy, Dr. Henry A. Reynolds, and Their Co-laborers: Embracing Also a History of the Women's Christian Temperance Movement*. New York: Henry S. Goodspeed, 1878.

van Dinter, Maarten Hesselt. *The World of Tattoo: An Illustrated History*. Translated by S. Green. Amsterdam: KIT, 2005.

Volo, Dorothy Denneen, and James M. Volo. *Daily Life in the Age of Sail*. Westport, CT: Greenwood, 2002.

Wachowich, Nancy, in collaboration with Apphia Agalakti Awa, et al. *Saqiyuq: Stories from the Lives of Three Inuit Women*. Kingston, ON: McGill-Queen's University Press.

Wade, Wyn Craig. *The Titanic: End of a Dream*. New York: Penguin, 1986.

Wallace, Frederick William. *In the Wake of the Wind-ships: Notes, Records and Biographies Pertaining to the Square-rigged Merchant Marine of British North America*. New York: George Sully, 1927.

Warburton, Christopher E.S. *Slaves, Serfs, and Workers: Labor Under the Law*. Pittsburgh: Dorrance, 1998.

Weekly, Ernest. *An Etymological Dictionary of Modern English: L–Z*. Vol. 2. New York: Dover, 1967.

Welsh, Frank. *South Africa: A Narrative History*. New York: Kodansha International, 1999.

Wennersten, John R. *The Oyster Wars of Chesapeake Bay*. Centreville, MD: Tidewater, 1981.

Whipple, A.B.C. *The Challenge*. New York: William Morrow, 1987.

White, William. *History Gazetteer and Directory of the County of Devon Including the City of Exeter, and Comprising a General Survey of the County*. London: Simpkin, Marshall, 1878–79.

Whiteaker, Larry. *Seduction, Prostitution, and Moral Reform in New York, 1830–1860*. New York: Garland, 1997.

Williamson, James A. *A Short History of British Expansion*. London: Macmillan, 1922.

Wilson, Derek. *The Circumnavigators*. New York: M. Evan, 1989.

Windsor, Justin, ed. *The Memorial of Boston, Including Suffolk County, Massachusetts, 1630–1880: The Provincial Period*. Vol. 2. Boston: James R. Osgood, 1881.

Wolf, Steve. *The Science Behind Movie Stunts and Special Effects.* New York: Skyhorse, 2007.

Woodman, Richard. *The History of the Ship: The Comprehensive Story of Seafaring from the Earliest Times to the Present Day.* New York: Lyons, 1997.

Zinn, Howard. *A People's History of the United States, 1492–Present.* New York: Harper Perennial Modern Classics, 1998.

Index

Numbers in **_bold italics_** indicate pages with photographs.